JAPANIZATION AT WORK

Japanization at Work

Managerial Studies for the 1990s

John Bratton

Foreword by
Huw Beynon

First edition 1992
Reprinted 1993, 1994

Published by
THE MACMILLAN PRESS LTD
Houndmills, Basingstoke, Hampshire RG21 2XS
and London
Companies and representatives
throughout the world

ISBN 0–333–54574–5 hardcover
ISBN 0–333–54575–3 paperback

A catalogue record for this book is available
from the British Library.

Printed in Great Britain by
Antony Rowe Ltd
Chippenham, Wiltshire

To my children, Amy, Andrew and Jennie
with love

Contents

List of Tables   viii

List of Figures   x

Abbreviations   xi

Foreword by Huw Beynon   xiii

Preface   xvii

Preface to the Paperback Edition   xx

1   Introduction   1

2   Perspectives on Japanization   17

3   Trade Unions and Change at Work   48

4   Patterns of Change   73

5   The Motor Components Company: Japanization in
    Large-Batch Production   103

6   The Drilling Machine Company: Japanization in
    Small-Batch Production   131

7   The Packaging Company: Work Groups and the
    Polyvalent Worker   160

8   Conclusions   201

Notes   220

Bibliography   223

Index   242

List of Tables

3.1   Aggregate union membership and density in the United Kingdom   49

3.2   Change in membership of the ten largest TUC-affiliated unions   51

3.3   Trade union model agreements   65

4.1   Employment by occupation in the twelve case-studies   77

4.2   Comparison of managers' and conveners' accounts of the effects of new technology on employment   81

4.3   Effects of technical change on the monitoring of job elements and employee performance   90

4.4   Trade union membership and density in the case-studies   94

4.5   Trade union density in relation to establishment size   95

4.6   Union membership arrangements for manual workers in the case-studies   95

4.7   Steward density in relation to establishment size   96

4.8   Trade union organization in the case-studies   96

4.9   Form of employee and union participation in technical changes   97

4.10   Extent and form of trade union participation in technical changes, by establishment size   98

5.1   Division of labour in the cells   108

5.2   Employment by occupation at Servo Engineering   116

5.3   Turnover and absenteeism rates (direct workers)   120

5.4   Union membership and stewards' organization   126

6.1   Results of cellular manufacturing system at Oil Tool Engineering   148

6.2   Union membership and steward organization at Oil Tool and Servo Engineering   157

7.1   Division of labour within the machine cells at Servo, Oil Tool and Flowpak   166

7.2   Changes in product design: mechanical components   175

7.3   Employment by occupation at Flowpak   177

7.4   Stewards' and workers' accounts of the effects of cellular technology upon the work of machine operators   182

7.5 Union membership and steward organization at
Flowpak, Oil Tool and Servo Engineering   198

List of Figures

2.1 The JIT production process 25
2.2 Core themes of the Japanese approach to people-management 27
2.3 A model of Japanese industrial management 32
3.1 Industrial disputes: working days lost and number of stoppages (UK) 58
3.2 Some TUC policy statements on technical change 62
4.1 Characteristics of twelve case-studies and number of employees 74
4.2 Changes in employment in each occupational group in the twelve case-studies between 1980 and 1985 78
4.3 Division of tasks by production unit size, number of employees and trade union influence 82
6.1 Management structure at the West Yorkshire plant 132
6.2 Occupational structure in the workshop 143
6.3 Intra-union organization at Oil Tool Engineering 158
7.1 Management structure at Flowpak Engineering 162

Abbreviations

ACAS	Advisory, Conciliation and Arbitration Service
AFL-CIO	American Federation of Labor-Congress of Industrial Organizations
APEX	Association of Professional, Executive, Clerical and Computer Staff
AUEW	Amalgamated Union of Engineering Workers
AEU	Amalgamated Engineering Union
ASTMS	Association of Scientific, Technical and Managerial Staffs
CBI	Confederation of British Industry
COHSE	Confederation of Health Service Employees
DGB	Deutscher Gewerkschaftsbund (German Trade Union Federation)
EEF	Engineering Employers' Federation
EETPU	Electrical, Electronic, Telecommunications and Plumbing Union
EITB	Engineering Industry Training Board
E&SEA	Engineering & Shipbuilding Employers' Association
GCHQ	Government Communications Headquarters
GMB	General, Municipal, Boilermakers and Allied Trades Union
LRD	Labour Research Department
MSC	Manpower Services Commission
MSF	Manufacturing, Science and Finance Union
NEDC	National Economic Development Council
NUPE	National Union of Public Employees
NUS	National Union of Scalemakers
TASS	Technical, Administrative and Supervisory Staffs
TGWU	Transport and General Workers' Union
TUC	Trades Union Congress
WEA	Workers' Educational Association

Foreword

Remarkable changes took place in British society during the 1980s. Often these have been associated with 'Thatcherism', and the powerful assault by successive Conservative governments upon the institutions which had ordered social and economic life since 1945. On reflection, however, it has become clear that a number of different processes were at work, some national, others more global in their scope. Arguably, these set the context for the 'Thatcher Revolution', and will outlive the politics that inspired it.

Technical change was one of the processes involved. To many, the microprocessor and its application to products and new productive processes ushered in a new creative era. Computer-aided design and manufacture were seen to offer the possibility of more flexible systems of production which were more generous than the old systems to the needs and capacities of workers and consumers alike. While social scientists talked of 'flexible specialization' and the potential it held out for a new order in industry, politicians, like Peter Walker, pointed to the future as an 'Athens without slaves'. Side by side with this went an alternative view, which highlighted the deskilling effects of previous periods of technical change, and questioned the generally beneficial outcomes of these latest developments. Unemployment figured strongly in these debates, with attention drawn to the ways in which the new technology replaced labour across a wide range of industrial and commercial activities.

The significance of unemployment and job losses as a feature of life in the 1980s, in and beyond the work-place, is clear. While unemployment levels remained below half a million through the '40s, '50s and '60s, they escalated in the 1970s and became an established feature of society in the 1980s, only to accelerate again in the 1990s. This pattern was made most dramatic by the severe cutback in manufacturing employment which ushered in the first Thatcher government. Between 1979 and 1984 the number of jobs in the manufacturing industry declined by 24 per cent. With this went a decline in trade union membership, a decline which (when allied with cutbacks in the public sector and the growing number of legal restrictions placed on their powers) gave credence to a view of trade union organisations as severely weakened and disorientated. To some this trend represented a change of historic proportions and with it the need for trade unions to adapt to the new times. For others, the changes represented a temporary setback associated with recession, a strategic period of quietude to be shaken awake with the next boom. Here, as with questions of technological change, interpretations diverge dramatically. While some have emphasized the transforming nature of the changes, others have given emphatic stress to continuity and the enduring nature of workplace relations. A similar disagreement has been associated with the arrival of the Japanese.

During the 1980s, the industrialized economies of the OECD became increasingly internationalized. Financial markets became linked through computers and satellites, and at the same time transnational corporations extended and intensified their operations beyond their home base. The growing presence of Japanese corporations – operating across a broad range of industrial and commercial activities – was the most significant development in this area. In Britain, these changes were positively encouraged by successive Conservative governments who saw in inward investment a much needed boost for the economy. Japanese managerial know-how would also, it was hoped, have beneficial 'demonstration effect', forcing British companies to adjust their activities in the face of increasingly efficient Japanese competition. This view was influenced by comparative studies of British and Japanese working practices, and latterly by accounts of the impact of Japanese car manufacturers upon the US industry. An MIT study stressed the effectiveness of the Japanese way of producing motor cars and the inevitability of a march toward 'lean production' and team work in Britain and the EC (Womack, Jones and Roos, 1991). Here, again, the changes were sketched out in terms which were compelling and attractive. In this view the Japanese approach to production is more efficient and ultimately more rewarding for both worker and consumer. However, as with the other changes, 'Japanization' has its detractors. For some it represents the re-emergence of 'human relations' theory. In this new guise 'Japanization' is seen to have the same limitations for effective management and to operate with similar practices which verge upon manipulation. For others, 'Japanization' is firmly related to work intensification and de-unionization, processes made all the more effective by unemployment and the location of factories on new greenfield sites. Perhaps the view of one experienced US car-worker offers the most balanced assessment of 'team work' and the operation of the new system of work. For him, 'the jury is still out'.

The need to evaluate carefully these changes and their impacts upon the working lives of workers and managers is urgent. It has been made the more difficult by the limited number of detailed accounts of work experience in the 1980s. The publication of this study by John Bratton is therefore to be welcomed. As a trade union tutor in the early 1980s, he talked with shop stewards about the kinds of changes they were experiencing in their workplace; often these were at odds with those published in academic journals. His interest in technological change led him to survey a wide range of engineering establishments and to follow this up with a number of intensive case studies. For these he visited factories regularly, talking with managers, shop stewards and workers, and observing changes as they were introduced. Through this interaction he became aware of 'Japanization' and the introduction of 'cellular production' techniques of manufacture. His investigation of these processes and the social dynamics which accompany their introduction produces a detailed and illuminating account of the incremental and variable nature of change. In this, Bratton re-examines the idea of different kinds of production and market arrangement, and the impact these have upon the position of managers and the decision-making processes within factories. Here and generally, the strength of his account rests upon its detail and upon his awareness of the many-sidedness of the processes which he observed. He shows how fear of unemployment and the 'demonstration effect' of plant closures was decisive in his cases, yet how workers came to value aspects of the new arrangements. Bratton discusses how decision-making was pushed downward toward the cell and the 'cell leader', but how workers complain that 'everything you make is monitored'. Similarly perplexing questions are raised about job losses and the skill composition of these newly automated 'Japanized' factories. Through all these changes trade union membership remains high, although the trade union organizations seem to play a different role, one which, on Bratton's account, could change again in the future as and when market circumstances alter.

In these ways, *Japanization at Work* provides a first-hand account of managerial strategies and their implementation. It will help in the task of assessing the issues involved in 'Japanization' and its effects upon managerial practice and the behaviour and attitudes of industrial workers. Most significantly, it provides us with an authentic document of industrial change in an English region in the 1980s.

HUW BEYNON
Manchester

Preface

Many Westerners are having a love affair with Japanese manage-
ment philosophy.
Richard Marsh, in Peter Wickens: *The Road to Nissan*, 1987:xi

This book is about two peculiarly 1980s phenomena: Japanese-style
management techniques, and microtechnology. It deals primarily
with the effects of both on the working lives of men and women
in three British factories in a period which saw substantial changes in
the UK economy. My interest in 'new technology' first developed in
shop steward courses in the late 1970s. As a trade union tutor, I
became involved in a TUC project to develop learning material for a
new technology course. The work involved me in extensive teaching
commitments; first piloting the material with full-time union officials
in the Manchester and Sheffield areas, and later on 'follow-on' new
technology courses for shop stewards. In 1979, I wrote a pamphlet[1]
for the health service union, COHSE, and addressed the union's
national conference on the issue of technological change. The book-
let, *New Technology and Employment*,[2] was written for union officials and trade union activists. It attempted to place the issue of
microtechnology within a historical perspective and raise some of the
wider economic and political issues absent in the TUC material.

It was during the discussions with engineering shop stewards that I
became aware of an apparent conflict between the experience of the
workers at the 'sharp end' of the labour process, and my own
deskilling perspective, which was strongly influenced by Braverman's
Labor and Monopoly Capital (1974). On the one hand, there appeared to be evidence of skill fragmentation and routinization when
some stewards remarked that such technology had made their work
more 'boring'. On the other hand, many stewards considered that
Computer Numerically Controlled (CNC) machine tools had resulted
in an increase in operators' skill and expertise. This anecdotal evidence highlighted to me that concepts such as 'deskilling' and the
analyses of technological change associated with the Braverman
approach may be too limited.

Shop stewards' experiences of new technology began to be more
systematically recorded and evaluated in subsequent years of part-
time research at the University of Manchester. Once I began visiting

factories and interviewing managers, shop stewards and workers in the mid-1980s however, my research became increasingly directed towards examining Japanese manufacturing and labour management practices. These practices were perceived by managers and workers alike, as having a greater impact on patterns of work than the hitherto, widely debated and documented, new technology. More specifically, the field investigations began to analyse the extent to which computer numerically controlled machine tools and innovatory capitalist management techniques altered employment levels, job content and social relations in the workplace. Skill enhancement, partly through CNC technology, but also by functional flexibility associated with Japanese-style teams or 'cells' became apparent during the investigation. In addition, shopfloor autonomy and skill enhancement were found to be influenced by trade union workplace organization.

The evidence on skill enhancement is in contention with labour process theorists, who either posit a view that deskilling is a central dynamic of technological change or consider that CNC and flexible production teams are bound to reverse the deskilling process inherent in the Fordist model. The empirical evidence on which my PhD thesis was based is drawn from engineering case studies in West Yorkshire between autumn 1985 and summer 1988. The evidence presented reaffirms the primacy of the social nature of the production process, and draws attention to the diverse and complex repercussions of Japanese-style production systems and technological change on the labour process, depending on social choices. This book is largely derived from my thesis and is written for managers and workers in the hope that it will help them to reflect on the arguments and implications of these changes.

I would like to acknowledge and record my thanks to those who, over the last ten years, have directly and indirectly helped me with my research and this book. I am deeply grateful to the managers and union representatives in the various organizations involved in the research who gave their time and invaluable data, and who patiently answered my unrelenting questions on technological and organizational change and industrial relations. The interviews I conducted with these people invariably lasted at least an hour and quite frankly without their assistance the research and this book would not have been possible. I am also grateful to the men and women who gave their time and answered my questions with patience and goodwill. I learned a great deal from them. Since information and opinion were often given on the understanding that it would not be ascribed to individuals, I am unable to mention the names of even those who helped me most. At Manchester University, my thanks go to Dr Julian Laite for advice on questionnaire design and to Professor Huw Beynon for recognizing the potential of my research data and for his encouragement and guidance on writing up my results. At Leeds Business School, I owe a debt to colleagues in the Work and Employment Study Group who have, by direct interest in my research, given me practical help and support: Steve Cockerill; Les Hamilton; Gerry Stewart; Brian Whittington. John Sutherland, Associate Head of Department, provided the support that helped the writing process along. And also, my thanks to the trade unionists attending my courses for providing a stimulating atmosphere in which to teach.

I am also indebted to long-serving members of the Halifax and District Trades Council for sharing their experiences of life on the shopfloor. Also I would especially like to thank Tim Enright of Halifax for reading the entire manuscript in draft and applying his sharp critical eye, thereby reducing the number of errors in the book considerably, and for his friendship over the years. That shortcomings remain is not to be blamed on any of those who have assisted me.

Most of all, I thank Carolyn Bratton for her support and encouragement, and our children, Amy, Andrew and Jennie, who have endured my absence whilst working on my thesis and this book.

JOHN BRATTON

Preface to the Paperback Edition

The search for remedies to improve productivity in British industry has led to Japanese-style working practices being studied as a model to give companies a competitive advantage. Some of the literature has focused on the usage of the term, 'Japanization'. Writers have also focused on the potential to transplant Japanese methods in Western manufacturing. Within this current debate the impacts upon the working lives of line managers and workers are largely ignored, and yet Japanese management techniques have the potential to intensify work and weaken workplace trade unionism. *Japanization at Work* seeks to make a contribution to the debate. Management can choose from a variety of manufacturing and employment strategies. This book provides an account of a particular management strategy and its effects on industrial workers. In 1993, twenty-five years after the publication of the Donovan *Report of the Royal Commission on Trade Unions and Employers' Associations*, it also provides an insight into the shop steward system and union–management relations in the late 1980s.

Soon after completing the book, I moved to the University College of the Cariboo in British Columbia, Canada. My new colleagues have been extremely supportive. Visiting Japanese companies during 1992 was made possible by a grant from the Scholarly Activity Committee. I would particularly like to thank Professor Tsuji, Ritsumeikan University, Kyoto – the discussions between us greatly informed my ideas on the Japanese labour process.

JOHN BRATTON

1 Introduction

Never in my twenty years in production management have we had such a mood for getting things done.

ICI Manager, quoted in Beynon, 1983:11

This book is about the current changes in the organization of work and industrial relations in a selection of case studies based in the North of England. According to Jenkins and Sherman (1979), at the end of the 1970s the advanced capitalist economies stood on the threshold of 'a new industrial revolution, based on developments in microelectronics'. It was judgements of this kind, together with intense media coverage on the implications of the 'silicon chip', which prompted governments, industrialists and trade unions to wake up to the significance of microprocessor-based technology. In the United Kingdom, the government commissioned reports on the state of the British electronics industry, the degree of awareness about the new technology amongst British managers, and the implications of the changes for British manufacturing (Sleigh, et al, 1979). The British trade union movement, already alarmed by rising levels of unemployment, issued documents, passed conference resolutions, organized education courses, and developed policies on technological change (TUC, 1979).

Much of the debate on technological change has been conducted at the 'macro' or societal level. Optimists describe the potential benefits of new technology in a 'leisure society', where the monotony and hazards of work are removed. Pessimists, on the other hand, point to mass unemployment, the degradation of work and new health hazards. Macro studies have examined the impact of microelectronics in particular sectors of British industry (Northcott and Rogers, 1982; Rajan, 1985). Research efforts have also been undertaken at the 'micro' or organizational level. Much of this work has been concerned with describing and interpreting the complex interplay of technical innovation, job characteristics, skills, patterns of work organization and social relations (Wilkinson, 1983; Batstone, et al, 1987; McLoughlin and Clark, 1988). The research foci may be divided into two categories: first, the effects on workers when new technology is introduced, and second, attempts by workers to influence the pace and scope of technological change. Much of this

1

research has been stimulated by Braverman's publication *Labor and Monopoly Capital* (1974), and the upsurge of interest in the labour process debate that followed in its wake (Thompson, 1983).

Running parallel with the diffusion of microprocessor-based technology in the 1980s however, is the influence of Japanese management concepts upon management in Britain, North America and West Germany. Here the emphasis is upon flexible specialization, just-in-time (JIT) and total quality control (TQC) systems of production. The newer debates on the organization of work and management strategies has highlighted the adoption by American and British employers of what is termed the 'human resource management' approach to 'people management' (Guest, 1987; Storey, 1989). For others, the adoption of a new package of measures to manufacturing and personnel management represented a shift to a Japanese paradigm of production and labour control. By the second half of the decade the term 'Japanization' was being used by academics to encapsulate the organizational changes at such British companies as Lucas Electrical (Turnbull, 1986) and Rover (Oliver and Wilkinson, 1988). However, Japanization in manufacturing has probably been pushed hardest in the USA. In automobile manufacturing, Chrysler, Ford, and General Motors have been pressing the United Auto Workers' union to accept a production system based on Japanese-style teams (*Business Week*, 24 August 1987). Again, flexibility and worker autonomy is a key element of the recent 'cultural' change at the US aircraft-maker Boeing: 'Boeing now talks of "empowering" the workers' (Oram, 1990:14). Similar arguments underlying the technological debates can be found in the current discourse on Japanization, such as the interplay of flexible cellular work structures and skill levels.

The primary aim of this book is to contribute to this debate on the effects of Japanization upon the working lives of men and women through three detailed case-studies. The cases show how both technological and organizational changes affect workers' skills and degree of shopfloor power, but also they illustrate the complex configuration of opportunities and constraints offered by innovation for managerial choice and negotiation. A second aim is to test empirically the popular thesis of 'flexible specialization': the thesis that the mass-production paradigm characterized by intense division of labour and the separation of intellectual and manual skills is replaced with a flexible production paradigm that utilizes workers' skills and combines conception and physical tasks; that such tendencies reverse the 'deskilling' process associated with new technology. Finally, the book aims to analyse trade union reactions to changes in the workplace. Before studying the case-studies, two separate chapters are devoted to exploring the theoretical debates on Japanization and technological change, and the fortunes and influence of organized labour in the 1980s. The aim of the remainder of this introduction, however, is to sketch the economic and political backcloth to these changes within work organizations. This is important, because in various ways the external economic and political environments have been used to explain employers' manufacturing and labour strategies, and the particular responses of workers to managements' initiatives.

THE BACKCLOTH

The research upon which this book is based was started during the second period of the Thatcher government, a critical time for British industrial relations. Indeed, the years 1983 to 1987 are seen by many observers as a 'watershed' in British industrial relations. Although the history of British industrial relations can cite a number of watersheds, what is not in doubt is that the 1980s have witnessed substantial contextual changes in industrial relations, including mass unemployment, major pieces of employment legislation, and a diminution of trade union membership and power. Fundamental changes in the industrial relations system was not an experience unique to Britain. In the United States the difficult environment of the 1980s has resulted in changes that have led to what some writers have called the 'transformation of American industrial relations' (Kochan et al, 1986). Although the transformation thesis is not universally accepted in the United States (see Block, 1988), American employers have, with government indulgence, persuaded or compelled a weakened labour movement to accept significant changes in collective agreements (Adams, 1989).

To summarize. Although the steep decline in the UK's GDP after 1979 began to turn in 1981, its upward path remained erratic and concealed the disappearance of large tracts of industrial landscape. High unemployment, falling levels of manufacturing output and, for millions of people, falling living standards marked the 1980s. In 1984, unemployment was 13 per cent and although many of the UK's competitors were also experiencing historically high levels of unemployment, only Belgium and the Netherlands surpassed the UK's unemployment rate. In the view of one academic, Government ministers had 'ceased looking for silver linings and the view is now commonplace that high unemployment is not only no fault of the Government but also a necessary price to pay for important, and lasting, economic benefits'.[1] Real income per head of the UK population was lower in the mid-1980s than in eleven other advanced capitalist countries. Moreover, there were significant shifts between different parts of the UK economy. The percentage of output (Gross Domestic Product) accounted for by service industries had increased while the proportion attributable to manufacturing had decreased. In 1950, manufacturing was 30 per cent of the UK's GDP; by 1984 it had fallen to 25 per cent. The UK's problems as regards trade in manufacturing manifest themselves in a number of ways. The UK's share of world exports of manufactures fell from approximately 17 per cent in 1960 to about 8 per cent in 1986. Whilst the volume of international exports of manufactures increased by almost 42 per cent between 1978 and 1987, the volume of UK exports of manufactures increased by only 23 per cent (Griffiths and Wall, 1989). The shift to service industries has been even more profound in terms of jobs: 35 per cent of the total in civil employment were employed in manufacturing in 1950; this had fallen to 26 per cent by 1981. During the same period, employment in the service sector increased from 47 per cent to 60 per cent of total employment. This structural change in the UK economy has been encapsulated in the term 'deindustrialization'.

Some observers question the wisdom of using the word, arguing that it has become a catch-all term often incorrectly used to describe the relative decline of manufacturing industry rather than industry as a whole which includes construction, gas, oil production, mining and quarrying and transport (Blackaby, 1979; Harris, 1988). Rhodes defines deindustrialization as 'the failure of a country or region to secure a rate of growth of output and net exports of all kinds sufficient to achieve full employment' (Rhodes, 1986:138). Deindustrialization has also been defined in terms of the economy's ability to export sufficient of its output to pay for imports, and to do this while maintaining 'socially acceptable levels of output, employment and the exchange rate' (Singh, 1977:128). Singh's definition establishes the relationship between the global trading position of the UK economy and the internal structure of the economy. Further, in the context of urban and regional economic regeneration most definitions of deindustrialization equate it with an absolute loss of manufacturing jobs (Massey, 1988).

The debate on deindustrialization forms part of a wider debate on the relative performance of the UK economy in the 1980s. Some observers argue that in the last decade it was at some kind of 'crossroads', and the dimensions of structural change are embedded in broader global processes of internationalization and multilateralism (Harris, 1988). Moreover, it is argued that we cannot explain or understand the structural changes in the UK economy without understanding the global forces that have acted upon it and which UK capitalism has itself helped to shape. Major structural economic change and a wider degree of exposure to the rest of the capitalist economies were features of the 1980s. In the words of Francis Green: 'the British economy in the 1980s is but a small unsheltered inlet on the edge of a turbulent sea' (Green, 1989:3). On the transformation of the British economy, Lash and Urry (1987) offer a contrasting interpretation. They argue that Britain and America amongst other capitalist societies are moving into an era of 'disorganized capitalism'. The increasing scale of industrial and financial corporations. combined with the growth of global market, means that national markets have become less regulated by nationally based corporations, and individual nation-states have less direct control and regulation over large transnational companies. As part of the transformation embodied in 'disorganized capitalism' there is a huge divergence in experience between manufacturing and service sectors. In manufacturing there is a fall in the absolute and relative numbers employed in manufacturing industry and in the significance of this sector for the modern capitalist society. Massey (1988) and Wells (1989) have similarly identified the extreme divergence in experience between UK manufacturing and services. Whatever the academic merits of the debate, to the men and women who were living in the UK in the 1980s the term deindustrialization has real meaning. In concrete terms it means that people experienced redundancy, long-term unemployment, immense upheaval and dislocation, poverty and despair. It also had considerable implications for trade union membership and collective bargaining traditions and practices. High levels of unemployment and structural changes shifted the locus of power in industrial relations: 'workers and their representatives become more tractable in order to preserve jobs; and managements find themselves more able to impose unilateral changes in working practices . . . a shift in the frontier of control'.[2]

During the 1980s we witnessed a fundamental shift in the role played by central government, via general economic management, labour law reform, and in its conception of 'good industrial relations'. The Thatcher government gradually and systematically eroded both the rights of employees and the collective rights of trade unions . The individual employment legislation, or 'floor of rights', established in the 1970s was increasingly viewed by the government as a constraint on enterprise and an obstacle to efficiency and job creation. The Employment Acts of 1980, 1982 and 1988 and Trade Union Act 1984 aimed, on the one hand, to 'deregulate' aspects of individual employment protection and support for collective bargaining and on the other to increase legal regulation of industrial action and trade union government (Lewis, 1986).

In terms of individual employment rights, amendments to the Employment Protection (Consolidation) Act, 1978, reduced unfair dismissal provision. The numbers eligible to apply to the industrial tribunals were reduced by extending the service qualification needed to make an unfair dismissal claim from six months to two years. For those workers who are in good health, not pregnant, and in a secure job, the changes in individual employment rights might seem to be of little consequence. But for those in the enlarged peripheral labour market, primarily female, curtailment of employment protection is not inconsequential and has implications for social security (Szyszczak, 1986).

A concerted ideological campaign against the trade unions by the Thatcher government preceded amendments to collective labour law. There were repeated assertions that the trade unions inhibited economic performance through strikes and restrictive practices, oppressed individual members through undemocratic practices and unrepresentative leadership, and non-members through the operation of the pre- and post-entry closed shop, or were above the law and wielded power which threatened constitutional government. The Government's industrial relations legislation sought to regulate industrial action by, amongst other things, narrowing the definition of a trade dispute in which industrial action is lawful. The phrase 'in contemplation or furtherance of a trade dispute' no longer fulfils the same function as it did prior to the 1982 Employment Act, and as argued: 'It now denies legitimacy to many disputes which are clearly about industrial relations issues' (Simpson, 1986:192). The policy objective of the statutes was designed to deter strikes and limit their scale, and to regulate membership discipline and recruitment policies of unions. According to Hyman, the legislation has marked 'a radical shift from the consensus underlying "public policy" on industrial relations during most of the past century' (1987:93).

According to the Secretary of State for Employment, the Employment Act 1988 seeks to give 'new rights to trade union members', notably protection from 'unjustified' discipline by union members and officials. The Government justified the statute in the belief that in recent years some British trade unions have meted out harsh treatment to thousands of non-striking union members (Gennard et al, 1989). However, the new 'rights' reveal the Government's individualistic conception of trade unionism. It is only a particular type of trade union member who is the beneficiary of these rights: the trade unionist who does not wish to take industrial action, and who wishes to restrain his/her trade union from embarking upon 'unlawful' activity. The purpose of the EA 1988 'rights' is to further discourage industrial action and reduce the likelihood of 'militant' union leadership (McKendrick, 1988). For many years Britain was one of a number of advanced capitalist countries most active in promoting the concept of international standards. During the 1980s, however, the UK played a largely negative role in relation to the improvement of international labour standards (O' Higgins, 1986). Denounced by Margaret Thatcher as 'Marxist interventionism', the Government's opposition to key elements of the European Community's *Social Charter* illustrated the negative role played by Britain in this matter (Buchan, 1989).

During the 1980s, an increasing number of British employers responded to the collapse of the manufacturing job market and a pro-management political climate, by introducing new strategies for conducting industrial relations. The approach to good industrial relations favoured by the 'pluralist school' and the Donovan Commission in the 1970s, that management should work *with* trade unions, implement organizational change through negotiation and agreement, became increasingly open to question (Marchington, 1986). It has often been observed that managers everywhere would prefer to manage without restraint. Thus it is not surprising that, given the new economic and political climate, managers in Britain have attempted to escape from the restrictions of collective bargaining practices in an attempt to create a more malleable workforce subject to greater managerial control, direction and diktat.

Management strategy in industrial relations appears to have been two-pronged. First, employers moved towards both greater centralization and decentralization in their control of industrial relations. Increasingly, strategic decisions are taken at a senior level within the

organization, while collective bargaining takes place quite separately
at a lower level (Kinnie, 1985:23). Such developments are facilitated
by the increasing tendency for firms to bring greater consistency
between their internal profit centres and their pattern of bargaining
units. In the private sector, multi-employer, industry-wide collective
agreements have given way to single-employer bargaining at company
or plant level. As Brown has pointed out:

> Single-employer arrangements have tended to become more for-
> mal, self-reliant and idiosyncratic as firms have developed their
> own particular employment packages and have achieved a better
> matching between their internal bargaining units and their internal
> financial control structures (1986:164)

Throughout the 1980s repeated criticisms of national pay bargaining
by Government ministers fuelled the debate about its appropriate-
ness. Researchers in industrial relations have clarified and chronicled
new developments such as decentralized collective bargaining (Millward and Stevens, 1986) and de-unionization (Clayton, 1989). Two
trends have been identified: a significant decline in the influence of
multi-employer, national agreements, and a shift towards single-
employer bargaining at establishment level and the decentralization
of pay negotiations to the level of business unit, profit centre or
factory (ACAS, 1987; IRRR, 1989a). It was reported by ACAS that:
'Increasingly, it seems, companies are organized into separate budget,
profit and product centres in which unit managers have responsibility
for all operations' (1987:12).

The move towards decentralized pay bargaining has been explained by the growing tendency of capital to devolve corporate
responsibities into separate product and profit centres, and the imperative to secure flexible working arrangements and link pay more
closely to performance (IRRR, 1989b). In multi-divisional companies,
portfolio planning methods also encouraged decentralized decision-
making and the formation of distinctive business units (Purcell and
Ahlstrand, 1989). In contrast to the developments in Britain, there
appears to have been no significant shift towards more decentralized
bargaining for pay in the European Community as a whole (IRRR,
1990). Union derecognition grew in the last decade. In all, fifty cases
of derecognition and four unsuccessful attempts at derecognition
were reported (Claydon, 1989).

In the early eighties there was also considerable discussion of a new generation of 'macho managers' and what was described as a 'managerial offensive' against elements of the pluralist industrial relations system inherited from the 1970s. The simple macho management model is characterized by the following elements: direct attacks on workplace union organization, an aggressive policy using the full power of labour law in the event of industrial action, neglect of workers' interests, and the reassertion of managerial prerogative. Some writers have pointed out that this employers' offensive was assisted by the Government's economic and industrial relations policies (Towers, 1982). An alternative, more subtle, management model plays down the overt attacks on shop stewards, but emphasises the re-assertion of managerial rights and a move to the use of joint consultation (Purcell, 1982). Although some managers have adopted some elements of a macho style, such as greater emphasis on employee 'involvement' in order to 'by-pass traditional negotiating channels', Edwards argues that on balance: 'the present results plainly contradict a macho style in which all these elements are observable' (1987:146).

Second, there is evidence that many organizations have been changing to a more individualistic approach to employee communications and participation. A number of surveys have provided evidence of such a trend within British industry (Batstone, 1984; Millward and Stevens, 1986; Edwards, 1987). One such investigation reported that between 1980 and 1984 there had been a large increase in the proportion of establishments adopting two-way communication between managers and workers, 'the management chain', without going through the medium of union representatives (Millward and Stevens, 1986). A survey by the British Institute of Personnel Management reported that organizations were devoting more resources to employee communication programmes: from an average expenditure of £8 per employee in 1977 to an estimated £15 in 1983. In addition, a growing number of organizations had appointed managers with sole responsibility for employee communications (Townley, 1989).

The eclipse of negotiation by consultation may similarly have been facilitated by the spread of quality circles, team briefing and various 'employee involvement' arrangements associated with the implementation of a 'Human Resource Management' approach (Guest, 1987), and Japanese-style management control strategies (Black and Ackers, 1988). The precise role of quality circles and team briefing has also been called into question. Some observers have argued that these

schemes are designed in order to circumvent workplace union representatives, and therefore reduce the unions' influence. However, it
has been argued that if the development of team briefing schemes did
coincide with a reduction in shopfloor union power, this does not
necessarily prove that this was an express or implicit aim of management (Marchington, 1989).

The strike-weapon is only one, albeit the most publicized, form of
industrial action. Whether it was due to high unemployment, amendments to collective labour law, or a combination of both, is open to
debate, but it is not disputed that the recorded number of industrial
stoppages fell substantially in the 1980s. The 1985 statistic of 903
strikes, for example, was the lowest annual total since 1936, and the
data prompted the Employment Minister, Kenneth Clarke, to pro-
claim that: 'Britain is enjoying its most strike-free year for nearly fifty
years' (Bassett, 1987:9). Parallel with the decline in strike frequency
some commentators perceived attitudinal changes amongst British
workers often expressed by phrases such as 'management beginning
to manage', 'a new sense of realism' (Bright et al, 1983) and 'new
worker'.[3] However, the longevity of this sea-change in worker attitudes, if they ever happened at all, was beginning to be questioned by
the end of the decade following an outbreak of strikes at that time
(Kelly and Richardson, 1989), with commentators warning of a
'summer of discontent' (Leadbeater, 1989).

Another notable development in the 1980s was that employers
were moving towards a more individualist approach to the wage-
effort bargain. A growing number of organizations appear to be
adopting performance appraisal, among both non-manual and manual workers. In one study, 82 per cent of the organizations surveyed
reported using some kind of appraisal scheme (Long, 1986). Employee appraisal has been defined as 'the formal process for collecting
information from and about the staff of an organization' (Randell,
1989:149). Its principal purpose is to improve the workers' performance in their existing job and forms a key component in the 'human
resource management cycle' (Storey, 1989). The rewards from employment appear to be increasingly emphasizing the individual; merit
pay, for instance, is increasingly replacing the traditional practice of
the rate for the job (IRRR, 1984). Also there appears to have been
an increase in the number of organizations offering profit-sharing and
share ownership schemes to their employees (Poole, 1986; Pryce and
Nicholson, 1988).

The flexible utilization of people, a key principle in the Japanese production paradigm, dominated much of management thinking in the 1980s. A whole new vocabulary sprang up around an influential flexibility model developed by Atkinson (1984, 1985), with terms such as 'functional flexibility', 'numerical flexibility', and 'core' and 'peripheral' workers. The reduction of traditional craft demarcation lines, with multi-skilled craftsmen prepared to be deployed on different work-stations as production requirements dictate – such as machine operators undertaking routine maintenance jobs or assembly work – is the feature of functional or task flexibility. Those workers on temporary or part-time employment contracts, sub-contracted workers and the self-employed constitute the numerical flexibility.

These arrangements facilitate 'a looser contractual relationship between manager and worker' (Atkinson, 1985:17), or to put it more bluntly, employers can hire and fire workers as circumstances change. Atkinson's 'flexible firm' model is a variant of the dual labour market approach by making a distinction between 'core' (primary) and 'peripheral' (secondary) groups of workers. The core group are the permanent workers – managers, technicians and skilled manual workers – who receive favourable conditions of employment in return for flexibility and loyalty. The peripheral groups are the workers on 'looser' employment contract, doing semi-skilled or unskilled jobs which can be filled easily from the external local labour markets. Sub-contracting, self-employment, homeworking, jobsharing and temporary employment have increased substantially (Brown, 1986:161). But part-time employment constitutes the largest element of the flexible workforce, covering 16 per cent of all jobs in 1971, to 23 per cent of the working population in 1987 (Hakim, 1987:555). The flexible firm model is controversial. Critics of the model have argued that the notion of core and periphery is confused, circular and value laden, and it fails to mention that the dynamics of the 1980s is undermining the bargaining strength of all workers, including the so-called core (Pollert 1988).

There is evidence to support the widespread impression of significant change in work organization. In manufacturing a number of surveys (Brown, 1981; Daniel and Millward, 1983; Chadwick, 1983; Batstone, 1984; Millward and Stevens, 1986; Edwards, 1987) revealed that the 1980s also saw substantial changes in working practices. Further evidence of change in working arrangements is provided by labour agreements. In the early eighties, it was reported that: 'right across industry agreements are being made that would have been difficult, if not impossible, in a milder economic climate'

(Fryer, 1981). In Britain and the USA a range of labour agreements specified flexibility in working practices, single status (common terms and conditions for all employees) and no-strike provisions (Bassett, 1986; Burrows, 1986; Wickens, 1987; Trevor, 1988). A recent agreement at Vauxhall, the UK subsidiary of General Motors, introduced a package of far-reaching reforms aimed against 'rigidities'. The major points of the labour agreement include: 'team working, with no restrictions on flexibility and mobility of labour; ability to use temporary employees if required to cope with peaks of demand' (*Financial Times*, 6 April, 1990). Cross (1988), reporting the findings of a study of 238 manufacturing establishments between 1981 and 1988, has argued that substantial changes in working practices have been rare. Others have argued that this result is not necessarily at variance with the other surveys, because Cross used a narrower definition of work re-organization. Moreover, his conclusion that radical alterations in job content have been rare is consistent with the widespread presence of 'less thorough-going change' (Edwards and Sisson, 1989).

These are some of the changing contexts and processes that impinged upon workplace industrial relations during the period of the research. As is clear from the above, the extent and interpretation of these changes have attracted widespread debate. Some writers argue that the cumulative effect of the changes has been to create a 'new industrial relations' model (Bassett, 1987). Other industrial relations observers have stressed the slow and uneven nature of the developments in UK industrial relations system and the continuation of some very traditional industrial attitudes (MacInnes, 1987; Kelly and Richardson, 1989).

THE RESEARCH

This book is largely devoted to an analysis of the vivid insights that can be gained from a study of the people directly involved in the labour process. This is especially the case when compared to the more general interpretation and evaluation of data obtained through establishment surveys. The companies investigated were selected following a postal survey of manufacturing establishments in the West Yorkshire area. In total, twelve were approached. In one case it was found that the new technology installed was outside the scope of the study. Of the eleven firms investigated, eight engaged in small-batch production, and three in large-batch. The majority of the establishments employed around 350 employees, although one, a sub-contracting, general engineering firm, employed fewer than twenty.

A three-stage research method was used. The first stage involved consultation with representatives from the Engineering Training Industry Board, and full-time trade union officials. The second stage consisted of a postal survey of 419 establishments. In the third stage, case-studies were carried out based on in-plant structured discussions. Over thirty taped interviews were conducted with managers, shop stewards and workers recently involved in decisions and negotiations over changes in the organization of work. Use was made of both management and shop stewards' committee documents and files. In addition, evidence was obtained by direct observation of the labour process on numerous visits. Preliminary interviews took place in autumn 1985, following the completion of the postal survey. However, the bulk of the empirical data was gathered between January 1987 and June 1988.

The survey provided a general assessment of how new technology affected the nature of work and employment levels. However, given the nature of the research instrument, a postal questionnaire, the results cannot hope to provide an accurate picture of all the subtleties and intricacy of the labour process.

Case studies, on the other hand, provide the following advantages. The source and accuracy of the information can be tested. The 1980 Standard Industrial Classification (SIC) defines industries on many bases, including custom and practice as well as more rational criteria. The West Yorkshire survey was based on mechanical engineering establishments listed under SIC 32. However, as became clear during the visits, the classification includes a wide range of firms from low technology 'metal-bashing' workshops, to high-technology precision engineering establishments. Equally it became clear that the respondents' understanding of terms like 'new technology', even when closely defined in the questionnaire, proved to be different, and visits provided the opportunity to verify the accuracy of the information previously supplied.

Another advantage of case studies is that they provide researchers with the opportunity to observe changes in how the labour process is organized. The questionnaire asked respondents to indicate in qualitative terms, the direction and extent of changes in skills, resulting from new technology. The interpretation of 'large decrease' in skill, evidence of increased flexibility of job tasks, and the erosion of craft demarcation can only be effectively done by interviews with the managers *and* the workers affected. Further, the significance of the way machine tools are grouped on the shopfloor cannot be appreciated by postal surveys. For instance, on one tour of a plant a woman machinist was operating two CNC lathes with the control panel providing program editing facilities blanked out. The machine, unlike the CNC lathe observed elsewhere, allowed no scope for operator intervention apart from stop and go.

Furthermore, information from postal questionnaires tends to be biased because the data are generated from a management source, usually personnel managers. In the survey the respondents were asked to describe changes in the labour process resulting from new technology. Information on the extent of trade union influence on the process of technical change, including benefits, for instance higher payments, were also requested. It became obvious through discussions that union officials' and workers' perception of change and union influence differed from that of their managers.

Data solely emanating from management must be evaluated with a good deal of care. Batstone's post-Thatcherite survey of British workplace industrial relations, for example, is based on information obtained from a small postal survey which he admits to be 'a very blunt instrument' (1984:193). During the entire research period Batstone did not interview the people most affected by the recession, the manual workers. The value of talking to both managers and workers is stressed by Nichols (1986): 'a . . . study which systematically samples both managers and workers is always likely to provide at least some snippets of information that rarely surface in other accounts and to suggest different lines of interpretation' (1986:260).

Extending this point a little further, the industrial relations system is analysed apparently scientifically, but industrial relations theorists, like labour economists, are inclined to adduce personnel managers' opinions to the exclusion of other participants in the labour process. The cyclical validating process is similar to empirical investigations into labour productivity criticized by Nichols (1986:243). When industrial relations theorists undertake studies they are apt to construct their investigation in the light of this received wisdom. The validating process comes full circle when yet other industrial relations theorists make reference to what are essentially managerial, rather than 'workplace' surveys, in order to add credibility to their own analysis (see MacInnes, 1987).

Postal surveys cannot show how changes in the labour process occur: they can only be a 'snapshot' of an organization. Wilkinson adopted a case-study approach, and tells us that 'only longitudinal studies which map developments over time and describe the social processes leading to the establishment of new ways of working can properly explain change' (1983:32). However, Wilkinson's analysis of the social and political processes involved in the introduction of new technology to the shopfloor is based on limited observation of the labour process. In one case, for instance, he acknowledges visiting 'only once' (1983:30). Wilkinson visited twenty-seven firms in a period of about eighteen months. One of his 'major and longitudinal' case-studies lasted less than six months, however (1983:55).

The absence of longevity in Wilkinson's study requires him to be cautious about the workplace processes he is seeking to explore. For instance, in his account of the influence shop stewards and workers have on the process of social and technical change he admits that: '*one must suspect* [my emphasis] that, at least at the level of shopfloor interactions, workers negotiate or "bargain out" detailed working practices' (1983:32). His conclusion is not based on any direct observations of the processes involved. In contrast, the study of Flowpak Engineering was carried out in the February of 1987 and the first few weeks of June 1988. It also involved observing several meetings between management and union representatives to negotiate an agreement on 'outside resources' or sub-contracting work.

The research instrument and methodology explanation of the case studies in this book emerged as a result of the analysis of the survey, further consultation, and informal preliminary interviews with managers and union representatives. The preliminary interviews were important in at least four respects. They helped the formulation of the research questionnaire. Also, they eliminated inappropriate firms – the fabrication or 'metal-bashing' workshops classified under SIC 32, for instance. Moreover, they established scope for access, particularly to shop stewards. Finally, the meeting with a full-time union official enabled the relative strength of different workplace unionization to be identified.

Case studies can represent an in-depth analysis of a real-life organization. But case studies have their limitations. Cases trade off generalizability for richness of detail and depth of data. A second problem is the question of organizational selection bias. It tends to be the 'better-managed', more 'successful' organizations that allow outside researchers to visit and conduct interviewers with managers and

workers. Therefore, the data do not provide a full account of management and labour strategies, because the selection bias operates against
studies in badly-managed organizations or multi-plant companies
rationalizing by plant closure (Batstone, 1984). To illustrate the
point, three firms initially selected for investigation had ceased operation since the postal survey in 1985. As such the case studies may be
examples of relatively 'successful' firms in comparison with others
which have closed down.

STRUCTURE OF THE BOOK

Reference has already been made to 'deskilling', 'division of labour'
and managerial 'control', and 'flexible specialization'. These concepts, which are important in understanding the empirical evidence,
are explained and located within the original text of Braverman and
post-Braverman writers in Chapter 2. The theory of 'flexible specialization' and its relationship to Japanese-style production and labour
management is considered. The chapter also examines two competing schools of thought on the analysis of technological change: the
'labour process' approach, and the 'strategic choice' approach. Chapter 3 outlines the state of British trade unions, and how they have
responded and influenced the process and outcomes of the changes.
Chapter 4 provides empirical evidence of workplace innovations at
twelve factories in West Yorkshire. The objective is to situate the
patterns of change in the engineering labour process within the
traumatic developments in the British economy in the first half of the
1980s. The cases are exemplars of technological and organizational
change, and the findings and analysis prepare the ground for the
more detailed case studies. Chapters 5, 6, and 7 examine three companies
separately. The chapters give the views of some of the men and
women in the labour process: managers, shop stewards and workers,
concerning the process of change in the 1980s. Three dimensions of
work organization are examined: division of labour, labour flexibility, and the scheduling and monitoring of shopfloor operations.
The final chapter seeks to pull together the arguments and findings
and relate them to themes discussed in Chapter 2, and outlines some
of the implications of the findings for managers and workers.

2 Perspectives on Japanization

Japanese and American management is 95 per cent the same and differs in all important respects.

T. Fujisawa, co-founder of Honda Motor Co.

Books such as Schonberger's *Japanese Manufacturing Techniques*, *World Class Manufacturing* and *The Road to Nissan* have captured the attention of British and Northern American managers. Since the early 1980s, the vogue managerial terms are labour 'flexibility' and a battery of 'Japanese' management techniques, including cellular technology (CT), just-in-time (JIT), total quality control (TQC), appraisal, and employee participation. It has been said that flexibility has become a managerial *cause célèbre*.[1] There appears to be a general consensus amongst engineering consultants and some managers that Japanese manufacturing management can be readily implanted into British manufacturing firms. Schonberger (1982) for instance, claims that such management techniques are 'a highly transportable commodity' (1982:1). And, in what is probably one of the most publicized 'models' of Japanese managerial control, Peter Wickens, Director of Personnel at the Sunderland Nissan plant, asserts that 'much that is good about Japanese management practices is transferable, with modification, to a western environment' (1987:38).

The term, 'Japanization' has several meanings: it describes the process of direct investment by Japanese multinationals in the UK, it encapsulates the notion that the British economy is reproducing Japanese forms of economic structure and practices, and it describes the attempts of British and North American managers to emulate Japanese industrial and labour management (Ackroyd et al. (1988).

This book explores the implications of the third process. Some writers have highlighted the problematic nature of the concept of 'Japanization' (Dickens and Savage, 1988), and the fact that many of the manufacturing techniques are not in themselves novel. Many were pioneered in the USSR and Scandinavia over twenty years ago (Graham, 1988). Empirically-based studies looking at the effects of Japanese manufacturing methods and labour-management practices

on the labour process in UK and US companies have been undertaken (Turnbull 1986, 1988; Giles and Starkey, 1988; Smith 1988;
Oliver and Wilkinson, 1988; Black and Ackers, 1988; Hague, 1989;
Jurgens, 1989). There has also been a surge of interest in Japanese
management and organizations amongst North American researchers
(Keys and Miller, 1984). For sociologists and industrial relations
scholars, some of the key issues include: skills, management control
and social relations. What is in contention is the nature of the
interrelationships and the direction of any causal linkages.

A number of researchers have argued that Japanese industrial
management will undoubtedly bring enormous opportunities for
enriching work, enhancing workers' skills and thereby raising the
quality of working life (Abernathy, et al., 1983). Others have made a
less sanguine assessment of the Japanese management paradigm.
They have argued that Japanese production regimes do not lead to
'upskilling' because of flexibility and job rotation, but result in an
intensification of the work process (Turnbull, 1987). Much of the
current debate on Japanization proposing alternative scenarios of
upskilling and deskilling models can be traced back to the question of
the impact of 'new technology' on skills which began to emerge in the
late 1970s.

The considerable current level of interest in Japanese management
concepts raises three important questions. First, why in the 1980s did
so many managers become interested in Japanese-style management
and the apparent enthusiasm for 'Japanization'? The second important question relates to the theory and practice of such management
techniques: what are the characteristics of the Japanese paradigm?
The third important question has to do with theoretical perspectives:
in particular, how have social scientists approached the analysis of
Japanese management concepts; what types of theory have been
used? A similar analytical framework can be identified to that used
for studying the implications of microtechnology.

This chapter attempts to answer these questions associated with
the Japanization thesis, and begins by examining some important
developments that have occurred in the capitalist 'global village' and
have caused many industrialists to reappraise how their manufacturing system is managed. The factors which have been identified as
creating an interest in Japanese management in America, Canada
and the United Kingdom seem equally applicable to explaining
another phenomenon currently receiving considerable attention,
'human resource management' (Storey, 1989). The second section

considers Japanese manufacturing and labour practices, such as cellular technology, just-in-time, total quality control, and personnel policies, and concludes by presenting a theoretical framework within which Japanese management can be analysed and looks at the newer debates on the labour process. In the third section two perspectives on the analysis of technological change are examined. This is important because the transfer of Japanese management concepts into the Yorkshire case studies occurred parallel to investment in new technology. An appreciation of the earlier debates on technological change is considered a necessary prerequisite for understanding the Japanization discourse. In the section below, however, the question is first posed: why the apparent interest in Japanese management?

FACTORS FUELLING THE DIFFUSION OF JAPANIZATION

Although many factors are doubtless responsible for the current academic interest in the Japanese approach to management, four can be identified as important in accounting for the adoption, the 'love affair', of so many North American and European managers with Japanese techniques and philosophy. These four factors are global competition, the limitations of the Taylorist-Fordist production paradigm, the application of new technology requiring a skilled and cooperative workforce, and the apparent success of the Japanese paradigm.

Global Restructuring and Competitive Advantage

Increased global competition stems from two processes which, it is argued, are simultaneously affecting international business. On the one hand, in the 1980s, capital, always agile, was restructuring itself and creating new economic divisions. The European Community was systematically moving towards a single integrated market, abolishing all social, industrial, technological, fiscal and monetary barriers to the movement of capital, commodities and labour by 1992. Similar developments have occurred in North America with the United States–Canada free trade agreement. The document promises to eliminate virtually all remaining tariffs on bilateral trade by the end of the 1990s. This realignment is in part a response to the competitive threat posed by Japan and the other industrialized countries on the Pacific Rim. These developments have created essentially three dominant technological and commercial trading blocs: European, North American, and Japan.

On the other hand, European and North American capital is moving towards an era of 'disorganized capital': the globalization and deregulation of capital and currency markets and a shift from Taylorist to a 'flexible' form of work arrangements (Costello et al., 1989; Lash and Urry, 1987). The intense global competition can be illustrated by the declining fortunes of the motor industry in the UK and the United States. The motor industry in Britain has been the barometer of the manufacturing sector's competitive performance. Between 1970 and 1983, automobile exports shrank by two-thirds, while the percentage of the British automobile market supplied by imports doubled from 27.4 per cent to 57.1 per cent. In 1988, although motor car sales in Britain increased by 10 per cent to a record 2.2 million, sales of British-built motor cars actually fell to 965 883, giving a drop in market share to 43.6 per cent. In the United States in the 1960s, the market was dominated by the US automobile manufacturers, and in 1967 only 9 per cent of all cars sold there were foreign-manufactured. In the 1980s, the situation changed radically, with imported cars accounting for approximately 27 per cent of US sales. Similar changes have occurred in other industries both in the UK and the US. The manufacturers of motorcycles, camera, television and video equipment have virtually disappeared in the face of superior quality Japanese products.

A growing number of managers consider that part of the solution to meeting the challenges of Japanese competitiveness lies in emulating their approach to manufacturing and managing people. Moreover, it is argued that competitive advantage can best be achieved by getting the workforce to contribute their intelligence and skill to the way in which the new microprocessor-based manufacturing technology is operated. According to Abernathy et al.: 'managers have lost touch with the notion that skill in production, not just in marketing or finance, could offer a real competitive advantage' (1983:8).

Limitations of the Taylorist-Fordist Model

In the 1970s, it became fashionable to expose the limitations of the Taylorist-Fordist model of manufacturing with its emphasis on job fragmentation and the transfer of skills to dedicated machinery. The barriers or, as the Japanese call them, wastes, in the Taylorist-Fordist model have been enumerated by Littler and Salaman (1984). They include the coordination and control costs, increasing cooperation costs, economic and technical limits. First, the old Fordist model of manufacturing characterized by mass-production and uniform mass-consumption carry high coordination and control costs. As the work is fragmented and the division of labour is extended, the coordination of physical and human resources becomes problematic. Coordination measures, such as production planning and quality inspection, need to be developed and extended. The cost of these formal structures of control tend to offset productivity gains from the extended division of labour. Second, the 'direct control' strategy associated with the Fordist model generates cooperation costs. If workers have only an instrumental approach to their work, then the price of worker compliance is increased when there is an upturn in economic activity and labour markets are tight. Moreover, the contractual core of Fordism – higher earnings in exchange for direct managerial control – is not cost-effective in product markets where non-standard, high quality products are demanded; such non-price factors place a greater emphasis on utilizing workers' problem-solving, cooperative skills. Third, Fordist techniques have economic limits; the fragmentation of tasks depends on the velocity of throughput. Finally, there are technical limits. Job fragmentation can be reduced to certain fundamental operations beyond which it must wait upon a transformation of physical technology. In the early 1970s, these and other factors led to the emergence of innovatory job designs associated with the Quality of Working Life (QWL) movement (see Littler and Salaman, 1984:74-80).

Application of Microtechnology

In the 1980s, microprocessor-based technologies began to influence every facet of organizational life, from the corporation office to the factory floor. At corporate level, microtechnology has spawned sophisticated computerized manufacturing systems with its own plethora of acronyms: DRP (Distribution Resource Planning), MRP II (Manufacturing Resource Planning), CIM (Computer Integrated Manufacturing), OPT (Optimized Production Technology) and so on. The objective is to match a more customer-driven business to the supplier-manufacturing side of the operation (see Leadbeater, *Financial Times*, 13 December 1989). On the factory floor, CAD (Computer Aided Design), CNC (Computer Numerically Controlled) machine tools, CAM (Computer Aided Manufacturing), and CAT (Computer

Aided Testing) are fast becoming the norm in modern manufacturing companies. To achieve the optimal utilization of the new technology further requires managerial and organizational innovations.

Models of Excellence

The current fashion for Japanese industrial management is also related to the stereotyped Japanese company portrayed by 'pop-management' publications, for example, *The Art of Japanese Management*, Pascale and Athos (1986), and *World Class Manufacturing*, Schonberger (1986). In Britain, it has been widely accepted that poor management was one important factor in the relative decline in the country's manufacturing performance. In the 1950s and 1960s comparisons were frequently made with North American industrial management theory and techniques. In the 1970s, parallel with the debate on industrial democracy and 'participative management', comparisons were often made with West German-style management. Today, there is a natural tendency among British and North American managers to look to the new-found competitiveness of the Japanese to explain the decline in the market position of their own businesses. Increasingly, attention has focused upon the 'obvious success of Japanese companies' (Richard Marsh, in Wickens, 1987:x). According to Sir Peter Parker: 'The message is not that only Japanese management is supreme; it is that success in enterprise depends on management above all, and what matters is . . . that it is excellent' (Introduction in Pascale and Athos, 1986:xiii). It is the competitiveness of such companies as Hitachi, Matsushita, Nissan, Sanyo, Toyota and others that has intrigued British and North American industrial managers, and compelled them to look to Japanese management practices as a role model and catalyst which would cause a resurgence of innovation and renewal (Gordon, 1988).

These and other factors seem to be behind the growing interest in Japanese management. The section below examines the main pillars of Japanese manufacturing management and the implications for workers.

THE JAPANESE PARADIGM

Japanese Manufacturing Techniques

The Japanese approach to manufacturing has three indivisible and interdependent elements: flexibility, quality and minimum waste. We shall examine each of these elements of the Japanese manufacturing paradigm.

Flexibility is attained in two ways: by arranging machinery in a group or 'cell', and by the use of a flexible multiskilled workforce. In conventional European and North American small-batch production, the machine tools in the factory are organized according to a machining process or function; for example, all the milling machines (which produce flat surfaces on metal) are grouped in one area of the factory. The functional machining configurations in larger workshops act as 'cost centres'. High variety and low volume production means that succeeding batches require different machining operations in different workstations in the factory. The components follow an erratic course, in a stop-go fashion; they spend time on pallets, in the stockroom, and sometimes they even get lost. The concept of cellular manufacturing, which derives originally from the Soviet Union (Graham, 1988), involves grouping together a configuration of machine tools for the production of a 'family' of similar components, rather than by function. All operations on a given component are performed in a U-shaped line or cell which reduces work-in-progress and increases the throughput of work by simplifying the flow. A cellular work structure forms new work groups. The specialized skilled machinist operating one machine tool, in one particular work station, is replaced by a generalized skilled machinist with flexible job boundaries. In small-batch environments, skilled flexible machinists operate all the machines in the cell, plan work within production parameters, and can undertake simple maintenance tasks. Cellular manufacturing deliberately seeks to demolish craft demarcation. According to Schonberger (1982), the cellular system of production has a number of advantages. First, functional and numerical flexibility: 'when volume is low, one person can operate *all* [my emphasis] machines . . . when demand picks up, add more labour'. Thus, the cell system increases worker adaptability and enables the work group to cope with fluctuating demand or deal with the absence of any of its members. Second, cellular manufacturing encourages cooperation

amongst the group, it 'forces problem-solving and quality improvements'. Third, the cellular layout improves quality control because
responsibility for substandard work is more easily identified as 'ownership' of a product. As a result of self-inspection by the operatives,
'rework should go to the original maker so that the maker cannot
evade responsibility for product quality' (Schonberger, 1982:66). Put
more simply, if a component is substandard the feedback from
another team member in the cell or the next cell is immediate.

At Nissan Motor Manufacturing (UK) Ltd flexibility means 'expanding all jobs as much as possible and by developing the capabilities of all employees to the greatest extent compatible with efficiency
and effectiveness' (Wickens, 1987:44). To achieve maximum functional flexibility the company has a minimum number of job titles. At
Nissan all manual tasks within the car plant are covered by just two
job titles, 'Manufacturing Staff' and 'Technicians'. In contrast, until
its 1985/6 negotiations, Ford (UK) had 516 different manual worker
job titles. A number of cells can be situated within the same plant,
but the cells are semi-autonomous, operating as 'mini-factories' with
an internal market, subcontracting or 'buying' work from other cells
within the same factory.

The goal of **minimum waste** is achieved by the second key element
of Japanese production management, just-in-time (JIT). Just-in-time
can be considered a concomitant of cellular production. In narrow
engineering terms, just-in-time refers to a system of organizing the
production system and buyer–supplier relations between firms. Just-
in-time is a hand-to-mouth mode of manufacture which aims to
produce the necessary products in the necessary quantities, of the
necessary quality, at the necessary time. Schonberger describes the
principles of JIT as following:

> Produce and deliver finished goods just in time to be sold, sub-
> assemblies just in time to be assembled into finished goods, fabri-
> cated parts just in time to go into subassemblies, and purchased
> materials just in time to be transformed into fabricated parts.
> (1982:16)

It is a system in which stocks of components and raw materials are
kept to an absolute minimum; they are delivered in a matter of days
or even hours before use in the production process.

There are a number of accounts as to the origins of the JIT
practice. One popular account claims that JIT was introduced into

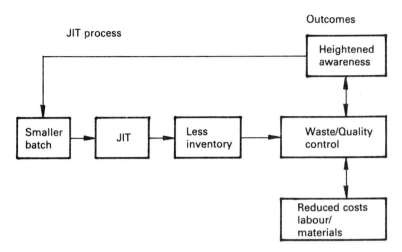

FIGURE 2.1   The JIT production process
Source: Adapted from R. Schonberger (1982).

Toyota after Mr Toyota visited a supermarket in the United States in 1937. Apparently, he observed how the supermarket was restocking the shelves just after customers bought the goods; they rang up and the supplier sent in new stocks. Toyota applied the principle in a manufacturing organization. Schonberger (1982) suggests that just-in-time came into wide use in the Japanese shipbuilding industry in the 1960s. For JIT production to operate effectively it is necessary that a number of conditions prevail: a relatively simple workflow, typically achieved by a cellular configuration (Burbidge, 1982); fast machine set-up times and total quality control (Schonberger, 1982). The JIT process and its outcomes is shown graphically in Figure 2.1.

The process is set in motion by batch-size reductions. The initial direct benefit is less inventory to store and control. In Schonberger's view more important are the waste and quality improvements that are likely to occur when batch sizes are reduced. A further outcome of JIT production is heightened awareness of defects or production problems. When components are produced in small quantities, just in time, any defects are discovered quickly and production of large batches of substandard work is avoided. According to Schonberger (1982), under JIT, when a substandard component is produced, the operator 'will probably not find it hard to guess what he [sic] did wrong . . . the worker's awareness of defect causation is heightened' (1982:27). By reducing stocks, warehouse costs (rent and wages) and interest, costs on variable capital are reduced releasing capital to be used elsewhere in the organization.

The Scottish Development Agency (SDA) calculates typical 23 per cent savings based mainly on transfer of inspection procedures from the customer to the supplier in return for a small increase in the unit purchase price.[2] Thus the benefits of JIT production depend not only on minimizing work-in-progress and stocks, but also on the transfer of quality control inspection from the customer to the supplier. In engineering journals, JIT is frequently described as simply an extension of existing production planning techniques referred to as Material Requirements Planning II (MRP). It is, however, far more than this. Just-in-time and its possible concomitant, cellular production, is a manufacturing system which deliberately seeks to break down craft cultures by eliminating craft boundaries, thereby augmenting managerial control over the labour process. It aims to modify and reshape the behaviour of work group members by fostering self-discipline and cooperation. With small JIT batches, it is argued, the need to avoid errors is apparent and this 'improves workers' feelings of responsibility' (Schonberger, 1982:28–9). Moreover, peer group pressures, such as withholding praise or reprimands, can correct deviant behaviour. A more critical interpretation of the effects of JIT on workers has been posited by Sayer (1986). The outcomes of JIT on the social organization of work, inter alia skills and management–labour relations are considered later in this chapter.

Quality control is the third key element of the Japanese manufacturing system. According to Wickens, 'Everything you hear about the Japanese attitude to quality is true. Commitment to zero defect product is absolute' (1987:61). The pursuit of 'zero defect' is through a manufacturing strategy referred to as 'Total Quality Control' (TQC). The basic concept of TQC, which can be traced to an American, J.M. Juran, in the 1950s, is 'production responsibility' which means assigning the primary responsibility for quality to the people at the 'sharp end' of production. If substandard work is produced, it is detected and corrected at the source, that is, where the defect arises.

In contrast to the principle of 'quality at source', in Britain and North America the inspection process is separate and performed by quality inspectors by statistical sampling *after* the batch has already been produced. In Japan, the T in TQC stands for 'total', which means *total process control*; every process is controlled by monitoring the quality during production. When quality control is at the point of production 'fast feedback on defects is natural'. In addition, with TQC there are savings on labour and raw materials: 'fewer rework labour hours' and 'less material waste' (Schonberger, 1982:36–7). There are two closely related goals of TQC: to inculcate the habit of quality and quality improvement, and quite simply to achieve perfection. Schonberger's view is that total quality control is a 'fundamental production function' and 'production, not quality control, must have primary responsibility for quality' (1982). Similarly, Imai (1986) maintains that *kaizen*, meaning improvement, is the single most important concept in Japanese management. In terms of quality control, employees 'kaizen-conscious build the discipline to achieve kaizen in their work' Imai, 1986:44). Total quality control may stand alone or may operate in tandem with cellular and just-in-time production.

Japanese People-Management

The one aspect of Japanese management philosophy that has most captured the attention of British and North American managers is the way the Japanese manage their 'human resources'. The Japanese approach to people-management has five unique characteristics: selection and development, lifetime employment contract, seniority-based rewards, consensus decision-making, and enterprise unions. These five core themes are summarized in Figure 2.2. This section

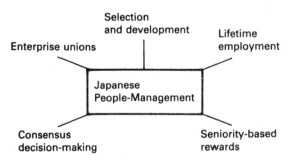

FIGURE 2.2   Core themes of the Japanese approach to people-management

will look briefly at each of these core themes of Japanese people-management.

The Japanese company aims to select people who will develop a long-term commitment to the organization. The rationale behind this approach to recruitment and selection is the assumption that committed long-term 'core' employees will be more satisfied, more flexible and more productive. Mowday et al. (1982) have defined 'commitment' in terms of attitudinal commitment, that is, 'the relative strength of an individual's identification with and involvement in a particular organization' (quoted in Guest, 1987:513). The Japanese company seeks to recruit individuals who will fit into the corporate culture, endorse the company's philosophy and values, and have company and job commitment. The theoretical proposition is that company commitment, together with job commitment, will lead to enhanced job satisfaction and performance, longer tenure and an acceptance of change (Guest, 1987:51).

The recruitment process is designed to obtain from individuals high company commitment. This is achieved in a number of ways. The overwhelming majority of employees are recruited direct from college. Resigning from a company is considered to be disloyal to the first company and therefore individuals who have been employed at another organization are generally regarded with suspicion by a new employer (Wickens, 1987). The screening process eliminates candidates possessing certain disqualifiers: 'inability to get along with others' or 'radical views'. The aim is to sustain a corporate culture where 'shared understandings act as a great facilitator in getting things done' (Pascale and Athos, 1986). Japanese training and development tend to be organization and task-centred, rather than, as in the UK, individual and career-centred (Trevor, 1983). Further, training goes beyond improving the competence of its employees' task related skills. It develops a combination of physical, cognitive and behavioural skills in order to increase performance and commitment to the organization's values and goals. According to Pascale and Athos, each new recruit at Matsushita is indoctrinated with the '"Matsushita way" from which little deviance is tolerated' (1986:52).

The Japanese notion of a 'lifetime employment' has received considerable attention in management literature. The origins of lifetime employment can be traced back to the incorporation of the *oyakata* (subcontractor) into giant corporations in the late nineteenth and early twentieth century (Littler, 1982). It is argued that lifetime employment engenders a high degree of commitment and loyalty; the sense of 'all being together in the same boat' (Kono, 1984:329), reduces labour mobility between organizations, and a willingness on the part of management to invest substantially in training in order to develop a highly skilled and flexible worker (Pascale and Athos, 1986). While this pillar of Japanese people-management may result in a number of these outcomes, what is crucial to realize is that the institution of lifetime employment is heavily qualified. In fact, only around one-third of the Japanese working population work for organizations offering lifetime employment. The arrangement is made viable by the large 'blue-chip' companies surrounding themselves with 'rings of defence' in the form of temporary, part-time and sub-contract 'peripheral' workers (Littler, 1982). In addition, even in the large most prestigious companies lifetime employees are expected to retire at the age of 55 and then often start work in another organization to 'make ends meet' (Wickens, 1987). Further, the institution of lifetime employment in Japan does not apply to women. Women generally form part of the peripheral workforce performing low-level jobs until they leave the workforce on marriage, since 'married women will devote themselves to the family' (Kono, 1984:319). Finally, lifetime employment is not a contractual or legal obligation, but rather 'a way of thinking on both sides'; neither does it mean that the number of employees cannot be reduced. A reduction in overtime, suspension of new recruiting, and voluntary early retirement are some of the methods used to cope with a fall in demand for labour-hours (Kono, 1984:319).

Another basic feature of the modern Japanese company is the seniority-based reward system. The *nenko joretsu* reward system means essentially that length of service and age play a more dominant role in determining salary than job performance and competence (Littler, 1982). It has been suggested that the *nenko joretsu* wage system serves to attract quality people to the organization, avoids internal competition, and encourages longer tenure (Littler, 1982). New graduate management trainees tend to move through the organization as a group, and it is not expected that younger employees will be promoted to senior positions to those occupied by older managers. A Japanese worker is inclined to feel uncomfortable if he/she is promoted more rapidly than his/her peer group. Not infrequently, this can result in individuals declining early promotion (Wicken, 1987).

Another key pillar of the Japanese approach to management is consensus decision-making. Japanese consensus can operate on a formal and informal basis (Wickens, 1987). The consensus approach involves multiple inputs and viewpoints from individual employees and work groups to ensure that decisions are made in the best interests of the company as a whole rather than in the self of any particular manager or group (Ouchi, 1981; Pascale and Athos, 1986). The consensus, or *ringisei* approach, aims to generate greater awareness and understanding of the problem(s)/issue(s), acceptance and total commitment to implementing decisions once they have been made (Wickens, 1987). The Japanese manufacturing practice of integrated work teams facilitates a high incidence of face-to-face communication in the Japanese organization.

A further defining characteristic of Japanese labour management is the *kigyobetsu-kumiai*, the enterprise union. In contrast to Britain's craft-based, industrial, general unions; West Germany's industrial unions; Canada's 'international' unions, and the United States' national unions, Japan's trade unions are not organized by occupation or by job, but by company. An enterprise union consists solely of regular employees of a single firm, regardless of their occupation, manual or non-manual. In 1975, 91.1 per cent of private sector union members belonged to enterprise unions (Okubayashi, 1989). Workers who have been promoted to supervisory or managerial positions have often previously been union leaders (Kuwahara, 1987). A worker leaving the company would automatically forfeit union membership. The presence of a company union is strongly associated with organizational size; in 1983 approximately 85 per cent of company union members worked in firms which employed more than 100 employees (Kuwahara, 1987). Company unions developed only after the suppression of independent trade unions in Japan (Littler, 1982; Morishima, 1982; Kuwahara, 1987). The enterprise union is the negotiating unit, and the union negotiators can concentrate on the situation in each firm, rather than any broader craft or national issue. However, it is argued that enterprise unions tend to develop 'company consciousness' rather than 'union consciousness' which weakens their ability to defend the interests of their members (Whitehill and Takezawa, 1978; Kuwahara, 1987). Full-time union officials are often company employees, seconded by the company to the union (Wickens,1987). It has been suggested that where Japanese companies have recognized trade unions *outside* Japan, they have insisted upon single union representation, often accompanied by agreements which include 'no-strike' clauses, and have explicitly given the union a collaborative, rather than an adversarial role (Bassett, 1987; Oliver and Wilkinson, 1988).

This section has aimed first, to identify the main components of Japanese manufacturing and labour management, and second to illustrate that the stereotype Japanese-style management idealized by Western managers is a sanitized version of reality. There is prima-facie evidence that significant numbers of British and North American business organizations are adopting variants, either 'hard' or 'soft', 'strategic' or 'operational', of the Japanese approach to the management of the employment relationship (Legge, 1989; Storey, 1989). The so-called human resource management approach with its 'unitary' frame of reference (Guest, 1987), signals a departure from the British 'pluralist' or Donovan labour relations orthodoxy (Storey, 1989). The following section draws together the diverse set of Japanese production and personnel practices to build a theoretical framework for examining the concept of Japanization.

A Model of Japanese Management

Our model of Japanese management is based principally on two recent contributions to the debate on Japanese-style management: Oliver and Wilkinson's (1988) theory of 'high dependency relationships' and Guest's theory of human resource management. As the model in Figure 2.3 graphically depicts, there are six major components: a set of manufacturing techniques; a set of dependency relationships; a set of human resource management policies; a set of supplier policies; a managerial ideology, and a series of outcomes or goals. We shall explore the main dimensions of the model – it may be more accurate to describe them as stereotypes – and assess the implications for managers and workers.

The set of manufacturing techniques are cellular technology (CT), just-in-time (JIT), and total quality control (TQC). The principles of these production methods have already been discussed. The outcomes or goals of the Japanese production system are: flexibility both in term of workforce skills and tasks, and product differentiation, minimum waste, and minimum quality defects as they arise in production. The realization of these goals is not dependent on advanced technology; most observers of Japanese industry conclude that the Japanese 'competitive edge' is based on levels of technology no different from those available to British industry (Jurgens, 1989; *Production Engineer*, September, 1987).

It has been suggested that Japanese manufacturing processes create a complex web of high dependency relations which requires greater interaction and increased coordination (Oliver and Wilkinson, 1988).

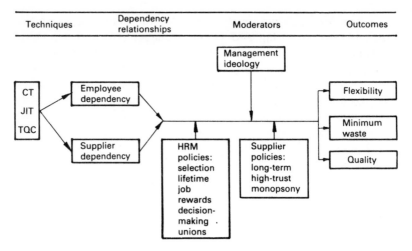

FIGURE 2.3   A model of Japanese industrial management

This is an important point and requires further consideration.

Cellular work structures create two problems. First, the more non-routine the tasks performed by the work team, the more processing of information is required and the greater the problem of coordination. Second, integrated work teams present a problem of 'substitutability'. Workers who are multiskilled, flexible and committed are not easily replaced. Therefore, the model implies a low level of substitutability and heightened dependency. Further, a system functioning on low or zero inventory is much more vulnerable to either 'sequential interdependence' – one cell depends on another for its input, but the dependency is only one way – or/and 'reciprocal interdependency' – where cells exchange inputs and outputs. The chain-effect of a failure of supply at any one point will quickly ripple through the whole manufacturing process. Hence, the importance of reliable machinery, in-process planning and controls, suppliers delivering on time, and orderly and stable labour relations. As Oliver and Wilkinson point out:

> A mere work-to-rule or overtime ban could be as disastrous for a company operating a JIT system as could a strike for a company not doing so. (1989:135).

The principle of total-quality-control (TQC) also heightens dependency. If the safety net of the safety inspectors is removed the organization is relying on its workforce to perform their quality control tasks conscientiously and correctly. Thus, total-quality-control offers the work group additional opportunities to cause disruption, whether it is by accident or design. In sum, the Japanese manufacturing paradigm heightens the dependency of the organization on its key agents, especially its workforce and supplier companies.

What control mechanisms are available for managing intercell and supplier relations? There are a number of options: formal rules and procedures, hierarchy, sophisticated computerized production planning. According to Oliver and Wilkinson, the organization must develop mechanisms that exert sufficient influence over its constituents in order to prevent them exploiting the organization's dependency: 'It is imperative that such organizations take steps to counterbalance this by averting the possibility of such power being used' (Oliver and Wilkinson, 1988:39).

The concept of dependency can be linked to the earlier labour process debate. For example, Blauner (1964) argued that highly automated production systems augmented worker autonomy and control, and therefore dependency. Similarly, Andrew Friedman's (1977) concept of 'responsible autonomy' implies a heightened dependence of the organization on its workforce, a reduced dependence on capital's agents of control, supervisors and middle managers. There is, Oliver and Wilkinson argue, a logic similar to 'mutually assured destruction': 'The high dependencies of the companies on their constituents appear to be balanced by an equally profound set of dependencies of the constituents on their organization' (1988:40).

Implicit in the Japanese model is the need to control the workforce, to avoid or obviate the need for trade unions and counterbalance the dependency on workers. There is another dimension to the Japanese model. In addition to a comprehensive corporate marketing, manufacturing and labour strategy, an ideological process pervades the Japanese labour process. The employment contract goes beyond 'a fair day's work for a fair day's pay' to mutual commitment and identification with the company's philosophy and values, and this tends to sit rather uncomfortably in a Western corporate culture. Advocates of the Japanese paradigm see loyalty and commitment as desirable and morally acceptable on the grounds that in the long-term everybody benefits. However, critics view Japanese management, especially managerial ideology, as instrumental, an insidious control strategy intended to carefully inculcate attitudes of cooperativeness. (Wood, 1986; Thompson, 1989).

Figure 2.3 depicts a further dimension to the Japanese model, a set of supplier policies. These are essential prerequisites because the success of just-in-time production is dependent on stability not only in the organization using JIT, but also in its suppliers. Supplier–buyer relationships are characterized by *long-term* commitment, a high-trust relationship, and monopsony. A unique set of supplier–buyer policies generates a reciprocal obligation between the core organization and supplier, together with a strong sense of obligation to assist each other and protect the other's interests, for example financial assistance for capital equipment. Further, the policies create an heightened dependency of the supplier on the core organization by the creation of a monopsony (single buyer) situation. In terms of supplier–buyer relations, goal homogeneity may also be achieved through interlocking directorships (Oliver and Wilkinson, 1988).

Some may question the model of Japanese management: is it a theory or a helpful way to organize a complex reality? In my view, the model is a useful framework for organizing the complexities of management practice and can be judged by its usefulness in identifying key aspects of management innovations. It is best conceptualized as an 'ideal-type' towards which Western organizations can move. It does not necessarily follow that all components of the model must, or can, be applied to every type of labour process. For instance, an organization may introduce cellular work structures without adopting the principle of just-in-time, and vice versa. And organizations may adopt Japanese production practices and choose to ignore Japanese-style personnel policies. Obviously, in such situations the dependency relationships, the moderators, and the outcomes will differ from those depicted in the model. Indeed, there is prima-facie evidence that transfer of Japanese industrial management into British and North American organizations has been highly selective (Jurgens, 1989), and many British firms do not fully appreciate the high dependency relationships implicit in the Japanese manufacturing model, and generally have failed to synchronize their personnel and labour relations carefully to manufacturing strategy (Oliver and Wilkinson (1988).

Finally, as many industrial relations scholars have noted, a mature capitalist society is a highly complex and dynamic arrangement of differentiated groups and cultures, attitudes and expectations, and institutional traditions and relationships. Consequently, any specific social phenomenon, such as 'Japanese management', cannot and should not be considered in isolation from its wider context. Management innovations and the relationships and outcomes depicted in the model will therefore be affected and constrained by economic, marketing and legal considerations and the social environment.

Japanization: Implications for Workers?

In terms of the possible implications of Japanization for workers, a number of conflicting outcomes have been posited to result from it. One theory extends the concept of 'flexibility' in the JIT system to develop what is referred to as the 'flexible specialization' thesis. This theory is associated with the work of Piore and Sabel (1984) *The Second Industrial Divide* and to a lesser extent that of Abernathy et al. (1983) *Industrial Renaissance*. It is suggested that Japanese production methods reunite conceptual and manual tasks and therefore are largely progressive in their implications for workers. According to Piore and Sabel, Japanese work arrangements exemplify 'the re-emergence of the craft paradigm amidst the crisis' (1984:205–8). After observing Japanese production methods first-hand, William Abernathy et al. (1983) arrived at conclusions similar to those of Piore and Sabel. They maintain that Japanese production methods have changed in a fundamental way the terms on which global competition must be carried out. In a manner similar to Piore and Sabel they argue: 'The imperatives of quality and productivity . . . are impossible to satisfy without the active, loyal, and committed participation of a well-trained and constantly improving workforce.' (1983:90)

They go on to argue that the Fordist model of production based on progressive deskilling was as a 'patent medicine . . . pure snake oil' (1983:91). It is argued that given heterogeneous, changeable and cyclical patterns in product markets the supreme challenge facing management and its solution lie in the flexibility and adaptability of labour, both at the point of production and in the market place. In other words, the flexible specialization paradigm is a reversal of the old Fordist paradigm and of the labour process theory (Thompson, 1989). The critique of the old Fordist mass production, mass consumption model has led to a much broader political discourse on 'post-Fordism' to explain where 'post-industrial' economies are, or should be, progressing, and what political (Left) strategies are most appropriate for a 'post-industrial' society (see Hall and Jacques, *New Times*, 1989).

However, the interpretation of the flexible specialization–Japanization paradigm, as one would expect, has its critics. Sayer developed a critical analysis of just-in-time production. He argues that the JIT system and its possible concomitants is designed to find new ways of extracting surplus value through 'elimination of idle time . . . plus the internalization of disciplinary pressure within work groups or production teams increases the intensity of work and associated stress' (1986:66). Like Sayer, Turnbull (1986, 1987) argues that the overall effects of the changes in manufacturing 'à la Japanese style' at the British Lucas Electrical plant was to 'reduce set-up time . . . thereby increasing the pressures of work and intensifying the production process' (1986:200). Tomaney also takes a less sanguine assessment of flexible specialization. He maintains that although the new forms of work organization can involve some 'requalification' on the part of workers this is 'often at the cost of intensification of the work process' (1990:43). Hyman offers a critical analysis of the flexible specialization thesis which at its most visionary, it is argued, promises 'a utopia where managements co-operate harmoniously with a polyvalent workforce' (1988:50). The danger of flexible work organization with 'core' and 'peripheral' work groups is that it undermines, rather than enhances, the position of labour market: 'flexibility entails intensified segmentation within the workforce, between the relatively sheltered and advantaged, and the vulnerable and oppressed' (1988:56).

Further, it has been argued that with the flexible specialization model a whole set of associations are assumed and not explored (Wood, 1989). The notion of the 'flexible workforce' is not a radically new phenomenon; the unskilled in British manufacturing have always tended to be subject to 'functional' flexibility (Nichols, 1986). Moreover, human flexibility is the defining characteristic of labour power and 'craft flexibility', 'flexible rostering', 'continental rota' and 'casualization' have been a feature of productivity bargaining and secondary labour markets since the 1960s (Young, 1986; Towers, 1987; Pollert, 1988). Finally, it has been argued that the flexibility–Japanization discourse is a well-worn route reproducing the 'same old romance of automation' (Thompson, 1989). Moreover, the flexible specialization paradigm repeats some of the mistakes made by earlier contributors to the labour process debate: unproblematic readings of skill; over-rationalistic conceptions of management strategy; and the failure to recognize that no qualitative change has been made in the organization of the capitalist labour process. Although the changes in the organization of work can be interpreted as 'a form of flexible Taylorism', Japanese manufacturing practices attempt to offer the capitalist labour process 'new' solutions on the back of the old (Thompson, 1989:228–9).

PERSPECTIVES ON TECHNOLOGICAL CHANGE

The aim of this section is to examine how various theorists have analysed technological change and in this the concepts such as 'skill' and 'control' are highly problematic but central to this debate. There are essentially three schools of thought on technological change. The first seeks to analyse technology as an independent explanatory variable. The 'contingency' theory, based on the work of Joan Woodward, argued that technology is a contingent factor exercising a primary influence on organizational structure and human behaviour. The second seeks to explain technological change in terms of the class-based conflict between capital and labour. Management introduces new technology as a means to control labour, this being facilitated by the long-term tendency of technology to deskill the workforce. This perspective is known as 'labour process' theory. The third school emphasizes the concept of 'strategic choice'. Whilst acknowledging that new technology has the potential to deskill, it questions whether under contemporary capitalist relations of production it must necessarily occur. It stresses that the technology and labour process interface is complex. This approach suggests that work patterns and skills are not determined by new technology *per se*, but by the outcome of social choice and negotiation. The focus in this chapter is on the labour process and the strategic choice theories.

Technology and Employee Skills

An operational definition of technology and skill is a critical issue in assessing the interrelations between technology, social relation and patterns of work. When social scientists use the term technology, they could be referring to either a physical device (e.g. a word processor or a CNC lathe), a technique or human skill (e.g. computer programming), a social arrangement (e.g. a factory; work teams), or some combination, or all of these. The research by Joan Woodward et al. (1970), for example, has shown that standard definitions of technology are problematic. Woodward defined technology as: 'The collection of plant, machines, tools and recipes available at a given time for the execution of the production task.' (1970:4)

This definition straddles a physical device and technique, 'recipes' (Buchanan and Huczynski 1985). Alan Fox makes a distinction between 'material' technology, that is the technology that can be 'seen, touched and heard', and 'social' technology, which 'seeks to order the behaviour and relationships of people' (1985:13). Material technology is the physical device and social technology is the social arrangement and includes authority relationships and reward systems. Eric Batstone et al. used a restrictive definition of technology; technology was defined 'less sociologically' in terms of 'physical pieces of machinery' (Batstone et al., 1987:2). However, to define technology so 'tightly' neglects the effects on the labour process caused by changes in the social organization of manufacturing over the last decade; in particular, by flexible specialization and the just-in-time system of production developed by Japanese capital.

The concept of technological change is rooted in the debates on automation (Sadler, 1980). However, given the heterogeneous nature of 'new technology', there is perhaps a need for a new standard operational definition (Sorge and Streeck, 1988). A better definition of technology has been proposed by Bell (1973) and quoted in Heller: 'the use of scientific knowledge to specify ways of doing things in a reproducible manner' (1987:19). Arising from this notion of technology, there is a social technology which would relate to the way systems are organized, e.g. cellular work configuration, and there is also a machine technology which would include process applications, e.g. CNC machines. In using the term 'technology' to cover social and machine technology, the problem of choice and substitution immediately become problematic (Heller, 1987). What is apparent is that the term technology is used with such a variety of meanings that it has become ambiguous. For the purpose of this study, technology is defined in terms of physical machinery, such as Computer-Aided-Design (CAD), Computer Numerically Controlled (CNC) machine tools, Computer-Aided-Manufacturing (CAM), and the social organization of work, which takes such forms as cellular work teams, just-in-time, communications, disciplinary rules, and payment systems.

The term 'skill' is not easy to define. Skills include such diverse activities as rock-climbing, driving, typing, and operating a CNC machine tool. Psychology literature has suggested that skills are inherent in an individual. The focus is on the learning of skills, that is, behaviours, through training, in which goal accomplishment is dependent upon the level of declarative knowledge (knowledge *about* a task) and procedural knowledge (knowledge of *how to do* a task) needed to perform satisfactorily (see Gattiker, 1990, for a brief review of the literature). Sociological analysis concentrates on the organization or job and suggests that skill is a multidimensional concept involving complex mental, interpersonal and manipulative tasks; discretion; and social factors. According to Beechey (1983), there are three aspects of skill: '(1) Skill can refer to complex competencies which are developed within a particular set of social relations of production and are objective competencies; (2) skill can refer to control over the labour process, and (3) skill can refer to conventional definitions of occupational status' (1983:63–4). More recently, a two-dimensional model of skill which combines technical complexity and discretion has been constructed (Rolfe, 1990). Further, writers have suggested that skill can be seen as a function of union strategies of 'social exclusion' in the workplace which succeed in enhancing the relative strengths of key employee groups (Beechey, 1983; Penn, 1983). The thesis in this book is that skill levels will be determined by changes in technical competencies and autonomy.

A key issue for sociologists and industrial relations theorists is to what extent CNC technology is being used to subordinate workers by decreasing the level of skill. Skill is important because it serves to maintain workers' control over the labour process (Burns, et al., 1983; Thompson, 1983). However, while skill may affect control, control is not always synonymous with skill. Unskilled workers may exert considerable control over some labour processes (Friedman, 1977; Nicols and Beynon, 1977). The study of the interrelationship between technological change and skill levels in the engineering labour process has centred around the stages in the metal-cutting process that still require human intervention. There are five stages: the generation of a set of instructions for the component to be machined, the program; the setting up of the CNC machine, which involves setting tools and attaching jigs; the varifying and editing of the program; the loading and unloading of the component, and making adjustments, such as speeds and feeds, to the CNC machine during the cutting process. The generation and distribution of skills will largely depend upon whether or not these five activities are combined or fragmented. In particular, whether engineering craft workers' skills are 'destroyed' or enhanced will, it is argued, depend upon operator access to program generation and editing functions.

The Labour Process Perspective

The concepts such as division of labour, deskilling and hierarchical control used by labour process theorists can be traced back to Marx's writings on machinery and the factory in *Capital*, Volume 1. Braverman (1974) revived Marx's theory of the labour process and applied it to twentieth century monopoly capitalism with its new forms of technology and structures of work organizations. Braverman is concerned to analyse the 'historical evolution which produced modern social forms' (1974:17), resulting from interface of capitalist priorities and the technology the system generates.

Braverman emphasizes three aspects of the labour process in a period of monopoly capitalism which stem from Marx's classic model. First, the necessity for workers to sell neither themselves nor labour services, but their labour power, the potential of labour, to the capitalist. The definitive problem of the capitalist labour process is, therefore, the translation of labour power into labour. This is the managerial problem of control which creates the basis for alienation; the capitalist breaks the unity of the labour process by separating mental – design, planning, coordination – from manual labour, or what Braverman called the separation of 'conception and execution' (1974:114). Second, the origins of management lie in the struggle to devise the most effective managerial instruments of control. Marx called labour power variable capital. The term 'variable' highlights the managerial function: the exercise of authority over an often recalcitrant workforce to ensure compliance, so that surplus value can be extracted from the labour process. The concept of 'managerial control' has led some writers to argue that control over work is the central issue in industrial relations (Smith, 1979).

Braverman (1974) argued that the translation of 'labour power' into 'labour' was achieved during the monopoly capitalism phase by Taylorist principles which would ideally involve the control of all work operations by management. The division of labour achieved by Tayloristic 'scientific management' techniques, epitomized the separation of conception and execution. Taylorism is a means through which workers' skill and knowledge is expropriated from the worker and placed into the hands of the employer. Braverman also argued that further advances in capitalist control could be achieved by new technology (1974:195). Third, within the capitalist labour process the systematic subdivision of work reflected the necessary principle for capital of dividing craft work to cheapen labour costs: the 'Babbage principle' (1974:81–2).

Critiques of Braverman

Braverman's general thesis has attracted numerous criticisms, (Schwarz, 1977; Elger, 1979; Littler and Salaman, 1982, for example) and a number of recent empirically-based studies of microelectronics refute it (Jones, 1983; Wilkinson, 1983; Senker and Beesley, 1986 for example). Still other writers have defended Braverman (Zimbalist, 1979; Thompson, 1983; Armstrong, 1988). Further, some contemporary studies contain evidence supportive of Braverman (Noble, 1979; Thompson, 1981; Cooley, 1980), while his critics have been numerous and prolific. Indeed, the refutation of Braverman became a major academic preoccupation in the 1980s (Hyman and Streeck, 1988). The intention in this section is to refer briefly to some of the work that is most relevant to this study.

An early criticism of Braverman's model was his treatment of labour as 'passive' and 'inert' (Schwarz, 1977). Braverman gives the impression that workers passively accept the deskilling of their work and offer no resistance to, or make little attempt to, shape management plans. A dynamic model of the labour process must take account of organized labour as an active and problematic presence within the process of valorization and accumulation (Brighton Labour Process Group, 1977; Stark, 1980).

The first major criticism relates to Braverman's treatment of management and management strategy: one dimensional, inadequate and vulgar. It should not be assumed that management is a homogeneous, unambiguous phenomenon whose actions are programmed by any single commercial objective (Knights and Willmott, 1986; Hyman, 1988). Whipp and Clark challenge the notion of a monolithic management, when they argue: 'It is just as likely that intra-management contests will cause fracturing as any which are generated from the frontier of control between management and labour' (1986:213). There is also a tendency to exaggerate the unity and rationality of management (Hyman, 1988:50). The Braverman model assumes that the prime *raison d'être* of management is to wrest control over the labour process from skilled workers, and that one particular strategy, 'scientific management', is the most appropriate means of achieving this. However, others have argued that management's primary concern is with product and market strategies, and manufacturing technology is selected in the light of these considerations; only then do labour questions attract systematic attention (Kelly, 1985; Sorge and Streeck, 1988).

Friedman (1977; 1986) attempted to correct some of the limitations in Braverman's analysis, by stressing that some workers are better able than others to resist managerial controls, and hence deskilling. Friedman has argued that the Tayloristic strategy of 'direct control' which is consistent with deskilling may be integrated with, or substituted for, one of 'responsible autonomy' which allows workers a degree of autonomy. The latter strategy goes some way in recognizing the value of moving beyond the cash nexus, with a cooperative workforce that taps the workers' problem-solving skills (Littler and Salaman, 1984). Edwards (1979) related the segmentation of labour markets in contemporary capitalist economies to the different types of managerial control strategies.

A 'dialectical' approach to the interpretation of managerial control has been put forward by Storey (1983, 1985). Underlying his argument is the recognition that numerous factors and forces mediate the relationship between the capitalist imperative of accumulation and control of work at the point of production. By extending the analysis outside the factory, it can be seen why what happens at the point of production does happen (Knights and Willmott, 1986). The planning of future investment, pricing policy, penetration of production markets, product market competition and 'market despotism', may exert greater influence than managerial controls *per se*, on labour processes at the point of production (Kelly, 1985; Child, 1985; Burawoy, 1985).

The third main criticism of Braverman's model is that it tends to ignore the social definition of what are 'skilled' and 'unskilled' jobs. The concepts used by Braverman in describing deskilling are the separation of conception and execution. However, it is argued, he fails to differentiate between the different aspects of the skill concept (Beechey, 1983), nor does he recognize the privileged position of craft workers and their numerical insignificance (Friedman, 1977; Stark, 1980; Littler, 1982). Further, Braverman neglects the ideological significance of skill and the fact that skills are often 'socially constructed' (Sadler, 1970; Zeitland, 1978; Penn, 1983; Phillips and Turner, 1980), and his analysis is 'gender-blind' (Beechey, 1983; Thompson, 1983; Bradley, 1986; Collinson and Knights, 1986).

The essential theoretical problems associated with Braverman's thesis may be synthesized. First is the excessive attention to Taylorism. Recent post-Braverman literature has stressed the diversity and complexity of social control processes within capitalist relations of production (Littler, 1982, 1985; Storey, 1983, 1985; Burawoy, 1985; Kelly, 1982, 1985). Control may be achieved with and without deskilling, e.g. the division of the workforce along lines of gender and race (see Thompson, 1983, 1989). It is recognized that management reaps benefits from actively fostering the cooperation and goodwill of workers (Littler and Salaman, 1984; Storey, 1986).

More recent contributions to the labour process debate focus on a variety of issues, including forms of control and resistance at the point of production (Kelly and Clegg, 1982); the deskilling of labour (Wood, 1983); the historical development of managerial strategies (Gospel and Littler, 1983); the design and restructuring of work organization (Knights et al, 1985); the role of management in the labour process (Knights and Willmott, 1986); gender at work (Knights and Willmott, 1986b) and industrial relations (Hyman and Streeck, 1988). In addition, some labour process theorists have attempted to answer the critics that 'the labour process bandwagon . . . is now holed and patched beyond repair' (Storey, 1985:194), by reconstructing a more adequate general theory, a 'core theory' for understanding the organization of work in advanced capitalist societies (Knights and Willmott, 1990; Thompson, 1990). What emerges from the current spate of empirical material is the need for attentive sectorial studies, which avoid generalizations, and appreciate the subtlety and detail of social processes within work organizations (Beynon, 1987). The next section considers a second influential approach which has attempted to address some of the 'social processes'.

The Strategic Choice Perspective

The 'strategic choice' perspective is based on the notion that the application of technology and the organization of work are not determined simply by the logic of capitalist imperatives or the external market, but by the processes of experiment and negotiation *within* organizations by organizational members. The following draws mainly on Buchanan and Huczynski (1985); Child (1985), and McLoughlin and Clark (1988). Child (1972; 1985) used the concept of 'strategic choice' to stress the role of managerial choice, rather than the technological 'juggernaut', in shaping work and organization.

The importance of the concept of 'strategic choice' is that it focuses on who makes decisions in the organization, and why . Child argues that the introduction of technology into an organization is a 'political process' whereby the strategic choices on the design of the technology, the goals that technologies are used to achieve, and the way in which work is organized around the technology are normally initiated and taken by a 'power-holding group' within the organization.

The notion of strategic choice also has significance for labour relations. Although strategic choices are likely to be made by senior managers, they can be altered by other organizational members: middle managers and the workers through collective action. According to Child (1985:264), 'existing economic, social and political institutions, together with the dynamic tensions between them, create the conditions governing the way technology is applied.' This view is supported by a number of post-Braverman empirically-based studies of technological change involving Numerically-Controlled (NC) and CNC machine tools.

Jones (1983) found that there is nothing 'inherent' in NC technology that would allow for the deskilling and surveillance assumed by labour process theorists. Wilkinson's (1983) studies suggest that managers and engineers can be seen as 'political beings' and act as 'creative mediators between potential and actual technology' (1983:19). According to Wilkinson: 'the technical and social organization of work can best be seen as an *outcome* which has been chosen and negotiated' (1983:20). Also, the study by Batstone et al. (1987) of a small-batch engineering company revealed that management considered 'craft ethos' important for the future viability of the company. Further, Burnes (1988) brought out the wide disparity in the way that CNC technology was used, and thus skill deployment: 'some of the jobs created were good, some bad, and some indifferent'. The interplay between complex socio-technical factors 'meant that within each company the process was inherently non-deterministic' (1988:109). McLoughlin and Clark (1988) have developed a model of the process of technological change that is said to capture its 'temporal element', focusing on 'critical junctures' in the process of technological change which are critical in shaping outcomes by formal and informal negotiation. According to McLoughlin and Clark, in the three companies investigated they found that managers developed different 'sub-strategies' which left 'considerable room for manoeuvre', and as such has 'a critical bearing on the outcomes of change' (1988:66–70).

The theory of strategic choice suggests that there are no automatic impacts in new technology. As Buchanan and Boddy argue, 'the capabilities of technology are *enabling*, rather than determining', and it is the processes of choice concerning its application, and not technology *per se*, which determine the outcomes of change (1983:255). McLoughlin and Clark, however, contend that 'an analysis of the independent influence of technology is a necessary *complement* to an examination of the way outcomes of change are socially chosen and negotiated' (1988:45). The case studies in this book provide an insight into this critical argument. Suffice it to point out that recent studies suggest that technology can have an independent influence on the outcomes of change.

Hartmann et al. (1983), for example, have emphasized the malleability of CNC technology and that the implications of CNC on workers' skills is contingent on, inter alia, batch size. Senker (1984) has pointed out that NC and CNC have crucially different characteristics. The distinction lies in their control systems. While NC punched tapes cannot generally be altered on the shopfloor, the more sophisticated CNC machines can be amended on the shopfloor by the operator. Thus, while in both cases direct machining skills are displaced, the potential for operator involvement is not the same. NC leaves little scope for levels of skill beyond tool changing and material handling. But the Manual Data Input (MDI) facilities of the new generation of CNC permit amendments which rely on the experienced judgement of the skilled operative. Noble (1979) also acknowledges that Computer Numerical Control (CNC) technology is much more amenable to operator control. In a manner similar to Hartmann et al., Noble recognizes that the way CNC machine tools are utilized varies between different countries. For instance, in a Norwegian plant, the operators routinely did all the editing (1979:46–47). Although Noble makes the point that in Norway the Iron and Metalworkers' Union is the 'most powerful industrial union in the country', he does not draw from these observations the inference that workers' skills and autonomy are determined, not by capitalist imperatives as such, but by managerial choice and negotiation with organized labour.

What these accounts suggest is that technology can have an independent influence on the outcomes of change; and a consideration of technical factors such as batch size and type of technology needs to complement an analytical model based on the concept of strategic choice and negotiation. Joan Woodward (1958, 1965) identified a similar relationship; for example, large-batch production was associated with a highly bureaucratic organization, while small-batch tended to have less clearly defined role-systems and make greater use of expert knowledge in meeting production exigencies. The relationship is explained on the basis of the 'situational demands' created by different technologies which affect informal relationships as much as the formal structure. The more recent contributions to the labour process debate may signal a renaissance of 'organizational theory', which for two decades has been in a 'backwater' (Beynon, 1987:252). Equally, what is apparent is that the analytical framework used for studying the implications of microtechnology has been utilized by social scientists for assessing the effects of the Japanese industrial paradigm.

Much theoretical terrain has been covered in this chapter. The concept of Japanization was examined. A theoretical model was developed which suggests that Japanese manufacturing and labour management is an interrelated coherent strategy. It was also emphasized that the model is built on stereotypes of Japanese management, a simplified version of social reality, and capable of being applied in part. This author considers that the Japanese approach to the management of the employment relationship constitutes a set of distinctive labour policies with an ideological underpinning, designed to shape attitudes and behaviour, in order to maximize capital's side of the wage–effort exchange.

Finally, two influential sociological perspectives on the analysis of technological change – the 'labour process' and the 'strategic choice' approach – were examined. The labour process perspective emphasized that new technology has no influence on the organization of work independently of management's need to control. The empirically-based critiques of Braverman indicate that the interrelationship between technological change and skills is diverse and complex. Strategic choice writers stress that the actual outcomes of technological change will be determined by *choices* made by managers, engineers, union representatives and workforce at critical points in the process of change.

The significance of the 'strategic choice' school of research and literature to the debate on Japanization of British and North American industry is this: the labour process needs to be understood within the context of managerial choice and constraint. Further, there is no uniform means of managerial control and it is important to have a more nuanced taxonomy of production regimes than direct control and responsible autonomy, suggested by Friedman (Wood, 1989). Management choice of control strategies will be influenced by prevailing 'fashion, emulation and consultancy' (Storey, 1985:204), to follow through the notion of managerial choice being influenced by fashion. Japanese management concepts are but one set of control strategies which coexist alongside an immense battery of other controls, including Taylorism, responsible autonomy, and advanced microtechnology. This book adopts a strategic choice perspective as a basis for examining the outcomes of Japanese manufacturing practices and new technology in a number of British organizations.

3 Trade Unions and Change at Work

Where unions are well organized, they face difficult decisions in how far to respond to employers' pressures for change.

TUC, 1988:7

Chapter 2 reviewed the concept of Japanization and two influential perspectives on the analysis of technological change. The analysis of Japanese industrial management was conceived as a coherent strategy designed to shape employee attitudes and behaviour and, where necessary, deal with trade unions. Having examined management strategies, we now turn to the role of the trade unions in technological change at work. It is clear that the diffusion of workplace innovations can be influenced by workers and their trade unions. Reciprocally, technological change and Japanese methods have repercussions for union growth, structure and bargaining power.

In the 1970s, British trade unions were considered powerful social institutions which merited close study. Clegg referred to trade unions as 'one of the most powerful forces shaping our society' (1976:1). Between 1968 and 1979 trade union membership increased by 3.2 million to 13.2 million, with union density exceeding 55 per cent. The sheer scale of union increase represented a 'decade of exceptional union growth' (Bain and Price, 1983:6). In contrast, since the election of the Conservative Party to government in 1979, the membership of British trade unions has fallen by over 3 million, standing at 10 million and union density around 40 per cent in 1989. This reduction has prompted commentators to call the 1980s the 'decade of non-unionism' (Bassett, 1988). The popular British image of unions as Luddite has not been substantiated by empirical research. Union resistance to technological change appears to be by no means pervasive (Willman, 1986; Daniel, 1987). There is a growing trend that British trade unions remain isolated from the centres of company decision-making (Kennie, 1987).

The chapter seeks to explain what happened to British union membership in the 1980s and why, and their response to technological change. In the first section British union membership and density

48

are considered. The rationale behind this is the assumption that union organization is a necessary condition, a prerequisite, for unions to influence the direction and form of work organization by collective bargaining. The second section outlines the response of organized labour to technological change, and critically evaluates the underlying assumptions in trade union policy statements and assesses their success.

TRADE UNIONS UNDER THE THATCHER GOVERNMENT

The significant decline in aggregate membership of British trade unions is shown in Table 3.1. In 1979 TUC-affiliated membership reached a peak of 12 769 000. Since then membership has fallen by 3 650 000, or 30 per cent, though this includes the loss of the electricians' union, the EETPU, which was expelled from the TUC in 1988. From the peak year of 1979, union density – that is actual union membership as a proportion of potential union membership – fell from 54.2 per cent to 40 per cent. The decline in aggregate union membership exceeded the decline in employment largely because of

Table 3.1 Aggregate union membership and density in the United Kingdom, 1979–89 (thousands and %)

	TUC unions only	All unions in UK	Density %*
1979	12 173	13 289	54.2
1980	11 601	12 947	52.8
1981	11 006	12 106	49.7
1982	10 510	11 593	47.9
1983	10 082	11 236	46.3
1984	9 855	10 994	44.5
1985	9 586	10 821	43.4
1986	9 243	10 539	42.2
1987	9 126	10 475	42.0
1988	8 652	10 308a	41.4[a]
1989	8 404	10 010a	40.3[a]

Source: TUC figures *TUC Congress Reports* and *TUC Bulletins* UK figures from *Department of Employment Gazette*.
* Density figure is calculated on figures for all UK unions and potential union membership (civilian employment plus unemployment).
[a] Author's estimates based on TUC membership decline 1987–9.

the continuing contraction of the private manufacturing sector which is the unions' traditional area of recruitment.

Surveys of different sectors of the British economy reveal significantly lower density figures. In 1985/86 the British Social Attitudes Survey found average union density was less than 20 per cent in private services. In business services the proportion of white-collar, part-time workers in trade unions was less than 5 per cent (Millward and Stevens, 1986). The figures produced by the TUC for 1987 and 1988 had provided evidence of a levelling off, but the aggregate rate of decline for 1989 was 2.9 per cent compared with 1.6 per cent in 1988, and 1.3 per cent in 1987.

In the European Community and North America trade union density in the 1980s has been highly variable. In three of the EC member states, Belgium, Denmark, and Ireland, trade union membership increased by 7, 12, and 2 per cent respectively, France and West Germany recorded no change, and Italy, the Netherlands and the UK record a 6 per cent decline between 1979 and 1985. In North America, trade union density increased by 1 per cent in Canada, but fell by 7 per cent in the United States over the same period (Kelly, 1988: 269).

To focus on the United Kingdom, the growth, or decline of the ten largest unions affiliated to the Trades Union Congress is shown in Table 3.2.

Interpreting Trade Union Decline

The aggregate membership of TUC affiliates fell by 3.7 million from 1979 to 1989. The two largest unions, the AEU and TGWU, lost members at a rate above the average, reflecting the growth in unemployment in their traditional industrial recruitment areas. Compared to the late 1970s there are now fewer large trade unions. In 1979, 26 unions exceeded 100,000 membership, in 1989 the figure was 19.

Although the general pattern clearly indicates that membership and density have declined significantly and continually since 1979, there is debate about the precise scale of the trend, its cause and likely duration. Part of the problem is measurement. Estimates of the decline in union density between 1979 and 1986, for example, range from as little as 8.3 percentage points to as much as 12.1 percentage points. These strikingly different estimates occur because the key statistic of union density can be measured in nine different ways,

Table 3.2   Change in membership of the ten largest TUC-affiliated
unions, 1979–89 (thousands and %)

Union	Affiliated membership 1979	1989	Per cent change, 1979–89
Transport & General workers'	2 862	1 270	−55.6
Amalgamated Engineering	1 298	741	−42.9
General & Municipal	967	823	−14.9
National & Local Govt Officers'	753	750	− 0.4
Manufacturing, Science & Finance*	691	653	− 5.5
National Union of Public Employees	691	604	−12.6
Shop, Distributive & Allied Trades	470	375	−20.2
Construction, Allied Trades & Technicians	347	258	−25.6
Confederation of Health Service Employees	212	209	− 1.4
Communication workers	203	202	− 0.5
Total TUC Membership	12 173	8 404	−30.1
Number of TUC Unions	109	78	−28.4

Source: TUC figures *TUC Congress Reports* and *TUC Bulletins*.
* Formed from a merger with Technical, Administrative & Supervisory Staff
(TASS) and Association of Scientific, Technical & Managerial Staff
(ASTMS) in 1987.

depending on which of three different data series for potential membership, and trade union membership, are used (see Kelly and Bailey, 1989).

Kelly (1988) using one estimate of 50 per cent density, argues that British trade unions face big problems but these are not sufficiently serious or novel to talk of a crisis or watershed: 'British trade union membership has held up reasonably well compared with previous recessions' (1988:271). The estimate is calculated by counting only civilian employment as potential union membership. In contrast, an estimate of only 39.3 per cent union density, counting the working population (civilian, plus unemployed) minus the armed forces, leads Bassett to argue that: 'Non-unionism is now dominant in Britain . . . and the real role models for British industrial relations are now no longer the consensual, unionised examples of ICI and Ford, but the dynamic, entrepreneurial and non-union examples of McDonald's and IBM' (1988:45–7). The different measurements of trade union density may be measuring different facets of trade unionism. To assess trade union influence on the government or wider society, for example, a broad measure of union density, including the unemployed as potential union members, is held to be more appropriate. However, it is argued that it is not appropriate to include the unemployed in a measure of union density if the object is to estimate bargaining power, because the long-term level of high unemployment has an insignificant impact on the bargaining process (Kelly and Bailey, 1989). Kelly's interpretation of trade union membership has a central political purpose, that of refuting the arguments of the 'Eurocommunist', that British trade unions have 'lost their way'. Bassett's account is also written with a clear purpose of demonstrating that the developments during the 1980s created an era of 'new industrial relations'.

One influential explanation of variations in rates of unionization over time, and differences at any one time between industries and occupations groups, categorizes the determinants under six headings: composition of potential union membership, the business cycle, employer policies and government action, personal and job-related characteristic, industrial structure, and union leadership (Bain and Price, 1983). However, although the Bain and Price approach is comprehensive, it is difficult to disentangle the relative importance of each of the six determinants in interpreting aggregate union decline in the UK since 1979. The 1980-1 recession, the 'business cycle' determinant, accounted for much of the decline in union membership, with substantial contraction of employment amongst highly unionized manual workers in large manufacturing organizations. Within the business cycle framework, Disney (1990) suggests the downturn in union density in the 1980s was caused by macroeconomic factors. Trade unions' traditional difficulties in recruiting and gaining recognition in the private services sector, smaller establishments, foreign-owned plants, and newly established greenfield sites have intensified. As a recent TUC document acknowledged: 'Unions are finding it generally difficult to recruit and bargain in the fastest growing parts of the economy'.[1]

Following the election of a Conservative government in 1979, public policy towards trade unions shifted against positive encouragement of trade union recognition. The suggested determinant 'government action' clearly can effect unionization. Public policies that create a favourable environment for union recognition will initiate a 'virtuous circle' of recognition and membership increase. The circle can be put into reverse by adverse policies and government 'example-setting' or role model (Towers, 1989). Freeman and Pelletier (1990) using a quantitative analysis of changes in union density, estimate that the Thatcher government's industrial relations laws reduced British trade union density by 1 to 1.7 percentage points per year from 1980 to 1986. This type of analysis, however, is fraught with problems; it is very difficult to disentangle cause and effect in dealing with trade union law (Disney, 1990).

Views differ on the question whether employers have in fact used the recession and trade union legislation to change radically the structure of workplace industrial relations. In 1983, one survey of large manufacturing plants compared the changes in British industrial relations since an earlier survey by the Warwick Unit in 1978. It found that there had been little decline in union density: 'the overall picture . . . is one of continuing high levels of membership' (Batstone, 1984:210). There had been no significant change in non-recognition of unions in the establishments. As regards shop steward organization, Batstone writes that there has been no significant change in either shop steward density, the number of senior shop stewards or full-time conveners (1984:217).

Edwards (1985) found in a study that half the manufacturing plants, with more than 250 employees, still reported 100 per cent union membership for manual workers. None had ended their closed shop or removed facilities for stewards, and only 3 per cent had reduced the number of stewards or conveners. Only 20 per cent of the plants surveyed had made any change in bargaining arrangements over the previous two years. The investigation by Batstone et al. (1986) into workplace trade unionism reached similar conclusions; they pointed out, for instance, that there had been no fall in union density in 50 organized plants covered by their survey. Making 'crude comparisons' with earlier surveys (Brown, 1981), they found that the number of members per steward had not fallen over the six years and may even have 'fractionally increased' (Batstone et al, 1986:77).

The survey by Millward and Stevens (1986) and the study by Beaumont (1987) provide evidence on trade union organization of a macro nature, for the period between 1980 and 1984. In 1979, trade union density in the UK reached a peak of 55 per cent; by 1985, it had declined to 43 per cent, during a period in which unemployment increased by 135 per cent. Explanations for this decline in union density have tended to focus upon structural hypotheses, such as changes in the industrial distribution of employment and changes in employment patterns. Beaumont argues that union organization in the UK is being shaped by factors that transcend the current recession. His contention is that the structural changes are no more than particular manifestations of the consequences of capital's changing preference for non-union labour.

Millward and Stevens (1986) found that the average union density for 51 manual workers in mechanical engineering was 66 per cent in 1984. However, the exclusion of firms employing fewer than 25 employees means that the density figures are higher than they would be if all establishments of all sizes had been included in the survey. They found a strong relationship between size and ownership and variations in union density. Those establishments employing 25–49 employees had an average union density of 26 per cent, and those employing more than 1000 employees had an average density of 72 per cent (Millward and Stevens, 1986:57).

Millward and Stevens' contention is that the basic fabric of workplace trade unionism survived the recession and the legal assault by the Thatcher government. Despite the substantial decline in the number of manual stewards in private manufacturing between 1980 and 1984, the shop-steward system remains intact. The number of stewards in manufacturing fell more slowly than that of employees in manufacturing. The data show however that the majority of stewards in the UK economy are employed in the public sector. The data suggest therefore that 'the stereotype of the trade union representative as a manual shop steward in manufacturing industry evidently needs revision' (1986:86). Millward and Stevens inform us that collective bargaining with unions has also remained intact.

Surveys by industrial relations theorists have been criticised. Batstone's postal survey has been described as a 'blunt instrument'. However, there are other reasons why the findings of Batstone and Millward and Stevens have to be interpreted carefully: Their surveys excluded small firms, and any employer offensive or 'macho' management may be more prevalent amongst these establishments. Also, the effects of the recession on labour should not be judged exclusively with reference to changes in the traditional industrial relations model as studied by industrial relations theorists. Nichols' contention is that Batstone, 'would have found more to surprise him had he considered more closely some developments taking place outside of the surviving "core" employment relationships on which he concentrates, developments such as subcontract' (Nichols, 1986:191). Besides, it seems likely that the respondents – personnel managers – would tend to under-estimate, or be reluctant to report, an employer offensive against workplace trade unionism.

In the United Kingdom, unlike the United States, collective bargaining is less formalized and legalistic and employers do not face legal constraints on derecognition. Bassett (1988) suggests that derecognition of unions is a small but growing trend in Britain. Of twenty-one known examples of derecognition, two – the government's intelligence centre (GCHQ) and British Rail's senior managers – were in the public sector; the others ranged from chemicals to book publishing. A survey of British-based companies in the UK found thirty-nine cases of either derecognition, threat of derecognition or an attempt to move to a single-union arrangement.[2] The spate of examples of deunionization has been associated with the growing adoption of the human resource management approach. Addressing the Institute of Personnel Management Conference in 1987, John Monks, deputy general secretary of the TUC, said that while most companies used to be at least neutral, and often favourable, towards unions, recent labour relations practice and theory, originating from the United States or Japan, in the main attempted to persuade workers that trade unions now no longer served any useful purpose (*Financial Times*, 23 October 1987).

The analysis of trade union decline in the 1980s emphasizes the 1980–81 recession and the interplay between long-term economic developments, the shift towards the service sector, the increasing numbers of peripheral workers, and the adverse political and legal environments. Against this background the British trade unions have devised five identifiable survival strategies: working for the election of a Labour government; recruiting in the fastest-growing parts of the economy; expanding membership services; appraising the role of unions; merging with other unions (Towers, 1989).

Energetic recruitment campaigns, in some cases using videos, have aimed at appealing to women, young workers and the growing army of temporary, part-time and self-employed workers. In addition, faced with a social climate which is unfriendly, even hostile, to trade unions, several unions have adopted a strategy of 'business' or 'market' unionism.[3] The strategy of 'new realism' – a pragmatic reassessment of the unions' role in the light of Labour's 1983 General Election defeat – has been closely identified with single-union, no-strike agreements, and has been most closely associated with the EETPU and the AEU.

To recruit from a broader constituency of full-time and part-time workers in new establishments, unions, often after holding a so-called beauty contest with several unions competitively seeking recognition, have negotiated such agreements. These new style agreements have become the focus of ideological differences between unions. For union leadership on the right wing of the political spectrum, such agreements are a fundamental element of the reappraisal of their role in an advanced industrialized economy. For many left-wing union leaders the agreements abdicate members' right to strike. The Electrical, Electronic, Telecommunications and Plumbing Union (EETPU), the principal advocate of new-style agreements, was expelled from the TUC in September 1988 for refusing to withdraw from two such agreements following a TUC ruling.

The Conservative government's industrial relations law has changed unions' attitudes towards the role of the state. In response to the ideological and legal attack by the Thatcher government, the British TUC has formulated new policies on industrial relations law covering union ballots and union democracy which seek to appease perceived public attitudes. According to Hyman:

> With remarkable speed for so conservative a movement both industrial and political wings of British labour have substantially revised their conception of the role of the state and the law in industrial relations . . . Though this change has been neither unanimous nor unambiguous, it symbolises far-reaching moves in the ideology and aspirations of the labour movement as it seeks an escape from the ravages of Thatcherism (1987:104).

Further evidence that trade unions in the advanced industrialized economies are taking a more pragmatic approach and re-orienting their political activities has come from a comparative study of the AFL-CIO in the United States, the Trades Union Congress in Britain and the DGB in West Germany. The study concludes that these union confederations in the 1980s began to move away from the high politics of influencing government policy, and towards reestablishing their support among their membership (Taylor, 1989).

In Britain a traditional response of the unions to falling membership and revenue has been mergers and amalgamations. Since 1979 the number of trade unions affiliated to the TUC has fallen from 109 to 78, almost entirely from mergers. A notable exception is the EETPU. The process of merger and absorption is sometimes seen as a prelude to further natural growth, to mitigate the effects of membership decline. Mergers allow for extensions of existing recruitment bases as the post-merger union is in practice regarded as organizing from the recruitment bases of the pre-merger unions (Waddington, 1988). For example, following the merger of ASTMS and TASS to form the MSF, the new union now recruits engineers, clerical workers, insurance and banking staff, tobacco workers, sheetmetal workers. The structure of British trade unions is recognized to be complex and diverse. The competitive scramble to seek membership anywhere has created trade union structures which are even more bewildering and incomprehensible.

There has been considerable debate on the effects of the decline in union membership and density on unions' bargaining power. The contraction of employment in the unionized manufacturing sector is widely assumed to undermine union bargaining strength. Various indicators of union bargaining power, strikes and earnings, appear contradictory.

Figure 3.1 illustrates stoppages and days lost in industrial disputes. Its most noticeable feature is the fall in the number of stoppages during the 1980s. In the 1970s, with both Conservative and Labour governments, the number of stoppages per year never fell below 2000; throughout the 1980s the figure never rose *above* 2000. The figure for 1989 was 701, which compares with 781 in 1988, 1016 in 1987 and an annual average of 1271 over the period 1979–88. The 1989 figure of 701 stoppages was the lowest recorded figure for any year since 1935 (*Employment Gazette*, July 1990). Although comparisons involving the number of strikes must be made with caution because of the exclusion of some of the smallest stoppages from the statistics, nonetheless the trend is unequivocally downward, and 'secondary' industrial action has virtually disappeared as a union tactic. The number of working days lost through strikes also plummeted in the 1980s; the 1984 figure was a result of the miners' strike. The reasons may be numerous: draconian fines meted out to the print unions (Kelly, 1988), the failure of the miners' strike leading many workers to doubt whether going on strike would be successful, and the pre-strike ballot provisions of the Trade Union Act 1984 (Bassett, 1987). But all earlier evidence suggests that the strike pattern is strongly cyclical: propensity to strike rises during economic booms and falls during a recession. Further, the strike pattern in the 1980s cannot be used as an unambiguous index of trade union power, nor does it mean that strikes are a thing of the past (Kelly, 1988).

However, trade unions through collective bargaining have been

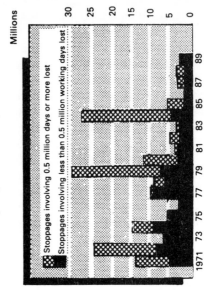

FIGURE 3.1   Industrial disputes: working days lost and number of stoppages (UK)
Source: Social Trends 20, March 1990. Reproduced by permission of the Controller, HMSO.

able to achieve rises in rates of pay equal to or greater than the rate of inflation. Virtually throughout the 1980s the earnings curve remained above the price curve (Kelly, 1988).

Evidence has been provided on trade union influence in technological change at work which suggests that unions were not able to exert much influence on the process (Batstone et al., 1987; Daniel, 1987). A contrasting interpretation, however, based on evidence from twelve case studies, suggests that workplace union representatives may be able to influence the outcomes of technological change (Price, 1988). Overall it is reasonable to conclude that the 1980-1 recession, high levels of unemployment, a Conservative government which embraced deregulation – the free market – and is less than sympathetic to (British) trade unions, have all combined to restrict the ability of unions to influence the outcomes of technological change and reshape work organization informed by Japanese production concepts. The influence of organized labour on the process of change is examined in the next section.

TRADE UNIONS AND TECHNOLOGICAL CHANGE

A number of writers have surveyed and commented upon the union response to new technology in the engineering industry in the 1980s. Some studies examine union response as part of a more general analysis of changes in industrial relations resulting from microelectronics (Bamber, 1980, 1988; Bamber and Williams, 1983; Francis and Williams, 1980). Others concentrate on specific industries (Martin, 1981; Gennard and Dunn, 1983; Davies, 1986; Willman, 1986; Batstone et al., 1986). The ideology and policies of unions have also been considered (Manwaring, 1981; Robins and Webster, 1982).

Since the early 1970s, trade unions throughout Western Europe have sought to confront the issue of technological change caused by developments in microelectronics. The research, information and education body of the European trade union movement, the European Trade Union Institute (ETUI), published a report in 1979 on *The Impact of Microelectronics on Employment in Western Europe in the 1980s* which examined the impact upon the quantity and quality of employment and trade union response, followed in 1982 by a report *Negotiating Technological Change* which reviewed the issues related to new technology that unions sought to negotiate. In 1983 the

European Trade Union Confederation (ETUC) held a conference on New Technology and Working Conditions.

Differences of approach towards technological change exist between European countries which have developed a centralized industrial relations system – such as Germany – and those with a decentralised system – such as the United Kingdom. Differences also occur between member states according to whether there is a legal framework for collective bargaining, as in Germany, or an essentially voluntarist approach, as in the UK. In contrast to Western Europe, where trade unions have taken a positive approach towards new technology and where in a significant number of countries some form of joint regulation over the introduction of microprocessor-based technology has increasingly become the norm, the unions in North America have conducted a debate over two basic policy approaches: a 'co-operatist' and 'militant' strategy. At the root of this policy debate are different assumptions regarding technological change and different ideological premises (Katz, 1988).

Since 1978, the British TUC has played a central role in initiating and coordinating the 'official' trade union response to new technology. The TUC's policy statement of 1979[4] indicated a desire to encourage microtechnology, while controlling any negative effects through the process of collective bargaining. TUC support for technical change can also be found in statements in the 1950s on automation. In 1956 the TUC concluded that trade unions had more to fear from 'too little automation than from too much'.[5] The safeguards demanded by British trade unions have been summarized: 'A demand for full employment . . . and [workers] should share in the benefits of industrial progress' (Mortimer, 1970:2–4).

At the 1978 Trades Union Congress, a resolution was carried calling on the TUC's General Council to formulate a policy on the social and industrial consequences of the diffusion of microelectronics, and prepare a policy statement. In its 1979 *Economic Review* the TUC General Council stated that it was:

> Fully committed to the promotion of technological innovation and change . . . the debate . . . is not about whether it should happen but about how it should happen. A greater danger to the trade union Movement is that it may not happen quickly enough (TUC, 1979:23–4).

The *Economic Review* examined the relationship between technological change, economic growth and employment levels. For the

TUC, Britain's relative industrial decline was rooted in its lack of competitiveness, stemming from low capital investment and low productivity. A final report, *Employment and Technology* was produced for the 1979 Congress and formed the basis for a lengthy composite motion. The report and motion, which the vast majority of affiliated unions supported, offer the fullest statement on new technology from the British trade union movement to date.

The 1979 Report reaffirmed the TUC's commitment to technological innovation and change and indicated a desire to encourage microtechnology while controlling undesirable employment consequences through joint regulation. The policy statement declares:

> Technological change and the microelectronic revolution are a challenge, but also an opportunity. There is the challenge . . . of the loss of many more jobs. Equally, there is the realization that new technologies also offer great opportunities . . . increasing the competitiveness of British industry . . . [and] the quality of working life (TUC, 1979:7).

Figure 3.2 illustrates the nature and longevity of the British TUC's analysis of technological innovation.

Many of the arguments expressed in the various documents remain essentially the same: the relationship between new technology, economic growth and employment, the joint regulation of change at organizational level, and emphasis placed on the need for government intervention. The debates on automation and microelectronics were, however, set within a very different context. The 1950s debate took place when there was virtually full employment, and when there was a consensus amongst the political parties to maintain the macroeconomic goal of full employment. In contrast, the 1970s debate took place against rising levels of unemployment and political vacillation towards achieving the post-1945 macroeconomic objective of 'full' employment.

Following the example of the Norwegian national agreement of 1974 on computer based systems,[6] the 1979 TUC Congress agreed to promote technological change through the negotiation of 'new technology agreements'. The TUC report on *Employment and Technology* set out a ten-point 'checklist for negotiators'.

These are summarised as follows:

1. No new technology should be introduced unilaterally: 'change must be by agreement'. 'Status quo' provisions are recommended.

1965	1979

Approach to technology

| The prospect of more rapid and more extensive technological advance is . . . welcome by the TUC (p. 30) | The TUC are fully committed to the promotion of technological innovation and change (p. 23) |

Basis of co-operation

| a good prospect of employment . . . is the chief condition for obtaining workers' ready cooperation in technological change (p. 19) | the basic imperative to secure full employment remains (p. 19) |

Effects on employment

| There is no inherent reason why technological change should cause large-scale and widespread unemployment (p. 8) | high rates of productivity growth need not lead to high unemployment (p. 14) |

Role of government

| Maintenance of full employment is chiefly the responsibility of Government (p. 11) | The successful pursuit of such a strategy requires a re-affirmation by Government of the commitment to full employment (p. 9) |

Sources: TUC, Automation and Technological Change, 1965; Employment and Technology, 1979; Economic Review, 1979.

FIGURE 3.2 *Some TUC policy statements on technical change*

Full consultation *before* the decision to purchase the technology.
2. Ensure that joint union machinery embraces all trade unions and that it is based on collective bargaining.
3. All information relevant to the process of technological change should be made available to union representatives. Union negotiators should nominate experts from outside the company to evaluate information.
4. Technology should be used to expand output or increase the level

of service in order to minimize negative employment effects. No redundancies if possible. Use of planned redeployment.

5. Mutually-agreed training and retraining schemes; training opportunities should be fairly distributed; principle of maintained or improved earnings during retraining.

6. Aim for a general reduction in normal working hours to the level of 35; elimination of systematic overtime.

7. Ensure present income levels are maintained and improved. Reward new skills; distribute the benefits widely; avoid dividing the workforce into a minority of highly skilled/paid and a majority of lower skilled/paid.

8. Measurement and control of operatives: union representatives should influence design system to avoid equipment being used to monitor work performance and increase managerial control.

9. Health and safety: specify regular breaks; unions should produce detailed guides; monitor health hazards.

10. Review progress: joint union/management study teams to monitor the effects of new technology; trial periods; disputes processed through existing grievance procedures.

The recommendations attempted to control the form and pace of technological innovation in a number of ways. First, the TUC sought to affect management decisions at the design and investment stage and therefore the choice of the actual technology, and help shape the work organization and the division of labour. Second, the TUC aimed to ameliorate any negative employment effects and influence the provision of training and retraining. Third, the model agreement aimed to determine regulatory rules and other controls exercised over workers by management. Fourth, through collective bargaining the TUC aimed to ensure that health and safety standards are established and maintained, and thereby regulate the day-to-day operation of the technology.

At national level, most affiliated trade unions either endorsed the TUC's advice to members or published guidelines which parallel the TUC approach to new technology. As negotiators union leaders aim to influence how technological change is introduced. As Bamber states, trade union leaders 'do not want to stop it, rather to control it, whether unilaterally, bilaterally or trilaterally' (1988:206). There was apparent consensus amongst both the left and right wings of the trade union movement that new technology should not be rejected. Ken Gill, general secretary of TASS[7] argued that: 'Britain should welcome developments that could provide higher standards, less boring work, more leisure'.[8] The EETPU argued it had no option but to 'enthusiastically foster the introduction of new technology in all sectors of the UK engineering industry'.[9]

The TUC and the employers' organization, the Confederation of British Industry (CBI) failed to reach a common understanding on technological change. Although there was some agreement on recommendations for access to information, more effective training, and consultation on health and safety, the majority of the CBI membership believed that a national agreement on new technology would be likely to impede investment in microtechnology.

The TUC approach received criticism from radical observers. Underpinning the views of most British trade unions was a commitment to Keynesian demand-management (Manwaring (1981), and the view that technology was an unproblematic, socially neutral phenomenon (Robins and Webster, 1982). Some critics argued that the policy statement was based upon an analysis rooted in Keynesian economic philosophy, an approach to economic management increasingly rejected by the government. Moreover, there was a contradiction; while microelectronics offered to heighten Britain's manufacturing competitiveness it also gave similar opportunities to foreign competitors. Further, the TUC and most British trade unions accepted technology as an unproblematic, socially neutral phenomenon. The notion that microelectronics can be designed and installed in the workplace to subjugate the workforce was not explored (Robins and Webster, 1982). It is suggested that, so long as technology is seen as an neutral product, then society is destined to accept technological innovation as a *fait accompli*. On the other hand, when technology is regarded as a social phenomenon embodying antagonistic social relations then, *inter alia*, interests served by particular innovations enter the agenda for social scrutiny and debate. It was, argued Robins and Webster, 'of real and practical significance that the social nature of technology is not apparent to the trade unions' (1982:13).

According to Manwaring, the TUC approach to the new enabling technology 'directly reflects the passive response which has characterised unions' role in British capitalism' (1981:20). However, given that the characteristic British trade union demand, after all, is for improved wages, not for the abolition of the wage system; for greater involvement in management decision-making, rather than the abolition of managerial hierarchical structures, it would indeed have been

Table 3.3   Trade union model agreements

Union	Job security	Training	Job control	Monitoring	Shorter working time	New pay rates	Health and safety
AEU							
GMB	*		*	*	*		*
EETPU	*	*	*	*		*	*
ASTMS	*	*	*		*		*
TASS	*	*	*		*	*	*

Source: TASS, ASTMS, EETPU, and GMB model agreements.

remarkable if the union approach had been anything but, essentially, defensive, pragmatic and short-term, concentrating on issues surrounding the wage-effort bargain.

Encouraged by the TUC, numerous trade unions formulated 'model' new technology agreements. The agreements have three aims: to provide for joint union/management determination of technological change; the amelioration of any negative effects of technological change; to distribute any productivity benefits arising from microtechnology. The specific response of a sample of unions is summarized in Table 3.3.

A survey of 'model' new technology agreements shows considerable differences of interpretation between unions on key negotiating issues. For instance, on the question of job security, TASS demand 'no reduction in the overall employment and no individual will lose his/her job' in the agreement. However, the union recognized that 'where union bargaining power is relatively weak, it may be necessary to accede to less satisfactory agreements.[10] On the other hand, the EETPU advises its negotiators to ensure that 'new technology does not involve redundancies', but adds 'this may be at the expense of job-loss in another plant owned by the same company'.[11] What emerges from the model agreements on the issue of job security is that in spite of their precise and uncompromising recommendations, numerous unions are prepared to make concessions on the principle of redundancy, providing certain conditions are met.

The specific recommendations of unions vary according to how they perceive microelectronics affecting the labour process where they recruit and organize. The EETPU's strategy was to try to 'capture' any new work arising from microelectronics. The AEU Executive Council recommended to its members that they should ask to be trained for computer-numerically-controlled programming, an area of work traditionally performed by TASS members. The Executive Council statement added: 'Our craftsmen members should be given the first opportunity to apply for and be trained for programming vacancies. It is essential, otherwise the position of our members in engineering will be undermined by staff and white-collar unions'.[12]

To what extent have union representatives at local level been able to translate model agreements into actual agreements? This will depend upon a number of factors, including the degree of workplace trade unionism within and between plants; the nature of bargaining arrangements; the complex variety of shopfloor policies towards technical change and the perceived balance of bargaining power. Early surveys of negotiated technology agreements were undertaken by Aston University Technology Policy Unit (AUTPU), Income Data Services (IDS) and Labour Research. Manwaring (1981) and Williams and Moseley (1982) also analysed a sample of technology agreements. Most commentators agree that stewards have experienced considerable difficulty in securing the terms of the model agreements in practice. More ominously, in the period of their research, Williams and Moseley (1982) found evidence to suggest that support for new technology agreements was waning and most new technology was being introduced unilaterally by management without any negotiation or agreement.

To date, the surveys have severe limitations as far as this study is concerned. The information collected and the analysis are biased towards the non-manual workers, and few technology agreements cover manual grades in manufacturing. Aston's sample of agreements included only 7 per cent from manual workers, and of the questionnaires received by Labour Research only 22 per cent (36) refer to 'general manufacturing'.

The survey of technology agreements by the Labour Research Department involved 255 agreements, making it one of the largest surveys yet published. However, only four per cent (eight) of the agreements covered manual workers. In the general white-collar area, LRD was able to report that in only forty-three cases (34 per cent) had management introduced new technology without consultation. This cannot be seen as a barometer of trade union power or influence, when many discussants on the labour process have stressed the importance of gaining workers' cooperation and goodwill.

While few technology agreements made explicit reference to the problem of deskilling, the majority of those examined did recognize the need to retain control over their own sphere of work. To achieve this objective, some union negotiators secured the agreement that new technology could only be operated by authorized users. The following clause was typical: 'work carried out by employees within the signatory unions' spheres of influence, prior to the introduction of new technology/systems will continue to be performed by such employees'.[13] Such clauses tend to defend traditional job demarcations, thereby protecting existing skilled jobholders at the expense of semi-skilled workers in the same plant. There are examples of unions securing agreement from management not to use new technology to measure, regulate or control their members: 'it is not the Company's intention to measure individual or collective work performances by computer based systems'.[14]

More recent case study and survey research in manufacturing has shown the extent of bargaining over technological change and the willingness of workplace union representatives to accept new technology in principle, whilst bargaining over the distribution of the rewards of increased productivity (e.g. Mueller et al., 1986; Batstone and Gourlay, 1986; Daniel, 1987; Batstone et al., 1987). The AUEW (AEU) welcomed new technology provided it was under their control or was introduced under conditions favourable to the long-term goals of the union, report Mueller et al. (1986:133). Batstone and Gourlay describe how patterns of bargaining over technology reflect the more general pattern of bargaining. In a national survey, Daniel observed that, in contrast to the conventional wisdom, 'the reactions of workers and unions to technical change were generally very favourable' (1987:182). In their case studies of chemical, brewery, engineering and insurance companies, Batstone et al. (1987) report that the unions' basic approach was essentially a cooperative one.

In a survey of over two hundred senior managers in manufacturing industry, Edwards (1984) found that union opposition was not a major obstacle to introducing technological change at the workplace. On the question of the threat of trade union opposition or resistance to technological change, Willman (1986) concludes that there is some evidence of opposition to change, but this is insufficiently extensive to justify the view that British trade unions are a major obstacle to technological change. Similarly, Dodgson and Martin argue that union policies on new technology are largely a product of the late 1970s, and conclude that 'managers do not perceive trade union obstruction as a major obstacle towards introducing new technology' (1987:17). Finally, in a survey of the UK mechanical engineering industry, Lintner et al. (1987) conclude that management did not perceive unions as acting in such a way as to impede the initial adoption of CNC or CAD. That particular survey, however, is susceptible to the charge that it focuses on employers' decision to invest in CNC/CAD technology which, given their 'reactive' behaviour, is atypical of trade union influence. Nevertheless, contrary to popular stereotypes and the role traditionally attributed to them by some economists, trade union attitudes and approaches to technological change have in general been positive. A study, carried out between 1981 and 1988, concluded that managers in British engineering companies, not shopfloor operatives, were more likely to be 'Luddites'. Managers remained suspicious and ignorant of computer aided design and their insecurity and obstinacy and prevented proper use of the technology (EITB, 1989).

Technology agreements tend to be more comprehensive in their approach to changes in work organization and job design than traditional types of collective agreement. Nonetheless, they have not been judged as particularly effective. Williams and Steward, in their review of new technology agreements, concluded that, 'both the adoption and content of technology agreements have been limited compared to original TUC objectives' (1985:71). Batstone et al., in their case study of engineering, reported that the AUEW's demand for a new technology agreement 'only had a small effect upon the way the new [CNC] machines were introduced and worked, since the agreement was not reached until *after* [my emphasis] they had been installed and were working' (1987:132). In the postal survey conducted by Batstone and Gourlay (1986) managers were asked: 'Over the last five years, has union influence over working practices and effort levels increased or decreased?' In engineering, 56 per cent of the respondents replied that the degree of union control was a 'fair amount' (1986:137–9). Daniel also identifies low levels of consultation: 'the extent of different forms of consultation was modest' (1987:115).

The research on trade union response to new technology has to be evaluated with some caution. As Batstone and Gourlay readily admit, given the research instrument – the postal questionnaire – they were dependent upon 'very crude subjective assessments' of union influence (1986:138). Further, much of the debate concerning new technology agreements and the influence that unions may have on technological change has been conducted in more or less an empirical vacuum. Also, the methodology of collecting and analysing negotiated agreements tends to place too much weight on formal agreements rather than the application, use and effects of the technology on individuals and groups of workers.

The absence of technology agreements indicates neither the absence of technological change, nor the absence of negotiation, nor trade union influence over the process of change. In many cases, even where union organization is strong and unions retain some bargaining power, unionized labour may rely upon traditional 'procedural' agreements. In Britain the trend towards decentralized workplace bargaining since the late 1960s has given rise to a substantial degree of 'organizational particularism' in inter-union relations, bargaining arrangements, and job control structure (Rose and Jones, 1985). Although new technology agreements were designed to provide a comprehensive negotiating framework within which to introduce microprocessor-based technology on an agreed and harmonious basis, the drive for such agreements lost impetus in the early 1980s. It was largely for this reason that Daniel did not examine the extent or content of new technology agreements, but focused upon 'what actually happened in practice, so far as consultation and negotiation were concerned, when particular major changes were introduced' (1987:113).

Daniel's point is important. There are difficulties in drawing firm conclusions about the overall picture of union influence on the process of technological change. In particular, the process of categorizing the topics covered by agreement divorces the terms of a technology agreement from the industrial relations context in which it was negotiated. Even where formalization is extensive, in many organizations some issues are not covered by formal 'rules' in collective agreements. Technology is introduced within an infrastructure of unwritten rules which influence the outcomes of change in work structures. It becomes difficult, therefore, to determine how a technology agreement will operate in practice, and how it relates to other collective bargaining arrangements and custom and practice within the organization.

A number of writers have commented upon the reasons why trade union response has been so apparently ineffective in the 1980s. The lack of thought, priority and resources given to the problem of technological change is considered important by Dodgson and Martin. They argue that, along with the recession, and the structure of unions, too few research resources have been directed towards identifying, quantifying, and speculating about the consequences of technical change which affect trade union members (1987:15). The

generally unfavourable economic and political context has constrained the role of unions (Bamber, 1988). As a result, few technology agreements have been negotiated, and most new technology
has been introduced unilaterally by management without any negotiation or consultation at all (Gill, 1987).

The interpretations of managers' responses to union influence,
however, perhaps neglect too much the obvious manifestations of a
'frightened' labour force, and the views being expressed by industrialists and trade union officials in the 1980s. In the winter of 1981, one
senior industrialist expressed the view that: 'On the industrial relations front, the effect of the recession has been to bring greater
reality into the bargaining scene.'[15]

There is, of course, one human aspect of the 1980–1 recession
which is not captured by postal questionnaire: fear. In the 1980s,
British trade unions in manufacturing industry were reported as
representing a frightened workforce. The fear syndrome was succinctly expressed by the then chief union negotiator at Ford Motor
Company (UK), Ron Todd: 'We've got three million on the dole,
and another 23 million scared to death'.[16]

TRADE UNIONS AND JAPANIZATION

The attitude of European and North American trade unions to the
transfer of Japanese industrial management concepts has been one of
suspicion, and they are monitoring their development (Bradley and
Hill, 1983). In Britain the growing adoption by British companies of
Japanese-style quality circles invoked a response from the TUC
Economic Department, in 1981. The Department produced a paper
on quality circles (QC), defining a QC as 'a system for harnessing the
expertise of employees in improving all aspects of the quality of
products and services'. It went on to suggest that QCs can be
presented as a form of 'participation', to answer the critics of British
employers' autocratic style of management while leaving managerial
authority intact. The report made it clear that, like any other alter-
ation in work organization, QCs had to be subject to existing bargaining procedures: 'Trade unions are likely to oppose QC structures
that are imposed unilaterally by management without reference to
these procedures'. It then went on to point out the danger of QCs
undermining workplace trade unionism: 'Trade unionists will be
opposed to the introduction of QCs if they challenge in any way

existing trade union machinery or practices'. Further, it argued that managers cannot expect trade unionists to see QCs as a substitute for other far-reaching forms of involvement in the areas of research and development, marketing and investment. Some of the trade union issues raised by QCs and other Japanese management concepts were incorporated into TUC teaching material, *Changes in Work Patterns*, in 1985.

A critical appraisal of Japanese-style labour management techniques at the Norsk-Hydro Fertilizer Plant, Humberside was undertaken jointly by Northern College in association with the Transport and General Workers' Union (TGWU). The study warned that the Norsk-Hydro New Personnel Package represented a critical attack on the workplace position of trade unions (Linn, 1986). Opposition to the Japanization process from unions at local level has been increasingly reflected in strikes over 'flexibility' (Wilkinson and Oliver, 1989; IDS, 1990). Significantly, in spite of empirical evidence and disputes over the Japanization process, the TUC has not attempted to formulate a 'model' agreement on Japanization. There has also been little debate on Japanization amongst TUC affiliated unions. Overall, the British trade union movement is remarkably complacent and is failing to confront adequately the broader and long-term labour implications of Japanese-style management techniques.

In the United States, Japanese-type quality circles are perceived by some managements as a prerequisite to decertification, or as a mechanism to help sustain non-unionized workplaces (Bradley and Hill, 1983). The cooperatist and militant wings of the labour movement differ fundamentally in their position regarding Japanese-type cellular manufacturing. The militants oppose cellular production systems. They argue that these work structures are essentially mechanisms to intensify work and are used by management to reshape workers' attitudes towards their union with the purpose of weakening workplace trade unionism. At the 1985 United Auto Workers (UAW)-Canada convention, the president, Robert White, warned that the agreement at General Motors' Saturn Plant in the USA was a dangerous step towards enterprise (and weaker) unions (White, 1985; see also Meyer, 1986). The cooperatists, on the other hand, are prepared to collaborate with integrated work teams. The opposing views are best explained by considering the views of the two camps towards worker participation. The militant view is that work teams and quality circles are designed to pacify unions, and the proper forum for labour–management interaction is through the social process of collective bargaining. To the cooperatists the new work arrangements enhance shopfloor autonomy and may create a form of deproletarianisation of workers.

To sum up: the approach of European and North American trade unions to technological change will depend upon the nature of the industrial relations system in each country, the legal framework for collective bargaining and the size of the country. Whether the trade unions can influence and shape the outcomes of technological change depends on a number of factors: union organization in the workplace; work group awareness of the issues associated with technological change; access to external information and support; a commitment to pursue a common approach; the state of the labour market; and bargaining power. In Britain the power of the trade unions to control the direction and form of work organization by means of new technology agreements has been limited. High levels of unemployment, reductions in public expenditure, privatization, deregulation, restrictive trade union law have all helped to undermine trade union bargaining power. To date, few employers have responded with any enthusiasm and since reaching a peak in 1983, relatively few technology agreements have been negotiated. One survey found that fewer than 100 technology agreements have been negotiated in the manufacturing industry (Williams and Steward, 1985). The survey findings, plus the rebuttal by the Confederation of British Industry (CBI) of TUC initiatives towards a joint approach to technological change, may assist in dissipating any illusions about the participative nature of British labour–management relations.

In addition, what this survey of the literature has shown, and it is reinforced in the case studies in the next four chapters, is that the diffusion and application of new technology and Japanese industrial management concepts have been greatly assisted by a new climate in British industrial relations, a climate characterized by fear and uncertainty amongst the labour force. Also, case study evidence suggests that workgroups and the infrastructure of unwritten rules on the shopfloor may be more significant than formal collective bargaining in determining the organization of work.

4 Patterns of Change

A quiet revolution has been occurring in Britain's manufacturing industry during the late 1980s. Cell manufacturing is rapidly emerging as one of the major tools being used in the drive to manufacturing competitiveness.

Ingersoll Engineers, 1990

Chapter 3 focused on developments in British labour relations occurring over the last decade at national level. Throughout the period trade unions have faced major challenges in coming to terms with industrial relations legislation and management-led initiatives. For much of the time trade unions were on the defensive, but they were not destroyed, and by the late 1980s there were signs of a more combative unionism. Some writers argue that trade unions have changed their approach and moved towards 'new realism' (Bassett, 1986). Other studies offer contrasting interpretations (Kelly, 1988). The state of the global economy, compounded by government economic policy and the long-term trend in British competitiveness has had a profound impact on British labour relations. As unemployment grew and union membership collapsed in the early 1980s there was a shift in the balance of power, certainly within manufacturing, towards management.

This chapter turns to the selected case-studies manufacturing to examine the effects of technology-induced change on employment and the nature of work. It draws on data gathered from managers and shop stewards to discuss the role of trade unions in matters of technology management. Furthermore, the chapter highlights inadequacies of earlier empirical work and also prepares the ground for the detailed studies later in the book of three of the companies: Servo, Oil Tool, and Flowpak.

THE CASE-STUDIES

The case-studies provided the opportunity to study the, process of change in different production processes: nine firms engaged in small-batch production, and three in large-batch. Six of the firms were selected for more detailed investigation: Flowpak, Oil Tool,

Batch size

Small	Flowpak* (317)	Pump Ltd (451)
	Oil Tool (450)	TMD (16)
	Precision Tools (250)	Engrave (71)
	Balance Instruments (301)	Fab Metals (33)
	Mining Power (787)	
Large	Servo (442)	Fanblade (775)
	Rads (339)	

Note: All names are pseudonyms.

FIGURE 4.1   Characteristics of twelve case-studies and number of
employees

Precision Tools, Pumps, Servo, and Fanblade. The twelve case-studies' characteristics are shown in Figure 4.1.

The case-studies were selected on the basis of their use of CNC machine tools. However, case-studies can sometimes produce the most surprising and rewarding results of research. Consequently, during the investigation it became apparent that some managements had also introduced Japanese production methods. The fieldwork revealed that managers had fundamentally transformed the social organization of work by adopting a Japanese-style manufacturing system.

This double process had not been elicited from respondents in the postal survey[1] and provides further justification for the case-study approach. The questionnaire used for the interviews was subsequently amended to provide information on the extent and effects of organizational innovation.

TECHNICAL CHANGE ON THE SHOP FLOOR

Large-batch methods of production were used in three out of the twelve firms visited. Large-batch volume refers to production runs of a thousand upward; the product is standardized and production entails dedicated automated machines, operated by semi-skilled or unskilled labour. In contrast, the majority of the firms visited, nine, employed small-batch methods of production. The term 'small-batch' is used to refer to products characterized by high variety, and production systems employing more skilled labour. The nine case-studies are typical of the British engineering industry since it has been estimated that over 70 per cent of all components being produced in Britain are in batches fewer than 50, and that components produced by conventional small-batch methods are more expensive than if they were produced by large-batch.[2]

Manufacture of components can be cheapened by speeding up the preparation and setting times on machines; by minimizing the input of skilled labour; and by the organizational realignment of machine tools to achieve more efficient flows of the batches from design to final assembly. Developments in CNC machine tools mean that adjustments in machining speeds and feeds can be made in the software, rather than in the physical setting of the machine itself. Of the twelve firms visited, there were marked variations in the extent of use made of CNC machine tools. The application of new technology is more prevalent in larger establishments. Six firms had within recent years introduced CNC lathes, milling machines and drills into their machine workshop. Five firms had sophisticated CNC machining centres capable of multi-functioning operations. One firm, involved in large-batch production, had a multi-pallet machining centre, capable of machining twelve components simultaneously. In all the case-studies CNC machines represented only a small proportion of the total machine population. Robots performing different types of tasks were in operation in three firms. In one case, however, the management used the term 'manipulator', clearly indicating their sensitivity to 'political' considerations – in particular, the fear of non-cooperation amongst certain well-unionized, employee groups: 'We don't use the word "robot", we call them manipulators; if we use the former, the shield goes up . . . employees don't like them so we talk of production units using manipulators.'

Developments in microcomputers have provided scope for integrating handling and machining operations: minimizing queuing times, monitoring work-in-progress and inventory control. The integration of discrete production activities is called computer aided manufacturing (CAM), and when linked to computer aided design (CAD) gives management direct control over all aspects of the manufacturing process. Industrial engineers have forecast that in its final form, 'total intersphere integration or computer integration manufacturing (CIM) would see the entire organization behaving as a single machine'.[3]

Eight of the firms visited had installed CAD. Three of the eight had undertaken large investment in a computerized system which attempted to integrate all aspects of the firm's functions: marketing, design, planning, purchasing, production, assembly and despatch. The extent of the integration and success of the system varied between the three firms.

ORGANIZATIONAL CHANGE ON THE SHOP FLOOR

Of the six cases selected for more detailed study, three had introduced cellular and just-in-time manufacturing within the last three years. Two were 'considering' doing so, and one firm was 'actively pursuing the possibility of switching to cellular production'. It has been stated elsewhere that just-in-time (JIT) is only appropriate for high volume production: 'as a system of mass production, JIT can only be used by a minority of manufacturing' (Sayer, 1986:57). The three case studies described here however, demonstrate that JIT is capable of being applied in a variety of types of labour process, large and small-batch and beyond the automobile and electronic industries. They show that such organizational innovations are evolving in ways which sever their roots from the particularities of Japanese culture and, as such, are likely to have enormous innovating potential for the majority of manufacturing firms.

The effects of introducing the cellular system into British manufacturing may have a more decisive impact on job content, job control and pace of change, than the familiar analyses of CNC technology. Since the seventies, the effects of new technology in engineering can be described as 'evolutionary'. A newly installed NC or CNC lathe for instance, alongside conventional machines, tended to affect a limited number of workers. In contrast, when management adopt a cellular system of production, the result can be described as 'revolutionary'. The pace of change is much faster. Traditional manufacturing methods can be in operation on a Friday afternoon; by Monday morning, the workforce can return to find a new organizational configuration in the machine shop, and totally new labour process arrangements in operation.

EMPLOYMENT AND THE TRANSFORMATION OF WORK

Table 4.1 and Figure 4.2 show the change in employment by occupation in the twelve firms visited. The numbers employed declined from 6240 to 4232, a fall of 32 per cent. Those employed in the six detailed case studies declined from 4429 to 2665, a fall of 39.8 per cent.

Among the six cases, the numbers employed had been reduced by between 17 and 51 per cent during the period 1980 and 1985. One case reported making more than half its workforce redundant: from 649 to 317, a fall of 51 per cent. The largest absolute fall occurred in a firm manufacturing turbine and compressor blades for the high technology industries including aerospace, power generation, where the numbers fell between 1980 and 1985, from 1305 to 755, a fall of 42 per cent.[4]

The numbers employed in the twelve workplaces declined in all occupations except managerial staff. Data from the case studies confirm industrial surveys showing that, in general, the less skilled an occupation, the greater has been the decline in employment in that occupation. For instance, semi-skilled and unskilled jobs declined the most, 44 per cent.

Survey results showed that there was a tendency for job losses to

Table 4.1   Employment by occupation in the twelve case-studies, 1980 and 1985

Occupational Change category (1)	Number		Percentage 1980–85 (4)
	1980 (2)	*1985* (3)	
Managerial staff	188	218	+15.9
Technicians including draughtspersons	456	387	−15.1
Clerical and related	650	430	−33.8
Supervisor	206	143	−30.5
Crafts workers	1110	772	−30.4
Operatives	1886	1059	−43.8
Total	6240	4232	−32.2

(N = 12)
Note: Totals do not reconcile because of absence of information on employees in each group.

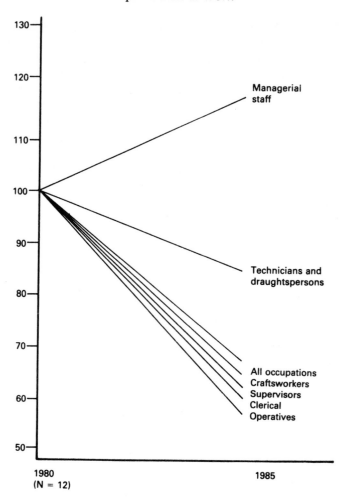

FIGURE 4.2   Changes in employment in each occupational group in the
twelve case-studies between 1980 and 1985

be associated with the introduction of new technology, but that CNC
technology causal effect was ranked very low by managers among the
range of reasons for reductions in the size of the workforce.[5]

In the follow-up interviews rarely did managers blame labour
reductions on the introduction of new technology. Of the twelve
managers interviewed, ten cited as reasons for manpower reduction
the economic recession, contracting markets, the introduction of cost

reduction exercises and foreign competition. Even in those cases where there had been heavy investment in new machine tools, and substantial manpower reductions, managers ranked technological unemployment low. Jones reveals that no manager cited labour costs as an influence in investing in NC. But as he points out: 'it is disingenuous to accept managerial statements that labour costs are not a prime reason for NC installation. This objection would presume that management is hardly likely to boast to a sociologist that NC is its way of cutting wage costs' (1983:191–2).

Technology was cited by two managers, and organizational change to cellular production was cited by one manager as a reason for labour reductions. To quote one personnel manager:

The machines must be labour saving. We have probably halved the numbers in the machine shop. I would say that half of our reduction is because of the order book, and half of it because of the changes in methods of manufacture.

In one case, a machine tool manufacturing company, one motive for investing in a CNC machining centre was labour savings. In a feasibility report submitted to senior management the production manager stated:

There would be an approximate reduction in manpower requirements of three. This does not include further savings to be made from unmanned operations. Estimated saving at present costs would be £32,400 per annum.

Reductions in labour costs obviously influence investment decisions, but in this example cutting wage costs was one criterion among six others. Thus it is difficult to assess the extent to which labour savings determine the decision to invest in CNC technology.

Interviews amongst manual shop stewards in the six detailed case studies revealed less unanimity. When asked: 'do you think jobs have been lost as a direct result of new technology?', only two AEU conveners attributed job loss to new CNC machines. One convener put it like this:

Management have never said it as direct as that, but there is no question about it. In the dye-milling section, you have this six-spindle

CNC machining centre, and we had four people got rid of in there.

AEU Convener, Fanblade Ltd.

The survey by Daniel (1987) concluded that where advanced technology had been introduced on the shopfloor, in most cases it did not have any short-term consequences as to the number of manual workers employed in the section affected. In establishments where manual unions were recognized, both managers and stewards reported that there was no change in over 60 per cent of all cases (1987:211–13).

This study found that there is a problem in interpreting the respondents' experience of technical change on employment. In all cases new technology was introduced by management in an acute recessionary period when the firm's markets were collapsing and managers, shop stewards and workers are often unable to distinguish the independent direct effects of new technology. In these cases, job losses are generally negotiated as part of a package involving voluntary redundancies, early retirement and natural wastage. Here there is a tendency for job losses not be associated with technical change, owing to perceived causes and the timing of the investment. In four of the six cases, investment in CNC machine tools came *after* the announcement of significant job losses.

Two cases provided evidence of negative employment effects associated with new technology and organizational change. In the first case, the AEU convener attributed job losses directly to recently installed robotic cells, and new multi-pallet machining centres. The robotic cell had replaced three semi-skilled operators.[6]

The two cases engaged in large-batch production had reduced their workforce by 42 per cent. This particularly affected semi-skilled operators. The disproportionate employment effects on the semi-skilled is the result of four main factors. First, the relative elastic supply of semi-skilled manual workers means that they tend to be laid off first during a recession. Given hiring and training costs, skilled labour may be viewed as a 'quasi-fixed factor' (Walter Oi, 1962). Secondly, there is a shift away from unskilled jobs, due to a policy of 'buying-in' components and/or new materials, for example plastic replacing metal components. Thirdly, in a union environment there is a tendency for skilled manual machinists to 'capture' the operation of the new machine for their own job security. Finally, it is easier for 'skilled' operatives to be flexible downward and undertake pro-

Table 4.2   Comparison of managers' and conveners' accounts of the effects of new technology on employment

	Managers	Conveners[1]
Technical change	2	2
Recession	10	5
Other (cell system)	1	

N = 12
[1] 7 out of the 12 cases allowed interviews with union representatives.

duction tasks previously the preserve of semi-skilled workers. The accounts of managers and manual stewards on the effects of new technology on employment levels are shown in Table 4.2.

The case-studies also provide evidence of direct and indirect employment effects resulting from Japanese production methods. Direct negative employment effects resulted from closure of the firm's stores department, and removal of first-line management on the shopfloor. In two cases for instance, adopting the cellular system resulted in the number of supervisors employed being reduced by 45 per cent, from 44 to 24. In one case, the firm made the four storekeepers redundant and adopted an 'open access', high-trust policy for parts acquisition. In addition, cellular production had an indirect impact on employment levels, due to increases in labour productivity resulting from greater functional flexibility.

As well as affecting the quantity of work available, new technology alters the quality of work, and introduces the question of the role of technology in the capitalist labour process. The case studies provided an opportunity to describe and explain the effects of CNC technology on skill levels in different workplaces according to batch and plant size, and trade union organization. The transfer of 'intelligence' and deskilling of the craft operator using NC/CNC technology is a central concept posited by Braverman and labour process theorists.

The evidence from the case studies is organized into five sections in order to examine the basic arguments associated with the 'destruction or enhancement' of shopfloor engineering skills. The approach is particularly influenced by the methods of Hartmann et al. These researchers used batch and plant size as a criterion for analysing the effects of CNC technology on skills levels. The relationship between batch size, number of employees and trade union influence on the division of tasks is shown in Figure 4.3.

	Trade union influence			
	Some		None	
Small-batch	*Company*		*Company*	
	Flowpak	(317) (E)	Pumps Ltd	(451) (E)
	Oil Tool	(450) (E)	TMD	(16) (W)
	Precision Tool	(250) (W)	Engrave	(71) (W)
	Balance Instruments	(301) (W)	Fab Metals	(33) (E)
	Mining Power	(787) (E)		
Large-batch	Servo	(442) (N)	Fanblade	(775) (W)
	Rads Ltd	(339) (N)		

Note: All names are pseudonyms.
Key: (W) operator writes programs. (E) operator edits.
    (N) operator has no access to program facility.
    Small-batch < 100; Large-batch > 1000.
    Trade union influence: consultation/negotiation.

FIGURE 4.3   Division of tasks by production unit size, number of
employees and trade union influence

Of the twelve firms using CNC technology, only two maintained a strict division of labour between programmers and machine operators. Both firms were engaged in large batch production. In the case of Rads Ltd, the 'pick and place' manipulator (robot) was programmed by the production engineering department. Servo Engineering observed a strict separation of mental and manual labour, between programmers, machine-setters and operators.

Out of the three firms engaged in large-batch production, only in one, Fanblade, did management utilize operator skills for writing and editing programs. However, this is a special case, for although the firm manufactured turbine and compressor blades on a large scale, the machine shop had all the characteristics of small-batch production. The principal function of the machine shop was to make dies for the presses, from which the blades were forged. The planning engineers calculated feeds, speeds and tooling requirements, and generated the more 'complex' programs using special software package.

But the skilled operators also generated simple programs for the CNC lathes. To quote the planning engineer:

If it's a straightforward job, they put their own program in. If it's complex, for instance aerofoils, it's three-dimensional and nobody

could write that in, it's too big and long a job. The operators are
quite capable . . . of doing their own programming . . . they are
all skilled men.

In addition the skilled operators routinely did editing of the more
'complex programs' according to their own criteria of convenience
and efficiency. They had sufficient skill and the facility on the CNC
lathes to adjust the sequence of cutting and the number of passes,
and adjust speeds. Management tended to turn a blind eye to this
unauthorized practice for reasons explained later.

The diffusion of programming and editing skills to the shopfloor
was most prevalent among the nine firms engaged in small-batch
production. In all of these workplaces the CNC lathe operators were
skilled, involved in verifying or 'proving' tapes generated in the
programming department or, in four cases, skilled operators actually
generating and proving their own programs on the shopfloor.
Whether firms were in the large-batch, large plant or trade union
influence categories, the differences between turning and milling and
multi-functional machining were noticeable. In the case of turning,
considerable shopfloor autonomy was retained, whereas for milling
programming was invariably performed in a separate department by
manufacturing support staff.

One firm, a machine tool manufacturer, had invested in two CNC
Japanese lathes in 1985, and a CNC Matsuira machining centre in
late 1987. The two CNC Moira Seika lathes were operated by two
recently qualified, apprentice-trained operators. Using the machine's
'menu-type' program system, the operator has total discretion to
write and 'prove' programs.

One of the operators, aged 22, with advanced City and Guilds in
mechanical engineering, had been employed at the firm since leaving
school at sixteen. During his apprenticeship he had operated bar
lathes, milling machines, centre lathes, and for six months an NC
lathe. Since 1986 he had operated the Moira Seika CNC lathe. He
described the changes in the nature of his work since transferring to
this new lathe:

You don't get as mucky . . . It's a lot cleaner machine. All the
swarf is going out into the bin. It's increased planning because you
have got to do programs totally different to what you can do on a
normal machine. Oh yes, it's a lot more interesting. You have total
control of that machine.

When the CNC lathes were installed at Precision Tools there had been no rules laid down by management for the technical staff and operators to follow. In the absence of management direction, the CNC lathe operators took on the task of programming their machines. Thus, management inertia was a critical factor in establishing shopfloor autonomy. The CNC project coordinator explained that 'Operators programmed the Moira Seika lathes because there was a lack of organization. It was left very much to run itself'.

However, operating programming was seen as a short-term phenomenon by the firm's production engineers. During the time of my investigation, management were examining the feasibility of direct numerical control (DNC). As the CNC projects engineer explained:

> What we are aiming towards is producing a program using our CAD/CAM, and then download them direct to the machine. At the moment they are producing the program on their own type CAM system, which is fine, but we have no control over it. We don't know what is happening.

Responsibility for programming the CNC machining centre had already been removed from the shopfloor operators, although they did 'prove the programs out'. Programs for the centre were generated by the production engineering office. The production engineers believed that programming was their domain, and the CNC operators would in the future be responsible only for proving tapes. According to the project coordinator, 'With the Matsuira [CNC machining centre] they don't actually do any programming. What they do is, they prove the programs out. At the moment we have a paper work system. I would like to run it with a DNC link-type system, but at the moment it's all paper work'.

In six of the case studies a supplement was paid to skilled CNC operators. The differential between skilled CNC machinists and conventional machinists ranged between £10 and £20 per week. One large-batch firm used individual piecework for its semi-skilled CNC operators. The setter-operators received the unit's average bonus. One workplace used a group bonus system and seven used a standard hourly rate. In five firms, the absence of individual or group bonus systems was considered important in encouraging labour flexibility. The works manager at Balance Machines explained:

In the machine shop they are capable of working any machine. We have no incentive scheme at all; they are paid a weekly wage and enjoy staff conditions. This is very important in terms of industrial relations. It is pragmatic . . . with any incentive scheme there tends to be confrontation all the time.

In six of the cases where CNC technology had been installed, shift-working was implemented. In four cases, two large-batch and two small-batch, a double-shift system each day and night was used before the introduction of either NC or CNC technology. In two small-batch firms double shifts had been introduced as a direct result of investing in CNC machining centres to shorten the payback periods of the technology.

The 'deskilling thesis', as applied to engineering, argues that employers reassert their control over the labour process by frag-menting engineering tasks, for instance, separating CNC production task skills between the programming and machine operation. All of the respondents, managers and those workers actually using CNC technology acknowledged that operator skills were affected by the new technology. But the evidence from this small sample is at variance with those writers who argue that 'as the machinery be-comes more complex, their own skills tend to decrease' (Thompson, 1981). These case-studies reveal that a universal deskilling thesis is difficult to sustain because of countervailing determinants in manu-facturing production. These included batch size, product constraints, machine innovations, plant size and internal organizational structures.

All the firms engaged in *small-batch* production preferred their CNC operators to be skilled, apprentice-trained, with machining experience on conventional machines. Where necessary the firms had a training policy, which provided for operators to be trained by the machine supplier or/and local colleges. When faced with a choice between 'button-pushers and responsible operators', management chose the latter for sound economic reasons. A CNC operator must still have traditional machining skills to diagnose tool wear or im-pending 'crashes'. As one owner-manager pointed out to me:

It's better to employ the best machinists on CNC. Labour costs are not a major consideration when you are paying £100,000 for a CNC machine. It's worth paying a skilled machinist to avoid mucking up the machine . . . although that is no guarantee.

In another case, it was common practice for CNC lathe operators to edit the programs written by production engineers. Management ignored this practice because by giving skilled operators a certain degree of discretion and autonomy it enabled the firm to run the machine more efficiently:

> If we have a program that is set to do a machining job in half an hour, I have no doubt a bloke can do it in 10 to 15 minutes cutting corners . . . I believe that ingenuity made this country great . . . I don't think we should discourage it providing they are not making scrap.

If management's long-term aim is to de-skill and fragment engineering tasks, and ultimately employ cheaper and more controllable semi-skilled labour, *product constraints* are an obstacle to such a strategy. Several managers pointed to the need to employ operators with both CNC and conventional skills because of the one-off nature of the work and complexity of the machining tasks. As a production manager expressed it:

> I have been in companies where they produce a tape with CAD/CAM and that's it. That's your tape. Push a green button. Well a monkey can do that. I don't believe that in our environment we can do that. In a mass production environment, producing nuts and bolts, yes . . . but not when you are manufacturing sophisticated machine tools like ours.

Developments in *machine tool technology* were also identified as a countervailing trend to the deskilling scenario. A number of managers explained that in contrast to the deskilling of the machine operative which took place with earlier generations of NC technology, the recent introduction of a new generation of user-friendly CNC systems is putting the operator back in charge of the machine. CNC lathes, such as the Japanese Moira Seika, has a visual display which facilitates manual data input (MDI) by the operator. The operator electronically in-puts into the machine the same data he would have conveyed manually using conventional machines. The machine is programmed from a graphic display on the screen or a drawing. Dimensions and cutting conditions are entered. The final stage is to run through and prove the program. CNC technology with a MDI facility has the potential to enhance operator skills. Some of the managers' comments illustrate the point:

> With the new CNC machines there is a swing to shopfloor control . . . the operator has more of a thinking job, he needs to know the machine functions.
>
> Manufacturing Systems Coordinator

> One was always told that new technology made life a lot easier and deskilled jobs. I don't think that this is the case. CNC has taken programming down to the shopfloor. It's a good development.
>
> Works Manager

Developments in CNC technology allowing operators to program the machine using menu-list software has enhanced operator skills but it could be argued that there is a tendency to de-skill the technician. As the project coordinator put it:

> When we say they are programming a machine down there, they never sit down and write a program. The actual system programs the job. What they do is to use the menu-list system . . . so they are not strictly speaking programming. They are doing the same as what we do on the CAD/CAM. You don't need to know how to program.

The majority of respondents acknowledged that *CNC operator* skills had 'increased a little', were 'different', required the worker to be 'literate and well numerate', needed a sound understanding of 'tooling management'.

The concept of deskilling, if used too generally, disguises the variety and fluidity of operator skills. This comes over particularly when interviewing CNC operators. When asked for examples of a task that requires less skill to perform on CNC, operators cited traditional manual machining tasks such as screw cutting. A CNC lathe operator, put it like this:

> Screw cutting on a manual machine you have to be watching it every moment. You have got to be able to take your tool out fast . . . wind your saddle back. You have to be careful you don't crash into the shoulder. So you have to have your wits about you.

But on CNC, the screw-cutting is done for you. All you have to do is to set the tool up, it works out how deep it's cutting; it's just generally easier.

The preparation and programming stage, however, was considered to be more skilful. Comments on a steward's questionnaire illustrate this: 'Programming the machine requires more skill as maths is used in the form of trigonometry for angles, and using the full scope of the machine'.

During the verification of programs, CNC operators require an appreciation of the technology greater than that expected of a 'button-pusher'. Unless there is a skilled setter-operator available, once the program has been proved, subsequent use requires further checking, as the lathe operator pointed out to me:

You need more skill to prove a tape. You have to make sure you don't go to sleep when you are proving it. You have got to know what the machine is doing. Although you can prove a tape, the next time the job comes round again it could slightly vary. You still have to check it.

Whether CNC operator skills were destroyed or enhanced depended upon two factors: operator access to program editing and/or the proving of tapes, and the approach of managers and operators to training. Perhaps equally important was whether managers and operators saw the CNC training as complementing previously acquired conventional machining skills. As one engineer remarked:

Skills are changing. I don't think they are diminishing at all. If you have been lucky and have been apprentice-trained on a manual machine all those skills are transferable and add to CNC skills. Therefore you have increased your skills.

Although in most cases the CNC technology was similar, the allocation of work, in particular a degree of operator discretion over programming, depended upon *plant size and existing labour arrangements*. For instance, where unskilled and semi-skilled workers were employed there would be a separate programming department and production engineers would generate programs. Skilled setter-operators could make minor amendments to the tape. In contrast, where CNC operators were recruited from an existing pool of skilled workers, their responsibilities tended to be far wider, ranging from editing and verifying tapes generated by production engineers, to actually producing their own tapes on the shopfloor.

Further, the degree of autonomy of CNC operators depended also on existing *internal organizational structures*. Within the firms CNC technology has to merge with the existing arrangements, especially when introduced in a piecemeal way over a number of years (Wilkinson, 1983:29). Of the firms using CNC technology, eight had separate programming departments. The justification for dividing programming and machining tasks was explained in terms of the lack of technical competence among the shopfloor skilled operators. Also, the division of tasks was justified on grounds of product and batch size. Some of the production engineers' comments explained this:

> The CNC lathe operators are not using it efficiently. For example, threading a bar. They might take twenty-four passes, when they could do it in eight. They always put that parameter in, they don't have the time to play with it at the sharp end.

> For simple components and small batches it's more economic and quicker for the shopfloor to write and prove a program. But for complex machining for large batches, production engineers can coordinate and plan tooling requirements, and it's better for programs to be written off-line.

Firms with complex organization structures installing NC technology in the 1970s used non-manual staff, often promoted from the shopfloor, for off-line programming. Design, planning and programming of machines tended to be viewed as hierarchical and discrete servicing activities. The differentiation of roles between non-manual staff and manual NC operators tended to be maintained after CNC was introduced (Hartmann et al. 1983). The different roles assigned to NC programmers and operators did sometimes lead to conflict, and experience of this conflict was given as one reason for choosing shopfloor autonomy by one manager. It was explained to me by a production director: 'At the previous company we had technicians programming machines. It was a constant battle. To the operator, the biggest thing was: you are going to kill me, the speed is too fast.'

In this particular case, a small company manufacturing a range of profile milling and engraving machines, all the shopfloor workers were 'time-served men'. The firm used one CNC Churchill lathe and three NC turret lathes. Organizational structures were simple and informal. The production director constantly supervised work on the shopfloor but left the NC/CNC programming to the operators. The production director elaborated: 'We find it better for the guy who actually runs the machine to actually program the work. Besides, it is more economical for a small company'.

Management Control

In addition to its potential to destroy or enhance operator skills, it has been suggested by labour process theorists that the decision to invest in CNC technology is motivated by management's desire to exert greater control over the labour process. Among those firms responding to the postal questionnaire, 50 per cent reported that CNC machine tools enabled a more detailed monitoring of the labour process.[7] Of the twelve case-studies with CNC hardware, six reported that the technology enabled a more detailed monitoring of job elements and employee performance (Table 4.3).

In four cases, management had invested in both the hardware and software systems, so that to a large extent progress-chasers had been replaced and elements of the work study process could be computerized. The rationale for introducing such a system was put in terms of improving 'efficiency', and minimizing human variability. The advantages of a management computer system was spelt out to me by a CNC project coordinator:

> I am looking for a DNC link system to measure the performance of any machine or group of machines . . . I don't want to employ a bloke to go down every two minutes to have a look at what Joe

Table 4.3   Effects of technical change on the monitoring of job elements and employee performance (absolute numbers)

	Not at all	*Limited extent*	*Large extent*
CAD	4	3	0
CNC machine tools	3	6	2
Computer testing	4	2	0
Robotics	4	3	0

(N = 12)

Bloggs is doing down there. I want to monitor it as it's going along.

In another case the investment in a computer system was justified on grounds of operator intransigence and lack of engineering expertise:

Having studied the situation down there, I don't believe they are using CNC lathes as efficiently as they could do. Not because they are idle; because they haven't had the education required. For example, threading a bar. They might take twenty-four passes, when they could do it in eight. I can put it on the CAD/CAM and simulate it on the graphics and then transfer it down there.

CNC Project Coordinator

Four cases demonstrate a diffusion of computer-based monitoring and manufacturing systems. In one case, design, technical services and production control were monitored through a central computer. The production manager explained the fundamentals of the system in this way: 'We are able to monitor performance all the way through the system to the very highest level. In the workshops, I know I can measure the performance down to a guy scratching his arse'.

Even in a small engineering firm employing fewer than a hundred, management utilize a computer system to monitor production and eliminate human variability, although the control over operators was considered 'not very important' in such a small workshop:

With CNC there is more control over how long that machine is on that operation . . . everything is fed back into the computer. You know what time was allowed and what time was taken . . . We can check and see that he's not cutting fresh air.

Numerous writers have examined how workers 'control' themselves in the labour process (Nichols and Beynon, 1977; Burawoy, 1979; Thompson, 1983; Fox, 1985). This implies examining the concepts of ideology and culture, and how they influence the relations between consent, coercion and labour resistance to management strategies. This small sample of case-studies provided evidence not only of a double process of technical and organizational change, but in those cases where cellular/JIT production was introduced, ideological processes of control pervaded the labour process.

In all three cases where cellular work structures were introduced a multi-union environment existed. There was no evidence of management recognizing or promoting only one union to facilitate change. This is at variance with scenarios presented by one writer (see Sayer, 1986:66). From the viewpoint of a long-term labour strategy it could, of course, be argued that these developments are as yet limited. In all three cases it was apparent that technical and organizational changes were accompanied by an ideological process directed at attitudinal transformation among shopfloor workers. There was evidence of new management initiatives associated with the 'human resource management' philosophy. There was, for instance, a strong commitment among the managers to extend direct communication and worker participation. The perspective on human resource management among the managers at the three firms can be summarized as follows: limited employee involvement is desirable, the aim of such a strategy being to promote workers' interest in the 'success' of the firm; machinery for involvement should be directed at the workforce as a whole, not just union representatives. At one level, it can be argued that improved communications and worker involvement act as an information transmitter. An alternative hypothesis is that it can be seen as an ideological process of getting workers to identify with production and management problems.

The Japanese manufacturing paradigm recognizes that it is inefficient not to use workers' capacities to the full. It is an acknowledgement that cellular production is a social process; it involves small groups of workers interacting together, within particular relations of production. Moreover, it recognizes that workers have potentially valuable contributions to make, and, working as a group, the potential to work more productively. However, the system also contains the inherent tensions between group autonomy and participation and the need for management control over the labour process. The enthusiasm for worker involvement in the three case-studies needs to be viewed, therefore, within the context of a mode of production which, to function most productively, requires a strategy designed to secure worker compliance and self and group motivation. Further, in a process that is vulnerable to stoppages caused by conflicts between individuals and competing interest groups, the strategy aims to counter the workers' potential power and minimize notions of collectivism.

TRADE UNION ORGANIZATION AND COLLECTIVE BARGAINING

The research on the case studies was undertaken in a period and in an industry where one would expect an 'employers' offensive' against union organization to have occurred. In order to pursue this theme, this section considers changes in workplace union organization, and examines the degree of involvement and influence of unionized labour on the processes of technical change. The intention is to refer to industrial relations surveys (see Chapter 3 for a discussion on these surveys) in order to locate and compare union organization and bargaining levels in the selected case-studies.

In describing the nature of workplace trade unionism in the selected case-studies, it is necessary, as is argued by Batstone et al. (1986), to consider a number of dimensions. First, the level of trade union density: there is likely to be a strong relationship between the proportion of workers unionized and union organization. Second, the disposition and capacity of unionized labour to influence the process of technical change also depends on the number and coordination of shop stewards. The relevant factors are steward density and the number of senior stewards 'quasi-elites', Batstone, (1977). Third, the successful coordination of union policies and action in a large plant with a large number of members and stewards will depend upon stewards meeting together to discuss and formulate a common approach to issues. An important facet of strong workplace trade unionism is therefore the existence of regular shop steward meetings. Union membership, the closed shop and union organization are discussed; then attention is turned to workplace collective bargaining. The discussion does not take in non-manual workers.

Union density refers to the proportion of manual workers who belong to a trade union. Table 4.4 shows that union density in the twelve case-studies is 70 per cent. In the 1986 survey by Millward and Stevens the comparable figure for the mechanical engineering industry was 66 per cent. However, if the three smallest firms were excluded, union density for the other nine cases is more than 90 per cent, and 87 per cent of the manual workers employed by the twelve firms were represented by trade unions. The overall picture is one of high levels of membership.

In more than half the case studies, union density among manual workers is over 90 per cent. At the other extreme, in only three firms (employing a total of only 74 manual workers) no manual workers

Table 4.4   Trade union membership and density in the case-studies, 1988

	Case-studies 1988	Mechanical Engineering* 1984
Trade union members (manual)	87.5%	36%
Average density (manual)	70.0%	66%
Average number of employees (manual)	209	101

N = 12 (* Millward and Stevens, 1986 survey).
Source: Manager and steward interviews.

are in a union. As in other surveys, size of the establishment and union density are strongly related. The contrast between the small 'jobbing', sub-contract firms, employing fewer than twenty-five, with no union membership, and the relatively large – in terms of West Yorkshire – companies having 200 or more manual workers and a membership between 90 and 100 per cent is striking (Table 4.5).

Legislation passed in the eighties concerning the closed shop could be expected to have changed the extent and the nature of the institution, suggest Millward and Stevens. Table 4.6 shows that 25 per cent of the firms operated a closed shop arrangement for manual groups. However, seven out of the twelve cases had 100 per cent membership among manual groups, and operated a *de facto* post-entry closed shop.

Millward and Stevens point out that most manual closed shops are comprehensive ones, in that they cover all the manual workers at the workplace in question. As a result, the *employee-coverage* of the closed shop follows the pattern of *establishment-coverage* (1986:105). The aggregate figure for manual workers covered by a closed shop in the twelve cases is equal to establishment-coverage: 25 per cent. The existence of a closed shop is related to other features of workplace trade unionism, senior stewards and stewards' committees. In two out of the three firms where closed shops operated, there existed a hierarchy of stewards, senior stewards and convener, high steward density, and there were regular stewards' meetings. Check-off the deduction of union subscriptions from members' pay, is one important facility that management may provide to unions. The check-off system has also been seen by some writers as an important aspect of management's attempts to incorporate shop stewards (Batstone,

Table 4.5   Trade union density in relation to establishment size, 1988

| | *Percentage of establishments with union density of* | | | | |
	0%	*1–49%*	*50–89%*	*90–100%*	*Average density*
All	25	0	17	53	70%
Size of establishment					
10–24 employees			17		
25–99			8		
100–199					
200–499			8	50	
500–999			8	8	

(N = 12)
Source: Manager and steward interviews.

Table 4.6   Union membership arrangements for manual workers in the case-studies, 1988, percentages

	All private manufacturing 1984*	*Case-studies 1988*
Establishments with closed shop	19	25
Proportion of manual workers in closed shop (per cent)	33	25
Check-off operating	30	42

Sources: Steward interviews
* Millward and Stevens, 1986

1984). Forty-two per cent of the firms operated a check-off system. This suggests that the system is more prevalent among the cases studied here than is given by the industrial figure provided by Millward and Stevens.

Where trade unions were recognized, there were one or more shop stewards present. In three workplaces, there were five or fewer stewards. In contrast, one firm had thirty-five stewards with a steward density of 12.8 per cent,[8] Steward density refers to the proportion of stewards to manual union members. Four other cases had a steward density between 16.6 and 19.1. The high steward density reflects the long-standing steward organization in engineering; it also indicates the unions' success in maintaining the number of stewards despite a

Table 4.7   Steward density in relation to establishment size, 1988

	Number of manual union members per steward, 1984*	Number of manual union members per steward, 1988
All cases	23	21
Size of workforce		
10–24	11	–
25–99	20	–
100–199	}	–
	}25	–
200–499	}	26
500–999	29	16

Sources: Steward interviews
* Millward and Stevens (1986)

Table 4.8   Trade union organization in the case-studies, 1988, percentage

	All private* manufacturing, 1984	Establishment size				
		10–24	25–99	100–199	200–499	500–999
Manual workers represented by:						
One or more stewards	98				58	17
Senior steward of two or more	46				25	8
Full-time steward	5				17	8
Regular stewards' meetings	33				25	17

(N = 12)
Sources: Steward interviews.
* Millward & Stevens, 1986.

fall in manual employment in the firms. Steward density figures are shown in Table 4.7.

There were senior shop stewards in a third of the firms studied, and in three firms a full-time steward was present; in five firms the stewards said there were meetings between stewards of the same union at their workplace. In one firm, the stewards had a formal meeting weekly,[9] two met fortnightly,[10] and two monthly[11] (Table 4.8).

Regular intra-union stewards' meetings are more prevalent in firms where workplace unionism is developed in terms of union density, and there are senior stewards and a full-time convener. This suggests that the greater the number of stewards in a plant, the greater is the need to 'coordinate' (Batstone, 1984) or 'control' (Hyman, 1979) stewards' activities. Coordination, as opposed to control, prevails when the formulation of union policy is a collective process which involves all stewards, not just a few senior stewards (Batstone, 1984:83). As one AEU convener told me: 'There is tight discipline but it's a collective decision. When you are talking about four unions and ten stewards, it's required'.

The preceding section has outlined at some length the evidence concerning union organization at the twelve selected workplaces. This evidence may be less than ideal, but it does help to compare and contrast the case-studies with industrial and national trends. The evidence does suggest that in nine firms with 'core' employment relationships, workplace trade unionism has survived largely intact. The section concludes with a consideration of case-study data which seek to verify managers' responses, and assess in more detail the extent and form of influence of unionized labour on the processes of technical change.

The survey found that the majority of managers reported that organized labour had virtually no influence on the processes of technical change.[12] However, managers may underestimate the significance of union opposition and influence. Managers may be either reluctant to admit that unions impinge on their decisions or they may be over-indulgent in their evaluation of their own success (Dodgson and Martin, 1987). The form of worker-involvement in technical change in the twelve selected case-studies is shown in Table 4.9. From the data it is clearly apparent that even according to the accounts of personnel managers, the extent of worker and union involvement was modest.

Daniel found that managers consulted or negotiated because they were required to do so, either by the trade unions at their work-places, or by workers' resistance to the changes. There was no

Table 4.9   Form of employee and union participation in technical changes, in these case-studies, percentages

Consulted	50
Negotiated a new technology agreement	25
Negotiated change using existing agreement	8

N = 12
Source: Managers response to postal questionnaire.

Table 4.10   Extent and form of trade union participation in technical changes, in these case studies, by establishment size, percentages

Form of participation	Establishment size, 1988					
	10–24	25–99	100–199	200–499	500–999	Total
No consultation	16	8			8	32
Consulted				58	8	66
Negotiated technology agreement				16	8	24
Negotiated change using existing agreements					8	8
Other						

N = 12
Source: Management and steward interviews.

suggestion that managers were committed to worker involvement as a means of generating enthusiasm for change (1987:113).

Evidence from shop stewards revealed that managers' commitment to worker involvement was minimal and pragmatic, a direct response to information from stewards or a reply to a rumour. This pragmatic nature was explained by another AEU convener; 'Management attitude is they go out of their way to consult rather than negotiate. But they consult by default. You go in to see management after hearing rumours, then they consult'.

Where unions were not recognized, there was no consultation with workers affected by CNC technology. Formal consultations were more frequent in those larger establishments recognizing trade unions (Table 4.10). However, the strongest relationship was between formal consultation and steward hierarchy and organization. The importance of workplace unionism is confirmed also by Daniels (1987); he found that union organization served as 'a context which encouraged managers to engage more in all forms of consultation, informal and formal' (1987:284).

In only three out of the twelve cases had management and unions negotiated a new technology agreement (Table 4.10). One agreement states:

New technologies would be introduced with the fundamental intention of saving cost, increasing productivity, providing a better product or service, but not as a deliberate attempt to reduce the number of people employed or de-skill or fragment jobs.[13]

In this case, there existed a sophisticated stewards' organization in the plant, including regular stewards' meetings and a full-time union convener. The senior stewards had attended TUC advanced shop-steward courses, and the stewards' committee had developed a common view on new technology. To quote the AEU Convener, 'We were all convinced that we needed a new technology agreement, and we were all prepared to take all measures necessary to get one'.

Negotiations for a new technology agreement started in October 1985. The agreement was finally concluded in February 1987 after two outside conferences and the threat of industrial action. The reluctance by management to negotiate was related to me by the convener:

> We were made aware that the factory was being computerised, by contacts in the admin side. When we queried management they were very evasive; in fact, on occasions they actually lied to us. Fortunately that manager and that style has gone. When the new managing director took over eighteen months ago, management were more prepared to come to terms with communicating with us, and recognizing the need for that.

In this particular case, employee involvement apparently amounted to more than management rhetoric designed to foster public relations or impress researchers. The new open, participative style had resulted in something more tangible. What is interesting however, is that throughout two extensive interviews, the process of negotiating and the threat of industrial action were never mentioned by the managers. The existence of developed steward organization is no guarantee that management will either consult or negotiate over new technology. At the other extreme, in one case, where CNC technology had been introduced in a large-batch environment, where management were allegedly 'giving more information' to employees and union organization was characterized by senior stewards, full-time official and regular steward meetings, management approach was to 'bulldoze' new machines onto the shopfloor without consultation or agreement with the union. As the personnel manager, put it,

> We didn't approach the unions. You would never get the damn thing in if you did. I know it goes against those people who say you should consult at every stage. I honestly believe that that's the biggest load of rubbish that anybody has ever come out with . . . If

somebody came to me and said there is a machine that does your job six times as quick, we'd have to negotiate. I would say, that thing is coming in over my dead body. It's like asking: 'can I chop your head off?'

Management's strategy in this case was to install the machine in the workshop and establish an elite group of skilled operators as an 'experimental team', to set and then operate the machines on a higher rate of pay. Install the new technology and then 'argue how much you are going to pay' was the way the personnel manager described his tactics. In this particular case the absence of any common view among the shop stewards is clearly apparent from a perusal of their committee minutes. Between February 1982 and December 1987 the issue of new technology did not even arise in the minutes.

Negotiations over new technology tended to be restricted to traditional bargaining areas, in particular enhanced payments for operating CNC technology, and health and safety: for instance, shift patterns. To quote one personnel manager: 'Yes, to an extent the unions influenced us. We recognized, for example, the classic that they don't work on Friday nights'.

None of the managers or stewards, for example, said that bargaining took place over investment strategy and the type of machines purchased. Enhanced payments to operators using CNC technology was therefore the most important area where the unions influenced technical change.

New technology agreements were commoner, the larger the size of the establishment (Table 4.10). The strongest relationship identified was between technology agreements and level of trade union organization at the workplace. What is striking is the unanimity of views over the desirability of new technology: all the managers, workers and shop stewards agreed that this was both desirable and necessary. The following comments were typical:

Our trade unions have always *encouraged* [my emphasis] us to bring in the latest equipment, so we don't have that sort of problems.

Personnel Manager

I don't think you can oppose it [new technology]. You have got to come to terms with it. But what you can do is to endeavour to distribute the benefits and try to get some job security.

AEU Shop Steward

The support from unionized labour for new technology supports Willman's findings that opposition to technical change from trade unions is 'insufficiently extensive to justify the view that UK trade union behaviour is a major obstacle in technological change' (1986: 59–60). This brief sketch of workers' attitudes to technical innovation further undermines the long-established view that Britain's relatively low labour productivity is largely attributable to workers' hostile attitude to change and new technology (Nichol, 1986). The evidence showed that workers and their representatives accepted the need for new technology and had become more sympathetic to management views; as one manager remarked: 'our stewards are more worldly-wise, there is a greater appreciation of financial and marketing aspects of the business and relations with customers'. Nevertheless, despite such favourable attitudes the levels of consultation and negotiation were conspicuously low.

In two cases where stewards had not developed a common view on new technology there had been *no* consultation or negotiation. Moreover, in these plants the stewards found it difficult to challenge managerial prerogative. In particular, without a union strategy, the incremental nature of technical diffusion proved difficult to combat. As one steward expressed it:

You see they are brought in so slowly and gently. The machine arrives, it is left for a while and before long he is operator for that machine: everything has gone by. He might get a bit more money, but it's just *crept in* [my emphasis]. It isn't a clear cut thing.

To summarize, Senker and Beesley (1986) warn against falling into what they call 'the rhetoric of the automatic factory', but there is a problem in interpreting the respondent's experience of the effects of technical change on employment. There is evidence of direct negative employment effects as a consequence of introducing CNC technology. Moreover, evidence was provided which shows that cutting labour costs influenced management's decision to invest in CNC machine tools. The assessment of deskilling among manual engineering workers has centred around the question whether CNC operators have been able to capture or have been allocated the task of programming. In small-batch environments management adopted a responsible autonomy strategy and skilled workers on CNC lathes performed both the programming and machining tasks: the unification of conception and execution. In large-batch production hierarchical divisions were apparent between white-collar programmers, skilled setters and semi-skilled operators, and management strategy was characterized by direct control. The choice between these two competing strategies was determined by existing divisions of labour, technical and efficiency considerations.

This small sample of engineering establishments provides sufficient variation to evaluate the degradation of work, in terms of engineering crafts, with a good deal of caution. Examples have been cited of CNC operator skills being transferred to the preparation stage, by the programming needs of a new generation of CNC machine tools. The introduction of CNC technology can be an opportunity to build upon traditional craft knowledge and skills. It can lead to an enrichment of skills and a degree of shopfloor autonomy. As such, the evidence is at variance with the destruction of skills thesis posited by some labour process writers. However, the case-studies did provide an insight into managers' attempts to obtain greater information and feedback on shopfloor activities by installing computerized monitoring and information-gathering systems.

Finally, evidence does suggest that in nine of the 'core' employment relationships, workplace trade unionism has survived both the recession and the legal onslaught by the Conservative government. The pattern of negotiations over the introduction of CNC machine tools tended to be restricted to traditional bargaining issues, such as extra payments for CNC operators. Contrary to managers' assertions of employee involvement, generally consultation was minimal. Formal consultation and negotiation were more frequent in those larger establishments with a developed steward organization and where stewards had developed a common view of new technology. No union representatives and, more significantly, no manager cited union attitude as an obstacle to introducing CNC technology. The next three chapters extend the analysis of the engineering labour process by examining in more depth three cases: Servo, Oil Tool and Flowpak Engineering.

5 The Motor Components Company:
Japanization in Large-Batch Production

Our people are the source of our strength. They provide our corporate intelligence and determine our reputation and vitality. Involvement and teamwork are core values.
Ford Motor Company, Quality System Standard (1987:iii)

In this chapter we discuss the changes in a large company engaged in large-batch manufacturing and marketing of specialist components: air-brake systems, vacuum pumps, hydraulics, for vehicle and agricultural tractor industries. The change to a cellular system started in 1985, and the following year the company invested approximately £5.5 million in CNC machine tools and production control software. By the time of the research visits in 1986 the changes had been completed, although some further developments were still occurring. The first section of this chapter gives a brief background to the company. This is followed by a section which discusses the investment in new technology and how the manufacturing system was transformed by Japanese-style work structures. The investment and restructuring cannot be understood without examining some global development in the motor-vehicle manufacturing industry, and this is discussed in section three. The fourth section discusses the effects of the changes on employment and manual workers' skills. In contrast to the other case-studies of similar size reported here, we find the union played an insignificant role in the process of change, and section five discusses the factors associated with the marginal role of the shop stewards in the plant.

COMPANY PROFILE

The company, Servo Engineering, was founded in 1897 to manufacture an improved miner's safety lamp. In the 1920s the company produced two-thirds of all miners' lamps and lighting equipment used in Britain. Thirty years later the engineering production facilities were re-organized to manufacture commercial vehicle components, mainly hydraulic valves and diesel injection equipment. In 1965 Servo Engineering became a subsidiary of Zipton Holding Ltd, which merged, in September 1977, with American Ensign. Servo Engineering then became part of American Ensign, with manufacturing companies in the UK, USA, and West Germany. In 1988 the UK group had four sites in Great Britain. The personnel manager at the West Yorkshire plant negotiated with union representatives at plant level on all aspects of pay and conditions of employment within centrally laid-down parameters.

THE PROCESS OF CHANGE

Technological Change on the Shopfloor

Between 1984 and 1988 the company replaced over half its conventional and NC machines with CNC. As in other firms the new technology had been installed alongside existing conventional machine tools. Of all the firms visited in this study, Servo Engineering had the most extensive and sophisticated technology, including hi-tech robotic machining cells. Such a development was the long-term management aims, for as one manager commented: 'At the end of the day the aim is to self-load, switch the lights off, and leave it. It's got to move to that sort of technology'.

In 1985 the firm organized production into six cells. What follows is a description of one of these, Cell 20, to illustrate how the company utilized Japanese manufacturing concepts and CNC technology.

Cell 20 is located in the 'basement'. The ceiling is low and the ventilation poor, and on entering one is struck by the heat and the strong smells from the cutting oils and general activities. The cell is one of the larger units in the plant, employing about forty people. The CNC machine tools are six lathes, five grinding machines, two drills and two pallet-loading machining centres, capable of holding forty-eight components. It was explained that to reduce the payback period of the machine centres they were used twenty-two hours a day, in theory only stopping for essential maintenance. The 'centre-piece' of machine tool technology in Cell 20 is two robotic machining units. One cell leader believed that a human operator could do the work of the robots more efficiently. As he commented, 'robots don't go on strike or take tea breaks, but they do break down a hell of a lot'.

Manual operators using the CNC machine tools believed that their skills were being enhanced because they were using 'new technology'. Andrew, a semi-skilled operator who had worked for the company twelve months and had no previous engineering experience described his work to me:

> I machine pistons . . . I've got a robot loader to load the turning machine . . . another machine that takes the component from the machine and puts it into an electronic gauging system (this is controlled by a computer). The robot then passes it on to a heat treatment unit. I have to load it. If the tools break or become worn, I have to replace them. A robot can't do that yet.

The long-term aim of management was to reduce their dependence on labour. But the hi-tech units can also play a commercial and political role. It was clear from discussions with the cell leader that visitors were often shown the robotic unit, and the prestigious investment was used to impress potential customers. However, the robots, despite their propensity to mechanical failure, can be viewed as a threat to workers to gain their compliance and cooperation.

Both external and internal pressures compelled Servo Engineering to adopt a sophisticated computer integrated system (CIS). The external pressure came from the Ford Motor company, a major customer. In the early 1980s Ford adopted a quality standard which they insisted their suppliers adhered to. This resulted in a change of emphasis from defect detection to defect prevention through the application of computerized control, employee involvement and training. This quality control standard is referred to as Ford Q101. To enhance quality the company adopted statistical process control (SPC). This system seeks to replace inspection with measurement and correction of the process which manufactures the product, and as explained it is carried out with computerized assistance by operators. The firm also invested in a software package called production monitoring control (PMC). To understand the significance of PMC it is necessary to discuss the previous system using progress 'loaders'.

The progress loaders 'chased' the work-in-progress as it moved from various workstations in the factory, for instance, from turning, milling and drilling sections, through to testing and painting. A job-card recording the completion of functions was attached to the work and a copy filed in the office. The old system of work-scheduling was described by George Wyke, the personnel manager: 'Progress-loaders chased it round and booking clerks sat in a middle office with their bits of paper. All that has practically disappeared.'

The new micro-computer based control system using production monitoring control (PMC), involved operators using their personal identification card to log on and off when tasks had been completed. PMC reduces inventory and reduces the gap between receiving the order and delivery by breaking down a master production schedule, based on orders, into detailed day-to-day production schedules. To do this, the PMC database must have knowledge of how much material is in stock or on order and, if appropriate, how many of the finished-goods. Thus for the system to work, feedback from the shopfloor is essential, so that it knows when tasks have been completed.

In the office of Cell 20 two terminals displayed data on work-in-progress gathered from operators scanning their card into a machine at the start and end of each shift. Information on productive and non-productive activities (e.g. trade union duties, waiting time) was electronically recorded. The external commercial pressure to improve quality control influenced the company's decision to invest in computer software packages. There were however internal pressures stemming from the firm adopting cellular and just-in-time production methods.

With a just-in-time system, if supplies deliver daily instead of weekly, five times as many transactions take place between customer and supplier. So as to minimize paper, financial and invoicing systems need to be computerized to facilitate the electronic exchange of data. As one commentator has stated, 'Arranging this two-way flow of information is a big task which, again, arises out of a genuine need, not just an urge to computerise'.[1]

In his study of a machine-tool manufacturer Wilkinson (1983) refers to computerized work scheduling as 'control technology'. The control of operators' work is evident, but the computerized system also controlled the activities of the cell leaders. The system had added stress to the cell leaders' role because mistakes could more easily be identified by senior management. According to one cell leader: 'Previously, mistakes recorded on paper could be destroyed but with this computer your mistakes are more difficult to retrieve in the system, and can be identified by somebody else and traced back'.

Quality enhancement was not confined to utilizing the latest CNC hardware and data processing software. Throughout the plant organizational changes had been directed to the same ends. A new level of supervision was introduced. the product coordinator. In addition, there was a strict division of tasks between machine operators, machine setters and programmers.

The Cellular System and Job Design

The company started to introduce cells in late 1985. The cells are product-centred, for example vacuum pumps, air compressors, or foot pumps. The cells were described as 'mini-factories' within a factory. Each cell had sufficient machining to complete the majority of the manufacturing stages. Processes outside the scope of the cell were subcontracted out, either to another cell, or to an external contractor. The principle was explained like this:

> If you need a special service like the plating process and you can't do it, it's subcontracted outside. If you need a service which is within the company, but not in your cell, then effectively you subcontract that work to another cell.

The number of workers in each cell varied between 12 and 50. The cells operated a three-shift system: 6 a.m. to 2, 2 to 10, and 10 to 6. New recruits were appointed not only to a particular grade but also to a particular shift. The physical layout of the cells varied immensely, from on the one hand Cell 20, which was humid and smelly, to Cell 60 where the designers appeared to take psychological perceptions into account by displaying growing plants around the workshop. A superintendent was responsible for three cells, and there was a night-shift superintendent for the whole six cells.

Labour process writers have highlighted the development of the capitalist mode of production in terms of fragmentation of tasks and division of mental and manual labour. Therefore a useful starting point is to consider the choices made by the management of division of labour within the cells. In each cell there was a graded hierarchy and pattern of social relations. The degree of stratification in the cells is shown in Table 5.1.

There were two supervisory grades concerned with the manufacturing aspects of the cell. The 'cell leader' or supervisor had overall responsibility for the cell; 'he effectively managed the cell'. The

Table 5.1   Division of labour in the cells

Supervisory grades
Cell supervisor
Product coordinator
Charge-hand
Manual grades
Setter
Setter-operator
Operator
Labourer

'product coordinator's' task was to ensure the supply of raw materials and parts to meet cell production targets, following just-in-time principles. The product coordinator and the 'charge-hand acted as progress-chasers in the cell. Below the supervisory grades was a hierarchy of manual grades reflecting different levels of training, experience and pay scales. There were two grades of 'setters', the majority being apprentice-trained and paid a skilled rate. At the time of the research this was £3.52 per hour. They also received the workshop average bonus. A setter-operator was classified as skilled, but they were operators who had shown some aptitude and 'come-up through the ranks'. They set a more limited range of machines and were paid less than the setters. The scope for upward mobility was stressed by George Wyke: 'There is nothing to stop a person coming to this company unskilled and becoming a setter. We don't close the door on them, and the unions don't close the door on them'.

Next in the hierarchy came the four grades of operators: 'standard'; 'experienced'; 'standard group'; and 'experienced group'. The standard operators looked after one or two machines. The tasks simply involved loading and unloading, and pressing the on/off button. Experienced operators ran the same machines, but had progressed onto the higher grade by having experience of a wider range of machines. Standard and experienced group machinists operated a group of machines, three or more, the latter receiving the highest rate among the operators for additional experience and acquired specific skills. The lowest manual rate was for general labouring. The setters played a key role within the cell and 'too few setters' was a frequent complaint from cell leaders. The job hierarchies within the cells reflected strategic choice by management to separate the functions of setting and programming. The large-batch nature of production at Servo Engineering also influenced management choice of a

Taylorist approach to job design. Volume production and high quality standards resulted in strict demarcation between the manual grades and virtually no scope for shopfloor autonomy.

Since the mid-1980s, conceptions of labour structure have been dominated by different types of 'flexibility'. The personnel manager explained the company's policy on flexibility:

> The people come into this company on the basis of full flexibility. That's for semi-skilled operatives . . . they are under the control of setters or charge-hands and senior management. The run-of-the-mill average semi-skilled operative comes into the company to do whatever we want . . . It could be assembly, painting or packing, testing, or sweeping the floor. We have full flexibility.

In December 1986, the company made over 100 workers redundant. But the following month it recruited about 100 operators. The new operatives were employed on a different' more flexible contract of employment. The timing of the redundancies and subsequent recruitment on new conditions only became apparent through discussions with shopfloor workers. Andrew explained:

> The management is definitely more aggressive . . . Since the Christmas of 1986, they got rid of a lot of the older workforce which was the old stalwart union men. And the new operators have been employed under a different contract. We have to work whatever shift they decide. I think they are supposed to give us a week's prior notice, but they tend not to do that . . . A lot of the lads are obliged to do it anyway because they are bothered about their jobs.

Full-time semi-skilled workers received little training. Maura had worked for the firm for nineteen years, and made the following observation about company training: 'Lately I haven't seen anybody training. A young fella lives near me. He started about a fortnight since. He was a miner and they just seemed to show him for an hour and that was it – which is wrong'.

Other workers made similar comments about inadequate training: 'It's a joke . . . as a setter operator you can be asked to do a job that you have never done before . . . the only training you get is maybe 15 minutes with a setter'.   CNC operator

The workers' remarks on training also give an insight into the narrow and unskilled tasks resulting from CNC technology. The firm had increasingly relied upon outside subcontractors, a practice which facilitates greater numerical flexibility.

For a long time the firm had contracted out some essential, but not firm-specific areas of work, for example canteen, cleaning and security, but more recently, additional areas were being considered. Hydraulic presses were to be sold off to a local fabrication firm, leading to the closure of the plant's press shop. The rationale for increased dependence on subcontractors was put in technical economies, labour savings and numerical flexibility terms:

> The press work we do is not of the volume it was ten years ago. We can well do with the space to do other things. The costs at Fabrication Ltd more than break-even with our costs. Subcontracting does two things. First, you are not paying to keep stuff in your own place on store. Secondly, it keeps down to the minimum the number of indirect workers, because at the end of the day everybody lives off the work produced by direct workers.

Gender divisions were also evident in the factory. Assembly work within the cells was predominantly undertaken by women, according to one cell leader the 'men don't like doing assembly work because its considered women's work'. This sustains the theme developed by Bradley (1986). Her study of the relationship between gender and technological innovation in the hosiery industry indicates that sexual divisions of labour can be related to employer and employee strategies. The labour process may reflect both the employer's aim to reduce costs and the determination of organized male workers to retain traditional work roles and privileges. Bradley concludes that:

> Processes of degradation and resegmentation are often intricately linked with the development of sex-typed jobs within a patriarchal division of labour.
>
> (Bradley, 1986:71)

To sum up, technological change may be associated with either skill enhancement or deskilling strategies, depending on the manufacturing system. The first strategy was more apparent in the firms characterized by small-batch production, for instance, Oil Tool Engineering and Flowpak Engineering. The second strategy was evident in the large-batch environment such as at Servo Engineering. At

Servo the direct control strategy resulted in greater division of labour. At one extreme, operators performed the simplest machining tasks with little or no formal training: workers were also expected to be totally flexible on job tasks and working times, and were closely supervised. Towards the other extreme, skilled setters, although they did not program the machines, undertook a range of tasks requiring conventional and CNC skills. Such divisions were facilitated by CNC innovations and were dependent on the strategic choice made by senior management. The policy of the management in this large and large-batch organization was to reduce manual labour as far as possible to the most basic form, unskilled and readily replaced to suit economic circumstances.

RECESSION IN THE CAR INDUSTRY

Why did these changes take place? In the early 1980s, the central problem for Servo Engineering's senior management was market contraction resulting from the collapse in the production of UK car and commercial vehicles. The firm is a major supplier of components to the motor vehicle industry: the investment, restructuring of production, and any assessment of management strategy, cannot be understood without first appreciating the external contextual changes.

Britain's motor car industry has been the barometer of the whole manufacturing sector's health. In the early 1980s, contraction of output and employment was the symptom of economic crisis and 'de-industrialization'. Between 1979 and 1983 output and employment in the industry fell by almost a half.[2] The contraction in the output of UK vehicles took place within the context of a decline in the relative trading position of the UK industry. From 1970 to 1983 UK car exports fell by two-thirds, while the percentage of the British car market supplied by imports increased from 27.4 to 57.1 per cent. These phenomena and restructuring in the global car industry had a profound impact on UK component suppliers, as noted by Fine and Harris: 'The British components industry had been based on relatively small scale production and model variety so that in the face of international competition a large number of its firms were forced to close'. (1985:273)

Excess car production capacity, price cutting, low margins in motor vehicle manufacturing, and the arrival of Nissan in the UK, demanded a fundamental reappraisal of the way Servo conducted its business. By 1984 senior management had become convinced that investment in new CNC machine tools, software packages and new organizational methods were the most effective way of resolving problems associated with unit costs and quality standards. To quote George Wyke again:

> In the initial stages there is no doubt that new technology was introduced in the company in order to lower unit costs. It was known that by using new technology . . . the quality standards were bound to be better *because you are not relying on the individual* and that was really why it was done [my emphasis].

Better monitoring of key performance indicators – quality, lead time, and productivity – were the central factors in Servo's decision to install CNC technology and a sophisticated computer-based control system. By primarily focusing on capitalist endeavours to control the unpredictable factor, labour, critics of Braverman (1974) have highlighted the reductionist nature of the analysis. This case-study suggests that to understand managerial practices and job redesign, it is necessary to move beyond the immediate labour process, and examine the contradictions inherent in capitalist production and product markets.

Cost reductions and competition in product markets continue to affect car makers and subsequently the suppliers of car components. Addressing the *Financial Times* Motor Conference, Ian Forster, Austin Rover's purchasing director, announced that in future the company's relationship with its suppliers would be based upon subcontractors meeting 'defined standards ensuring their total competitiveness'.[3]

The decision by Servo's management to change production and quality control methods stemmed not simply from a desire to lessen their reliance on human activity in the labour process. Impinging upon management choice was commercial pressure from the firm's major customer, Ford. George Wyke held that 'When Ford Motor Company decided to do a deal with people who have quality standard Q101, it forced this company in turn to new technology. It was felt that better quality would come out of the new machine tools.

External pressures also influenced the decision to adopt just-in-time production methods. Said George Wyke:

A certain number of our customers have forced us into it [JIT]. Ford have, Massey have. Because what they are saying is, when we've got it it's stock, and it's money. We are the same. We will say to a supplier, we are pig-in-the-middle, who have all been fat and lazy in past times: we want 200 of them by next Thursday, at 2 o'clock . . . I have seen vehicles turned away. A guy was told to park up and we would take it tomorrow so that it goes on next month's accounts. It's as tight as that . . . We are *forced* to influence our suppliers [my emphasis].

Evidence from the Servo case-study suggests that labour control is not the only, or even the principal, interest of the firm's senior management. However, that does not mean that there is no juncture, even though it is not articulated by management, between corporate strategy and labour control. Several factors suggest that the criteria which enter the investment equation are not solely economic or technical, but in Wilkinson's terms, 'political': the management wanted to minimize the human factor in the manufacturing processes in order to improve quality standards. In addition, there was a six-weeks' strike at the plant – referred to by the Personnel Manager, George Wyke, as the 'debacle of 1983' – during the depth of recession in industry.

Computerised Control

The installation of production monitoring control (PMC) and statistical process control (SPC) have important implications for management control over the labour process. In response to the postal questionnaire the previous personnel manager had reported that CNC machine tools, robotics, and computer-aided-tested had to a 'limited extent' enabled a more detailed monitoring of job elements and employee performance. He went on to describe how the new technology had enabled greater monitoring of workers' tasks and performance: 'You can monitor more closely because of new technology . . . Because of the tally system there is very much tighter control over efficiency of machine tools, test rigs, assembly areas'.

Discussions with the incumbent personnel manager suggest that one motivating factor in investing in computerized testing is what Noble (1979), refers to as the 'ideology of control', according to which, worker intervention in the labour process is seen as a potential for 'human error'. Improvements in quality standards were to be achieved by minimizing labour involvement. As the personnel manager asserted: 'it was known that by using new technology the quality standards were bound to be better because you are not relying on individuals'.

The management tools of PMC and SPC were supplemented by more traditional bureaucratic forms of control, 'In fact we disciplined a guy who didn't check work properly', said George Wyke. A cell leader provided further insight into the control process: 'We monitor . . . the job goes out and we keep up the pressure . . . If my production controller has chased and can't get anywhere, I will go in all guns blazing: "Why haven't I got my stuff? You are letting me down! This kind of thing – in a proper manner.'

A sample of workers were asked how effective in their view were management in terms of control and the monitoring of workers' performance. Their comments concur with management's regarding the effectiveness of the system:

> I would say they know from day to day every move everybody makes . . . Every move you make is monitored. When you clock on the computer, they know how many components good or bad you have turned out. Basically they know what you are capable of.
>
> June (operator)

> We used to have time sheets and book-on using cards. A lady in the office booked you on and off. But now with the computer you do it yourself.
>
> Maura (operator)

> They keep a track of them here. If your bonus drops they know that quantity is down and they ask why. It's done every day.
>
> Cliff (setter)

The notion that such a control system leaves the worker powerless, and control in the labour process is a zero-sum concept, is a theme explored by post-Braverman critics. Although it could not be investigated and substantiated, the system apparently offered scope for some manipulation by the workers as this frank comment from a semi-skilled operator makes clear: 'We put into the computer whatever we want. The operator can fiddle the computer because it's up to him to tap in how many he has done.'

The vulnerability of manufacturing software has been acknowledged by another source. Describing the advantages of a software package, Manufacturing Resource Planning (MRP), one writer admitted that 'the information about what is in stock, what is on order and what is already on the shopfloor as work-in-progress must be accurate'.[4]

To conclude this section Braverman's assumption that management is preoccupied with labour regulation is an over-simplification of management practice. By extending the analysis beyond the labour process, to include contextual changes outside the organization, such as contracting product markets and imposed quality standards, it is apparent that numerous factors, not labour control *per se*, determine investment decisions.

EMPLOYMENT, SHOPFLOOR AUTONOMY AND SOCIAL RELATIONS

This section first examines the effects of the charges on employment manual workers' skills at Servo Engineering. It then goes on to consider the new pattern of social relations in the plant created by changes in job redesign.

Numbers employed in the Leeds plant fell from 772 to 442, a decrease of 42.7 per cent; between 1980 and 1985. All occupations, including management, declined, but the largest fall occurred among the semi-skilled operatives, from 543 to 287 – a decline of 47 per cent. The numbers employed are shown by occupational category in Table 5.2.

The introduction of micro-based technology in the machine shop did have a negative employment effect according to the reports of two personnel managers, and the AEU convener Philip Redman, who completed the postal questionnaire, reported that reductions in manpower had resulted from a combination of the economic environment, technical change and 'reorganization' of production. He also revealed that output in 1985 was equal to the 1980 figure while employing 330 fewer workers. On the shopfloor the AEU convener had little doubt that new technology had provided the opportunity to reduce labour; 'The new machining centres can do the work of three or four machines,' he thought.

In addition, the robotics cell had replaced three semi-skilled operatives. The firm reorganized the stores department and installed a new micro-computer based control system in each cell. This

Table 5.2   Employment by occupation at Servo Engineering,
1980 and 1985

Occupational category (1)	Number 1980 (2)	Number 1985 (3)	Percentage change 1980–1985 (4)
Managerial staff	12	9	−25
Draughtsmen	6	4	−33
Technicians	21	14	−33
Clerical	72	46	−36
Supervisors	24	18	−25
Craftsmen	94	64	−32
Operatives	543	287	−47
Total	772	442	−43

Source: Questionnaire return from personnel manager.

investment made four or five storekeepers redundant. Further, the computerized system for production and quality control and cellular methods had led to direct job losses among non-manual staff, according to the MSF senior steward Geoff Tanner: 'Yes, jobs have been lost. Production control was centralized and a computer was installed; five or six people went; five or six people doing progress chasing went, also.'

Operators used up to four CNC machines. This 'flexibility' was a direct result of the simplification and improvements in machine tool technology.

Job Redesign

The Servo case-study provided the opportunity to analyse the effects of new technology on operators' skills in a large-batch, unionized workplace. The question of deskilling and shopfloor autonomy centres on the control of programming. All the managers and cell leaders stated they preferred a strict division of labour between operators, setters and programmers. This is in contrast to managers interviewed in small-batch workplaces. Neither was there any apparent disagreement over programming between unions, the AEU and MSF, on this central issue, and this is in contrast to the findings of Wilkinson,1983; Brady, 1984; and Batstone et al, 1987.

Each cell had a graded hierarchy. Operators had no access or discretion over the running of the machines; their task was limited to loading and unloading them and 'pushing buttons'. Setter-operators and setters were not allowed to write or amend tapes. This was despite the fact that setters were skilled and most of the younger workers had experience of generating their own tapes in previous employment. Prior to March 1988, setters were allowed to adjust and prove tapes. But in order to increase quality standards further, setters received written notification that their intervention was prohibited. As one CNC setter explained: 'you can't just go in and change a program or alter it . . . I can prove a tape but not alter it without permission'.

Work was characterized by a restricted type of 'implicit control' (Watson, 1987), and a 'low-trust' relationships (Fox, 1974). Mistrust of the employees became a justification for the direct control strategy and the rationale for the separation of programming and setting of the CNC machines. It was expressed by Don, a cell leader:

> If you had a setter-operator on every damn machine, we would be having different levels of quality because you would have people altering programs willy nilly; reducing feeds and speeds and God knows what. Getting round for bonus. Getting a quick way round and everything that goes with it.

If there is some ambivalence about the effects of technical change on setters' skills, this is not the case with operators. For this large group of manual workers there was universal acceptance that innovations in machine tools had further reduced their skills. To quote one cell leader:

> Most involves just loading and pressing a button.There is nothing else there. That's why we do employ semi-skilled people. These people come from all walks of life, they have no formal apprenticeship. These machines, I wouldn't say they are idiot-proof, but they are as near as you can get.

Another manager considered that CNC machines had reduced the tasks of operator to simply loading and pressing buttons: 'you could train a monkey to do it'. The skilled setters also considered that CNC technology had further deskilled the machine operator's work. As Cliff pointed out, 'Everything is geared up to make thousands of things here . . . The only thing operators do now is press the button.

Walter the AEU convener, also concurred with this view: 'I think new technology has deskilled the semi-skilled by a large amount. Take DB4 tests, you just put the valve into the machine and press a button and it automatically tests itself'.

When it came to examining operators' opinions there was clearly a problem with defining the meaning of skill. Most operators equated skill with versatility in machine operations and tasks. Some of the operators' comments illustrate the point:

> When I came first they used to put valves in with a hammer . . . now it's done with a machine. There's a lot more machinery. [Skill has] probably increased because I can do many things that I couldn't before. Generally the machines are not hard to work.
>
> Rick

> My skill's remained the same . . . I consider myself versatile. I can do most jobs they give me.
>
> June

The division of labour and the Taylorist approach is a function of large-batch production, with stringent quality standards, and the choice of management to employ largely unskilled labour. It also depends upon existing organizational arrangements. The separation of programming and operating was established in the 1970s, when NC machines were introduced onto the shopfloor, and the size of the operation warranted the creation of a programming section. Programmers, most of whom were recruited from the skilled manual group, were granted white-collar status. These working practices were accepted by the unions and continued when CNC machines were introduced in the mid-1980s.

Job Design and Social Relations

New technology and cellular/just-in time methods can embody different social relations, and one consequence of the changes in work organization at the plant was the new role of the cell leader. Cell leaders had responsibility for the manufacturing and related planning and problem-solving, requiring extensive knowledge of the machines and processes in their cell. But among the new skills expected of cell leaders was labour management within the cell. As one described his new role:

My function is to co-ordinate the work-flow. I am dealing with suppliers and customers on a one-to-one basis. I also to deal with the overall discipline. I am also responsible for quality within the unit. I have to visit companies if we should get anything wrong. I have to go and face the flak. In other words the old-fashioned idea of the foreman has long gone.

From an industrial relations aspect it is the additional labour management responsibilities that are most significant. Discipline within the workplace has been defined as 'action taken by management against an individual or group who have failed to conform to the rules established by management within the organization'.[5] The cell leader had the traditional foreman's responsibility for initiating formal disciplinary action against cell members deviating from the company rules. In 1984, 90 per cent of workplaces surveyed had written procedures for dealing with discipline and dismissals (Millward and Stevens (1986:170). The dismissal procedures are normally under the auspices of the personnel manager. An important reason for this practice is the relatively recent development and influence of unfair dismissal legislation. The company gave cell leaders considerable discretion for labour management. To quote George Wyke, the Personnel Manager:

What the cellular system has done as far as man-management is concerned, it has pushed that responsibility further down the chain, into the cells. So where somebody wants disciplining, they don't say to the personnel manager: 'I want to sack this bastard. What can I do to get rid of him?' They know what they have got to do. The only time they will come to me is to seek advice on whether they are doing it right or wrong.

The rationale for the additional labour responsibilities given to cell leaders was that each cell was 'a factory within a factory'. Because as the personnel manager argued, 'at the end of the day, unlike the old structures, the person who will take the stick for not getting the work done is the guy controlling the cell. The buck stops on his desk, OK.'

The cell leader had complete responsibility for production together with the task of liaising with both suppliers and customers. Appended to these tasks were responsibility for aspects of human resources' management, with the authority to dismiss deviant cell members. This has allowed senior management to focus on strategy issues and to shift some management problems onto cell leaders or, as the personnel manager put it: 'Managers have become more street-wise . . . they know they have got to be looking up the course, and not fire-fighting, and leave the fire-fighting to cell organization'. Moreover, the cellular system, by giving cell leaders wider discretion over labour relations, offers senior management the potential to resolve some of the problems of labour management by abdicating them.

Changes in work organization did cause problems for recruitment. In addition, there was evidence in the plant of informal resistance to job redesign, which had increased management control of produc-tion, further deskilled an already semi-skilled workforce, and made operators easily replaceable. Job redesign had removed operator discretion, making tasks become more routine. These factors, coupled with the firm's reputation for low wage-rates in the district, made recruitment a problem. In the early months of 1988 the company experienced a 'serious shortage of skilled setters' and was, according to George Wyke, 'paying the price of not recruiting and training apprentices five or six years ago'. Four reasons for recruit-ment difficulties were given by personnel: the shift system ('people don't like them'); finding it difficult to commute to work due to inadequate public transport; relatively poor rates of pay; and inflexi-bility ('people are reluctant to change'), said the personnel manager.

When George Wyke referred to the recruitment problem as 'dig-ging holes in sand', he neglected to link it to the nature of most manual work in the plant and low levels of manual workers' commit-ment. The figures on turnover and absenteeism shown in Table 5.3 indicate worker discontent and the type of industrial conflict that Hyman (1972) describes as 'unorganized conflict'.

The apparent low level of commitment among direct workers can be explained in two ways. During the interviews with stewards and workers it was clearly apparent that there was considerable discon-tent over the bonus scheme: the standard time allowed to complete a

Table 5.3   Turnover and absenteeism rates (direct workers), per cent

Turnover rates, 1988		Absenteeism, 1988	
January	34.4	January	5.3
February	20.4	February	5.7
March	27.5	March	8.0

particular task was not considered adequate to earn a 'decent' bonus. The following comment from Maura summarizes the widespread view: 'The old times in the jobs that have been going a few years, now those times are not so bad. People are happy with them. It just seems to be the new jobs. You have nothing to work for.'

An additional drawback with work organization was that it resulted in manual operatives performing narrow, repetitive tasks, closely supervised. As Fox (1974) has argued, such management strategies are likely to be reciprocated by low commitment. Thus the firm's management faced a familiar dilemma. The essentially antagonistic nature of employment relations compels management to control the labour process. Competitive pressures force manufacturers to reduce unit costs, enhance quality and exert more control. The relations between management and labour deteriorate further, thereby making it necessary for management to use additional controls over the quantity and quality of workers' performance. In turn the intensification of control leads to further withdrawal of commitment by workers. This downward spiral of management and worker relations has been described by Fox (1974) and Littler and Salaman, (1984).

This case-study provides evidence of negative employment effects resulting from CNC technology, progressive deskilling division of mental and manual tasks, and greater managerial control through new hardware and software manufacturing systems. The Servo study also highlighted different social relations stemming from changes in work organization, in the form of the cellular mode of production. Job redesign gave the cell leader new powers which impinged on labour–management relations. Evidence was also presented which shows informal worker-resistance to the changes in work organization.

UNION INFLUENCE AND THE 1983 STRIKE

This section considers the degree of involvement and influence of organized labour within the plant upon senior management's decisions. The union played a marginal role in the process of technical change, which is explained in part by the extent of plant-level union organization, and the impact of a major dispute in the plant in 1983. The section begins by discussing the collective bargaining arrangements in the firm.

Three unions were recognized by the firm for collective bargaining purposes: AEU, MSF and APEX. The AEU was the largest union at the plant; it had 200 members out of a total of 351 manual workers, a union density of 56.9 per cent, the lowest of all the case studies. The non-manual technical staff, including the cell leaders, were organized by MSF, and they had 50 members out of a possible 70, a density of about 71 per cent. Both management and union representatives for manual and non-manual constituencies considered that plant bargaining by stewards was very important in determining wage rates.

For the manual workers, earnings were made up from the basic rate, shift allowance, overtime, and individual output-related bonus payments. Apart from the annual negotiations for basic pay rates, the main problems faced by the stewards related to challenging job-times set by work-study engineers. On some jobs it was possible to earn £30–40 a week bonus on top of the basic rate. But there was a general opinion among the long-service workers that management were trying to get them to work harder by imposing tighter time-limits on the jobs. It was also expressed that the stewards were ineffective in defending established job-times, and winning relatively fair times for new jobs.

Maura was in her late forties; she had worked at 'Servo's' for nineteen years. Currently she was working in Cell 60 as an assembler and she described the increase in work intensity and the union's incompetence:

> The new jobs' times are ridiculous. I think it depends on the union's blokes, it doesn't seem strong somehow. We once had a women convener, and any of your problems, she would fight them . . . I worked in the assembly before; if we weren't satisfied with the times, we use to have union in and play pop and all that. The new people, they don't want to fight.

June was twenty-five; she left school at the age of fifteen and had worked at the factory for four years. She was a semi-skilled operator and this was her current grievance over job times:

> Some of the new jobs now . . . There is no incentive. I would work harder if I had a better time for the job. I'd know at the end of the week, for going berserk, that I was going to get something out of it.

She believed that the union was ineffective and that workers only joined 'to cover themselves in case they have an accident'. Rick was fifty-eight. He had worked in a number of industries including gas, carpet manufacture and road haulage before starting at the plant in 1984. He told me how the pace of work had increased in recent years: 'They are trying to get us to work harder. I'm off with cold a lot, sweating a lot . . . Our Union is a wash-out'.

Andrew had only worked at Servo's for twelve months; prior to that he had done a number of jobs, including three years in the RAF. Like the rest of the shopfloor workers he recognized the inequitable nature of the bonus scheme:

> We have lads in our department who can work at 170 per cent, so they are doing 70 per cent more work then they have to do. For that 70 per cent they are getting £10 a week extra . . . that's no incentive. Not for doing nearly twice as much work. The shop stewards don't appear to have much contact with management.

The AEU did represent the majority of the production workers at the plant, and might therefore be expected to seek to influence the form and pace of technological innovation. It was acknowledged by management, stewards and workers alike that the unions in the plant played an insignificant role in these key bargaining areas. In particular, the AEU stewards' influence was largely confined to additional payments for workers operating groups of machines. The union had no input regarding choice of technology or design of the cells. They were-informed after management had decided to go ahead with the investment. To quote George Wyke, Personnel Manager, again:

> I don't think the company ever asked whether they wanted to do it, they were told this is what we have to do if we are to survive. And remember, people were bashed a bit by the long strike. It was by acquiescence more than by an agreement.

This interpretation of the degree of union participation in the decision-making process was shared by the AEU convener: 'Management told us what they were doing . . . we knew we had to have it'. There was no evidence that the AEU shop stewards influenced management on division of labour. The setting and programming procedures for the CNC machines, for instance, were neither jointly determined nor even the subject of consultation: they were unilaterally determined by management. Nor did the stewards negotiate changes in manning levels, changes in work tasks, or flexibility within the cells. The focus of plant negotiations centred around the re-muneration part of the wage–effort contract.

No new technology agreement was negotiated, neither was there agreement with the manual union covering Japanese-style manufac-turing methods. The only item to be negotiated was the premium payment for shift working. On the management side it was felt that a new technology agreement was unnecessary because it was 'natural and right' that new technology should be installed. On the union side, no agreement was sought from management: there was a sense of technological determinism. As Walter remarked, 'they just informed us they were bringing the machines in . . . most people realized that it had to come'. There were, however, certain areas where the union still managed to exert some control within the factory. For instance, traditional craft demarcation prevented management achieving func-tional flexibility in the tool-room. It was admitted that the firm would have 'a problem with our manual union' if they tried to place an unskilled person in the tool-room.

Health and safety is one of the largest categories of decision in which trade unions are involved in technical change, although there is no evidence to suggest that reductions in manning levels, multi-machine manning and increased work intensity caused an increase in accidents. During my discussions with stewards and workers the only comments about health and safety on the shopfloor were negative. Andrew described the health and safety hazards to me:

> There is a fair amount of oil contamination on the floors. Ventila-tion is poor. It's far too hot. There is a build up of fumes. We get people complaining of headaches. Dermatitis is a problem; that's been linked to the coolant we use . . . We are supposed to have safety reps but its become so lax.

In summary, the stewards kept a low profile and their leadership was weak. The AEU shop stewards had given little consideration to the changes; neither had they discussed nor developed any strategy for new technology or cellular/JIT production. The manual union's influence within the plant was negligible and generally restricted to pay-bargaining.

If nothing else, the workers' comments on management's attempts to intensify the level of exploitation further invalidate the findings of those industrial relations theorists who assert that the effects of the recession on workers is marginal. When assessing the impact of recession, labour legislation and 'macho' management on labour, it is necessary to go beyond the superficial data on industrial relations structures generated by management surveys.

Bargaining power and union organization explain why the union played such a marginal role within the plant. Technological innovations had further deskilled labour, making it easy to control and be replaced. The workers' capacity to establish and maintain job controls had diminished, and George Wyke frankly admitted, 'In general terms the bargaining power has got weaker, particularly on the shopfloor. Because, coming back to deskilling, we are not reliant upon experts. You can put anybody on a machine and we do. You can put students on'.

Power also reflects the external labour and product markets, and the level of workplace union organization. The AEU had achieved formal recognition some time in the late sixties. There was just one bargaining unit for the manual shopfloor workers. In the seventies the stewards were considered 'militant', and their intervention and conflicts over job times gave them a high profile. Table 5.4 shows the pattern of union membership and shop steward organization in the plant in 1983 prior to the strike, and in 1988.

What is striking is the fall in union density between 1983 and 1988, and the collapse of union organization. The events after the six-and-a-half weeks' strike in 1983 demonstrate the vulnerability of workplace trade unionism.

The strike is critical in explaining why union organization collapsed at the plant. Trevor Jones was elected AUEW convener six months prior to the strike; after it, Trevor was in the first group of workers to be made redundant. Since then he has successfully studied for a politics degree at Bradford University. Information here on trade union organization prior to the strike comes from an interview with Trevor in June 1988.

He described union membership and steward organization before the strike as being 'up and down'. However, stewards had a lot of control over prices for jobs, and 'that's what builds up your relationship with the members'. There were regular disputes over job times, as Trevor explained:

Almost daily . . . there was something going on. If it was a new job you just didn't agree a time until it was a good one. Sometimes they would give you a big time so as to get the bloody job done . . . If they altered any tiny aspect of the job at all, you used to have a

Table 5.4   Union membership and stewards' organization

	1983	1988
Union density (manual)	98%	57%
Check-off	Yes	No
Closed shop	No	No
Steward constituencies	15	9
Stewards elected	12–15	4
Steward density	1:23	1:50
Full-time steward	Yes	No
Senior stewards of two or more	Yes	No
Regular stewards' meetings	Yes	No

Source: Steward interviews.

re-time . . . So you used to stick out for a bit more. Sometimes a lot more.

Workplace union organization in the early 1980s was relatively sophisticated. There were on average 12–15 AUEW stewards: 'We never had less than eight and that was really low'. There was also a full-time convener who was assisted by a deputy. Any steward could sign off a job at any time, and book on union duties; 'we always refused to ask permission from management to do that, we always regarded that as a right'. In addition, there were informal but irregular contacts with stewards in other plants in the company.

By the late 1980s, AEU organization within the plant was virtually non-existent as Table 5.4 shows. There were four stewards, one each, in assembly, Cell 60, Cell 20 and the night shift. At the time of the research there were five unfilled stewards' positions, and this, as stated elsewhere, is an important factor limiting intra-union sophistication (see Batstone et al., 1987:72). There were no longer a full-time convener, senior stewards or stewards' committee meetings. The check-off system no longer existed. The management had demolished the convener's office a number of years ago. It was also clear that inter-union coordination at the factory was virtually nil. There was no contact either formally or informally with other stewards in the company, and the virtual absence of coordination of stewards' activity at plant level left them relatively isolated.

Lack of coordination and discussion meant that problems relating to technological innovations were treated in a one-off, ad hoc manner. Moreover, the absence of inter and intra-union sophistication meant that there was little opportunity to develop a common approach on the changes and widen the scope of bargaining. The stewards' perspective towards the changes within the firm in turn affected the members. If the stewards had played a more pro-active role on the shopfloor, it might have encouraged an increased union awareness on the part of the members. A full-time union organizer maintained:

> People will only join a trade union if they can see something in it for them; if there is some activity going on. If it becomes moribund and no one is having meetings with management, reporting these to members . . . then the union disappears.

When a payment-by-results system exists, conflict over control is often a permanent feature of work. The division between line managers and workers has been described as a 'frontier of control': management rights versus workers' rights. In a society where workers sell their labour power to employers, the most basic and fundamental conflict occurs over how much work workers get paid for and how much work they do (Baldamus, 1961). The price of labour power was at the heart of the 1983 strike. The union claimed parity for basic wage rates with other plants in the Group. Further, it was recognized that the bonus system which had been in existence for over fifteen years had 'fallen into disrepute'.[6]

The stewards' decision to strike was influenced by the restructuring within the company, and the investment in new plant and machinery. It was explained by Trevor like this:

> The company decided to do all the manufacturing at Servo's. They started investing. Because we saw all this new machinery coming in, we decided that now was the time to take them on and get a real increase in wages, because Servo's was always pretty badly paid.

The company made an offer of 8.5 per cent, but emphatically refused claims for parity. In the words of the managing director: 'The Company will not, at this time or at any other time, consider claims for parity for wages with companies inside or outside the Group'. A glimpse into how a multinational company conducts its industrial relations strategy is offered by the personnel manager's account of events:

128   *Japanization at Work*

When you are organizing a strategy, you do various calculations. Possibilities of industrial action, whether it's disruption or all-out war. What you are prepared to stand and not stand. That goes off to the group. If American Ensign approve it, we will stand the strike for ever.

The stewards issued a 'failure to agree,' at a domestic conference in November 1982. At a mass meeting the shop stewards asked for, and received, support for their recommendation of immediate strike action. Three hundred and fifty AUEW workers were on strike for over six weeks. The strike was 'official' and had the support of the District Committee. The strike was apparently well supported by the members. About half the strikers were 'actively involved in the strike, either going out on delegations, visiting other workplaces, going to other factories within the group, or picketing', recalled Trevor. The strike committee also published a weekly bulletin. The strike at Servo Engineering was, claimed the *Socialist Worker*, 'a testimony to union solidarity and organization'.[7]

The workers were unsuccessful, and in April 1983 the membership accepted a management offer of 10.1 per cent to run over eighteen months. Trevor gave three reasons why they lost. They did not get the support from other plants within the group; their attempts to persuade car workers to boycott Servo's products failed – 'people were reluctant to put blacking on'; and excess capacity in the car industry undermined their bargaining position.

What happened after the workers went back was described by George Wyke:

We had lost so much business, we had too many people. So the Company reorganized its groups. It was unfortunate that Mr Jones [convener] found himself in a department that was going to be defunct, and he was got rid of . . . [The workforce] went down to 250. People began to think, 'I'm on my bike here if I'm not careful'. So the strength of the union went away.

The collapse of union organization at Servo Engineering was based on fear and anxiety over job security. Trevor explained the situation: 'When somebody has got such a high profile as a full-time convener – its like getting rid of Derek Robinson at Leyland – the workforce say: "Well, if that happens to *him*, I don't want to be a bloody steward".'

Following the strike the company reviewed their approach to industrial relations: a combination of winning some degree of commitment from workers, and coercion. Meetings were arranged for workers to receive information on 'the state of the Company'. The management removed the check-off facility but continued to tolerate shop stewards: the latter played a functional role for the company. George Wyke had worked for the company twenty-five years. Prior to becoming the personnel manager, he was, an AUEW shop steward and convener at another plant within the group, He described the company's new approach to shop stewards in the following way:

> Now it's a more open style . . . There is always the view that if somebody starts jumping up and down, 'he's a bolshie bastard – get rid of him'. Management have learnt that if there is a groundswell, they [stewards] will tell you – they can be our eyes and ears.

There are prima facie grounds for believing that management at Servo influenced the choice of shop stewards to ensure that they got a person defined by them as 'responsible', a ploy discussed by Lane (1974). For example, Andrew was elected as a steward in December 1987; he had been accepted by the union's district committee but was not acceptable as a steward by the management: 'I don't know why the management won't accept me, I've never been in a union before in my life. It's not as if I have a dodgy record '.

Management refused to recognize Andrew as an AEU steward because he was considered to be a potential militant: 'A bit left-wing and we don't want him as a steward', said George Wyke.

It has been argued that the shift in the balance of power has been caused by the general state of the labour and product markets, progressive deskilling of the workforce, and the collapse of union organization since the 1983 strike. Although there is no evidence to suggest that the strike prompted the investment in new technology and Japanese-style work structures, the changes did have a profound impact on labour regulation. The resulting intensification of work and control, and the weakened bargaining position of organized work groups within the organization, were thus a by-product, rather than an imperative shaping management strategy. The bargaining that did occur was restricted to improving the 'cash nexus'. The case study provides ample evidence of unrestrained managerial prerogative on the key question of workplace innovation, and the restructuring of the labour process to restore profitability. It also illustrates the relationship between different production systems and organizational structure (Woodward, 1958 and 1965). In this case, implanting a Japanese production system in a large organization with large batch-size influenced the relatively bureaucratic structure and promoted a deskilling strategy towards manual workers.

6 The Drilling Machine Company:
Japanization in Small-Batch Production

Somebody decided that this cell system was working for the Japanese and it's got to work for Oil Tool.

This chapter examines the introduction of new technology and a cellular production system in a small-batch, unionized environment. The company, Oil Tool Engineering, manufactures a range of equipment and valves for the oil extraction industry. In November 1986 the company introduced a package of new production and labour practices: a cellular work structure, just-in-time, total quality control, and direct worker communications. Details of the company in terms of structure and ownership, product range, and management are first outlined. The chapter then goes on to examine the changes in the labour process and management motives behind the transformation in work. The next two sections examine the effects of the changes on shopfloor workers at the plant, and the company's employee relations strategy. The final section considers the degree of joint regulation and union sophistication.

COMPANY PROFILE

Oil Tool Engineering was established in West Yorkshire in 1950, and four years later became part of Oil Tool Incorporated, an American multinational company engaged through its subsidiaries in designing, manufacturing, and marketing a broad range of oil tools, ball valves and forged products through its two operating divisions, Oil Tool and Forged Products. The West Yorkshire plant is part of the Oil Tool division, manufacturing pressure-control equipment used at the wellhead in drilling for and production of oil and gas, both onshore and offshore.

The company, whose corporate headquarters are in Houston,

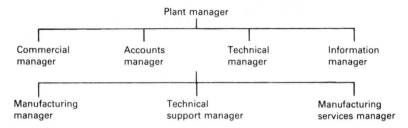

FIGURE 6.1   Management structure at the West Yorkshire plant

Texas, has other manufacturing establishments in Scotland, Germany, France and Mexico, and employs 4500 people throughout the world. The West Yorkshire management operate with considerable autonomy from the corporate management. While the plant manager had to achieve three corporate goals: forecast on profit: maintain spending levels to prescribed limits; and maintain inventory levels within forecast levels, working within these parameters he has complete autonomy. The management team consists of seven people, and is represented in figure 6.1.

The plant manager, Bill Dorfmann, indicated his preference for a 'flat' structure and revealed something about his approach to labour management: 'you want real flat organizations, you want good dialogue with people, you want to remove as many physical differences between groups of people as you possibly can . . . ' Below Bill Dorfmann are four managers responsible for sales, finance, quality control and information systems. Reporting directly to the plant manager is the manufacturing, technical support, and manufacturing services manager. The manufacturing manager, Doug Meyer, has responsibility for all the technology on the shopfloor and the maintenance. As Bill Dorfmann said, it is the manufacturing manager who 'really calls the shots on priorities, where the effort goes'. The most striking feature of the management structure is the absence of a personnel function, the industrial relations function being undertaken by the plant manager. The removal of personnel specialists from the firm is considered later.

THE PROCESS OF CHANGE

This section looks at the way key aspects of Japanese manufacturing philosophy were rigorously applied to reduce costs and improve quality standards at Oil Tools. It begins by outlining machine tool configuration and job design before 1984 and goes on to analyse the application of cellular technology, just-in-time, total quality management on job design.

Pre-Cell Job Design

The firm had invested in NC machine tools in the late 1970s and CNC machines in the 1980s. The works manager believed that the existing CNC machines were in fact a little out-dated because of the rapid developments in machine-tool technology. Prior to 1984 the machines were distributed around the workshop according to 'families'. That is, all the machines of a like nature were placed together: the milling machines were located in one part of the shop, there were two long lines of small and large lathes, and NC and CNC machines as well as radial drills were put together. Comments from the plant manager highlight the uncertainties, and the absence of planning associated with such a system:

> Before, the part kind of bounced around the shop. It went from one horizontal borer mill that happened to be empty. It went to another that happened to be empty . . . materials queued up for the machining centre. After, it went to another horizontal boring mill, and it queued up there . . . We really ran without any system for a while.

The NC and CNC machine tools were installed alongside existing conventional machines. Management had chosen not to invest in the latest CNC technology, and instead operated the cellular system with far less sophisticated machinery. As the plant manager explained it, 'We may opt for two less sophisticated machines, to have the ability to parallel processes, rather than one all-singing, all-dancing CNC machine. The tool-makers may be worried a lot more than we are at the moment'.

A large proportion of the plant's manual workers were skilled and this determined the way NC and CNC machines tools were utilized. Only grade one workers who were apprentice-trained could operate grade one machines, that is, NC and CNC machine tools. There were two semi-skilled groups, grades two and three: grade two workers operated radial drills, grade three undertook deburring and stamping. General labourers were classified as grade five. Drilling, for example, was considered a semi-skilled task and was performed by a grade two worker. The actual marking out, indicating where the holes were to be drilled, was done by a skilled, grade one worker.

There was a separate programming department in the plant and programs for the NC and CNC machines were generated by industrial engineers. The NC and CNC operators set up the machines, mounted the tools, edited and proved the programs. When the first NC machines were installed in the plant in 1978 the industrial engineers union, TASS, insisted that programming was their sphere of work. The AUEW argued that the NC machines should be programmed by the operators on the shopfloor. There was no direct confrontation with the TASS membership, but a separate department was established because, to quote the manufacturing manager, 'The battle was fought and won by TASS'.

Operators' received instructions from the twenty-two supervisors employed on the shopfloor about the components to be machined in terms of quantity and priority. The supervisors also 'chased' components necessary for a particular assembly. This involved checking that work-in-progress was on schedule for final completion by the date it was due to be assembled in the fitting shop. Whether operating a conventional or a CNC machine tool, skilled machinists normally remained on the same machine; in some instances, this could be for years. The job design in a cellular work structure was quite different.

Cellular Configuration and Job Design

Simplify, and goods will flow like water.

Schonberger, (1982:103)

One steward remarked on how in the initial period of change managers at the factory were walking around the shopfloor with Schonberger's book tucked under their arm. The management had made some moves towards cellular methods in 1984, when the spool cell was set up in one part of the plant. The skilled and semi-skilled workers within the spool cell constituted a semi-autonomous work group within the factory. There was complete flexibility of labour within the cell which resulted in significant increases in productivity. To quote the manufacturing manager, Doug Meyer:

> We got 50 per cent reductions in throughput time. We had complete flexibility of labour in there, we had trained the people accordingly. The people more or less ran their own department; we didn't have much supervisory input to it. They were given the schedules for the month, they worked out the priorities, and they got on with them.

Joe Greenwood is fifty, he is a radial drill operator by trade, and he has been employed at Oil Tool for ten years and in the AEU for thirty. A steward for nine years, Joe was elected full-time AEU convener in April 1985. When he gave his job-title as 'driller', Joe was quick to point out that he was a 'class one', rather than semi-skilled class two, radial driller. He described the impact of flexible working in cell one on traditional craft demarcation: 'You have people in there, they'll do bloody anything – anything at all. They have taken on this responsibility of stamping and deburring, labouring for themselves: it's just crazy'.

In November 1986, senior management extended the cellular/JIT model to the manufacture of the sub-sea block valve. According to Bill Dorfmann that product was central to the future of the company. Management broke up other processes and transferred machines into a main cell and three smaller sub-cells capable of performing the whole enlarged task to engineer a block-tree valve. The main body cell contained two horizontal borers; five NC lathes; two CNC lathes; two CNC machining centres; and two radial drills. The three sub-cells made internal components for the block-tree valve. Each cell was designed to be self-contained, and each had a mixture of conventional, NC and CNC milling machines (3); lathes (10); radial drills (2); grinders (4). In total there were thirty-seven machine tools in the four cells. There were thirty operators working in the four cells, on either day or night shift. Following the cellular concept, machine tools are dedicated to specific functions, as the manager revealed; twenty-two out of the thirty-seven machines are unused in each shift. Within each cell there was established an inspection area to facilitate self-inspection. The cellular organization of work only affected one third of the workshop, the other two-thirds remaining untouched. Technical problems did arise with the new layout. In the main cell, there were problems with components U-turning and going back to processes previously done in the machining operation; 'they kept doubling back so you weren't getting a true linear flow'. Owing to the complexity and the non-standard nature of the components, sub-cells two and three could not achieve a linear flow.

Management did concede that with hindsight they had 'probably bitten off more than they could chew', and 'it was a major blunder'. Apparently the failure of the sub-cells came as no surprise to the manual workers. According to Joe:

Our view of the cell system as it was set up in Oil Tool, it wouldn't work. It couldn't work: manpower for one, machining on the other . . . We outlined this right at the beginning . . . [recently] I had a meeting with some of them [management] and they said: 'Cell two and three aren't working'. You know, that's no big secret, everyone knew that.

An industrial engineer was brought in from the United States to analyse the flow, and a statistical process control team to examine the process capabilities in the three cells. In February 1988 the main cell was considered to be 'under control . . . we have proved that the cellular system can work with small-batch', said the manufacturing manager.

Work undertaken outside the cell was 'subcontracted' to another cell or workstation within the factory. Thus the cells operated as 'mini-factories'. The manufacturing manager explained:

If we have to go out of the system, we would charge the cell with the cost of the machining. It is a mini-factory or product line of its own, and it's measured like that. We completely separate it from traditional manufacturing.

The plant manager envisaged that in the future the company would be moving towards two enterprise units based around two products within the one factory. In other words, a full cell accounting system would be established by allocating to each cell costs attributable to its product. As the product left the cell a notional sales value would be allocated to calculated a net cell profit.

Just-in-Time

Schonberger informs us that the *kanban* or JIT system with total quality control (TQC) is 'an imperative to continually improve' (1982:45). These two interrelated strategies accompanied cellular manufacturing at Oil Tool Engineering. Prior to introducing a cellular/JIT system, twenty-six steel racks were used on the shopfloor to store in-progress inventory. The JIT philosophy was practically demonstrated when these racks were removed: 'we took them all outside and cut them up for scrap, and we haven't needed them since', said the Manufacturing Manager.

The adoption of the JIT inventory system reduced work-in-progress considerably. To quote the plant manager,'Overall inventory has continued to move down in huge increments; we are talking about £7 million, 30 percent reduction in inventory last year (1987); we are talking about another 10 per cent this year, and in both cases our sales are increasing, so you would expect our inventory to be gradually increasing.

As stated in Chapter 2, JIT is more than an inventory control system. The just-in-time mode has a cause–effect chain; it improves quality by placing additional responsibilities on operators, while allowing management to control the pace of work. The manufacturing manager told me:

> Traditional manufacturing will tend to batch-up on production, so say you have fifty as a batch, they may also run an extra five for fear of scrap or rework. In cellular manufacturing you only run what is the requirement. The emphasis is on the throughput time, and the quality is paramount. If the component goes down you have no safeguard.

Therefore work is intensified because the worker's awareness of defect causation is heightened.

Total Quality Control (TQC)

> *Production, not quality control, must have primary responsibility for quality.*
>
> Schonberger (1982:82)

Criticisms of the Western practice of separating producing from inspection focuses on two areas: cost and workers' attitude. Employing large numbers of inspectors increases indirect labour costs. Also, traditional inspection methods encourage an attitude of mind among operators, that if they do produce defective parts the fault(s) will be picked up later (Wickens, 1987:3). Oil Tool's management followed Schonberger's third lesson and introduced their interpretation of the Japanese concept of total quality control (TQC). Operators were given responsibility for validating the quality of their own work, and greater emphasis was placed on defect prevention, or the 'zero defect' ethos. The manufacturing manager explained the principles: 'Within cellular manufacturing you have to have the commitment of the operators. They will also do process capability studies, and measure the actual quality of the machining aspects that they are doing . . . So, the actual operator is doing the in-process measurement'.

As was the case at Lucas Electrical (see Turnbull, 1986:198), management at Oil Tool Engineering emphasized the necessity of fostering a new engineering ethos to achieve quality improvements. Workers were given training in inspection techniques and the company invested in additional quality control measuring equipment.

The quality control department in the plant has been reduced in size and most of the QC inspectors dispersed into the cells. The QC department has become a facilitator, monitoring operations, QC training, and generally promoting the ethos of zero defects. I was told that 'the inspector plays the role within the team of doing random sampling, *with* the team, supporting the operators'.

As a result of switching to the cellular and JIT/TQC system and adopting a responsible autonomy strategy significantly higher productivity and quality were recorded. Schonberger argues that the 'real power of JIT/TQC is that it has amplification properties . . . temperament: co-operation, dedication, harmony, and group-thinking decision processes' (1982:13–14), although at Oil Tool there was no evidence that workers at the plant 'carry their concerns – about defects, breakdowns, and so forth – home with them, or to bars . . . where they meet fellow workers' (1982:29–30).

An education exercise preceded the introduction of Japanese-style manufacturing innovations in June 1986. The Quality Education School and the Zero-Defect Day were designed to shape workers' attitude towards greater commitment to the company's objectives and new manufacturing philosophy. Peter Turnbull, in his article 'The "Japanisation" of British Industrial Relations at Lucas' writes:

> The success of module production is dependent on a social organization of the production process intended to make workers feel 'obligated' to contribute to the economic performance of the enterprise and to identify with its competitive success. (1986:203)

At Oil Tool Engineering the process designed to make workers feel more 'obligated' started with a Quality Education School. Senior management invented a game called 'cellmonopoly', which involved players (manual operators: supervisors or 'team leaders'; managers) drawing cards from a pack and responding to various manufacturing scenarios, for instance, how the participants would respond to a machine breakdown, excessive queuing for a process, or an operator absence due to illness. Apparently the manual operators beat the production engineers on many occasions. The shop stewards thought that the exercise was a waste of time: 'In our opinion it was a waste of money. Ninety-nine per cent of the items introduced, they have never been taken up. You put ideas forward, its forgotten'.

The company's Zero-Defect Day was based on the zero defects (ZD) concept initiated in the United States in the 1960s. In essence workers are 'indoctrinated with the notion that a defect is not normal, that perfect conformity to design specification is realistic and should be the goal', writes Schonberger (1982:54). Oil Tool's ZD day involved all employees, both manual and non-manual listening to corporate management speeches on the quality imperative. The Labour MP, Merlyn Rees, addressed the workforce on quality, as did guest speakers from British Aerospace, and major oil companies' management. At the end of the day all the workforce were asked to sign a pledge that they were committed to the quality improvement process within the company. Over four hundred and fifty workers signed the following statement: 'We, the undersigned, pledge to establish Zero Defects as our personal performance standard'. Various slogans also adorned the workshop: 'We can beat the competition', Oil Tool Engineering and Quality'. The workers did not respond positively to slogans exhorting quality standards and beating the rivals, and the banners have since come down. The exercise has similarities with those of other firms inspired by Japanese management philosophy (see Smith, 1988).

Changes in the Management Structure

Industry does not need specialists: production managers and workers can do it themselves.

Schonberger (1982:198)

If anybody had to be the last person here, I would have bet on the Personnel Manager.

Joe Greenwood, AEU Convener

Japanese management stresses the central role of the line manager and the workteams. Additional staff are only justified if they help the direct workers to produce more product or the sales personnel to sell more product. Ford Motors reduced their administrative staff by 26 per cent between 1979 and 1981 (Schonberger, 1982:196). In Britain, the competitive climate has forced many companies to change from 'empire-building to empire-demolition', writes Michael Dixon.[1]

There is a growing trend to judge company performance by new criteria, the strength-to-weight ratio as measured by productiveness per permanent employee. Companies are seeking to limit their full-time staff to the minimum core of people directly required to produce and sell the firm's products. Other activities on the periphery of the business, requiring professional expertise, such as training, or recruitment are subcontracted to consultancy firms.

The plant manager at Oil Tool Engineering, referred to non-producing employees as 'that elephant – administrative cost . . . a lot of administrative cost is a burden'. In April 1986, the company dramatically resolved the firms perceived over-specialization problem by making the staff of the personnel department redundant. The plant manager had taken over responsibility for negotiating with the shop stewards, including annual pay negotiations, and line managers were given responsibility for their own people-management, including the employee-relation function of hiring and firing.

MANAGEMENT MOTIVES: CQMPETITION AND CONTROL

This section looks at the reasons why management at Oil Tool Engineering introduced such a radical package of innovatory manu-facturing practices. The first point to make however is that the new cellular/JIT system was not local management initiative. The company's annual report for 1987 makes it clear that the radical shift to Japanese-style manufacturing techniques is a corporate trend, not confined to its UK operations: 'Dramatic improvements throughout the world have been realized by using . . . statistical process control and cell manufacturing configuration'.[2]

The rationale behind the radical organizational changes can be explained in terms of corporate strategy to reduce costs in the face of external competition. The plant manager provided an insight into the company's corporate strategy:

> This is now our biggest manufacturing operation in the world. But, it would only be a question of months before another operation could be bigger. We have moth-balled several of our operations . . . and the French, and the Germans in particular, have very flexible working practices.

This quote exemplifies the nature of manufacturing operations within global companies with the potential to transfer production across national boundaries. This was one reason for the adoption of new work structures; to quote from the same interview:

> We did it because we were afraid that if we did not improve our ability to manufacture block-valves, they would go to another plant within our organization which had a lower cost structure. And given that you can't change the wage structure here, the other answer is to improve the process time in the shop.

Cost reductions through improvements in labour productivity and inventory reductions were the overriding objectives of the new cellular/JIT system. The changes in 1986 followed operating loss of almost £6m for the West Yorkshire plant, mainly the result of dramatic falls in oil-field activity, which in turn was related to the collapse in the price of crude oil. Another commercial reason for introducing organizational change was the fear of competition, particularly from the Japanese. The plant had to be more cost-competitive in an important market sector, the manufacture of block-tree valves. This objective was put to me by the Plant Manager: 'In 1981 we were afraid that the Japanese would move in on our markets . . . If prices hadn't fallen I'm pretty sure that the Japanese would have moved in'. The block-tree valve was 'at the heart of the operations' at the plant, and local management was concerned that this product would be transferred to another location, thereby leaving the plant vulnerable to closure.

Computerised Scheduling

The cells were supported by a computerised scheduling function, a modified materials requirements planning (MRP) system, which provided instant data on work-in-progress, priorities, operator logging activity. The shopfloor computer data collection and transmission stations were located throughout the workshop and the production control department updated the screens every twenty-four hours, depicting priorities at any particular time, so as the priorities changed, they changed also on the screen. All the standard tooling requirement for a product was down-loaded onto the screen. At the time of the investigation, management were planning further modifications to the MRP system so that when the operator keyed in his work number and part number, and logged onto the job, the VDU printed out all his tooling and scheduling details, thereby giving management considerably more scope for monitoring the operator and controlling work-allocation, machining functions and pace. The main computer was linked to the computer at the plant in Scotland, and there is no reason to assume that information was not directly down-loaded to the corporate headquarters in Houston, Texas.

The computer workstations had subsumed some control functions previously undertaken by the skilled machine operators. Moreover, it was felt by both managers and shop stewards that the work-scheduling system had increased management's ability to monitor workers' performance. It was not the operator who was being measured, but the process, claimed one manager. Some of the comments from managers and shop stewards illustrate the point:

> Measurement is viewed as a bad thing by most people because if someone measured me, I would feel hurt about it. But in this particular case we are not measuring the person, we are asking the person to measure himself in the process. If you can eliminate the person out of the measurement, then people will respond and do it quite freely.
>
> We have had complete employee support in doing it, although we have had to do a lot of communicating . . . people have this in-built fear that you are measuring them, and some form of action will be taken on them, and that's not the case.
>
> It's a team approach with a complete open environment, where if something does go wrong, and the operator highlights it, he is praised rather than criticized. That's the actual trick in doing it.
>
> Manufacturing Manager

> Control over workers? Oh, that's improving. They're getting better at that. They are logging people on the job, bookings, tape-proving, machine break-down and whatever. They keep a log of that. Your efficiency, your productivity.
>
> Joe, AEU Convener

INTEGRATED TEAMS AND THE TRANSFORMATION OF WORK

This section begins by examining the division of labour and the new pattern of social relations on the shopfloor. After considering the employment effects at the plant, the section goes on to analyse the effects of new work-structures on manual workers' skills.

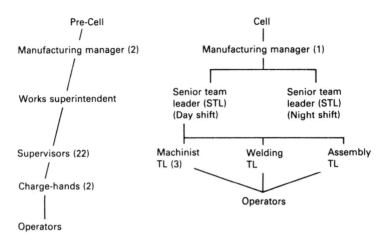

FIGURE 6.2   Occupational structure in the workshop

Division of Labour and Flexibility

Japanese-style labor flexibility is the key to effective resource management.

Schonberger (1982:155)

We already have a situation in the first cell where grade one men are doing semi-skilled and labouring work.

Joe, AEU Convener

The division of labour on the shopfloor differed significantly before and after the adoption of cellular production. Figure 6.2 shows the changes in the occupational divisions.

The new supervisory structure illustrates how responsible autonomy strategies are cheaper: over two-thirds of the supervisors were displaced, the numbers being reduced from twenty-two to six. When cellular/JIT work structures are operating, writes Schonberger, there is 'no particular need for supervisors steeped in behaviour-modification lore to provide pats on the back' (1982:27). The manufacturing manager pointed out the new management strategy in this way:

In the traditional days of manufacturing, we had twenty-two supervisors. They were viewed by the vast majority of employees as being policemen, and I can see the reasons why they were viewed as policemen, progress-chasers, standing at the bottom of the line. If a man went off his machine to go to the toilet, they were on his back, that sort of thing.

So we had to eliminate that first of all . . . So we reduced the number of supervisors to six, and we called them team leaders. We sent them away on rigorous training, and we looked into Japanese manufacturing techniques.

The team leader's role within the cell was more restricted than the cell leader's role at Servo Engineering. The team leader did not have responsibility for disciplining cell members, that was left to the manufacturing manager. Neither did the team leader have direct contact with suppliers or customers, although he met customers during in-plant tours. In other respects the team leader had similar responsibilities to the cell leaders at Servo Engineering. They scheduled work according to priorities established by Production Control, defined tooling requirements and the working of overtime. Each cell had its own cost-centre budget and the team leader was responsible for monitoring and staying within the cell budget. Team leaders were categorized as staff; none was a member of a trade union.

The team leader was viewed with suspicion by the shopfloor workers; essentially this role was still seen as that of traditional foreman, rather than 'team leader'. The problem of workers' acceptance was expressed by the plant manager: 'There is still a lot of mistrust. There is still a lot of feeling that this guy really wants to be the gaffer rather than the coach'. Part of the problem was that the skilled workers believed that the team leaders appointed were incompetent and lacked shopfloor experience. As Joe Greenwood said: 'They [team leaders] can't do the job. You can't go to them and ask them any questions because they can't answer you . . . People in charge don't know their arse from their elbow. Its as simple as that.'

Within the cell the team leader and Quality Control (QC) inspector reported directly to the manufacturing manager, but they worked as a team, neither had authority over the other. To emphasize the importance of the quality improvement process the team leader was unable to compel the QC inspector to accept his ruling; the QC person was an 'autonomous agent' within the cell structure. Although not officially recognized within the new management structure, chargehands assisted the team leaders in their work and stood in during the team leaders' absence. Unlike the latter, charge-hands were members of the AEU.

Below the team leaders were four manual grades corresponding to different tasks, skills and pay. Among the skilled, grade one, workers there was considerable horizontal and vertical flexibility in the established cells, with skilled operators not only using the full range of machines in the cell, but also undertaking drilling and deburring tasks. In practice, flexibility meant that skilled workers undertook as many jobs as possible within the cell, compatible with efficiency. Most of the skilled workers wanted to learn new skills in order to enhance their earning potential and provide some protection against redundancies by allowing them to be reassigned to another task if demand for their particular product contracted. The management were proud that they had 'knocked down a lot of cultural barriers'. Evidence that the new work groups were encouraging cooperation and 'teamwork' came from one worker returning my questionnaire: 'We tend to work together and look after each others' problems with the job and the machines.'   (NC lathe operator)

The extent of labour flexibility and its advantages to workers was spelt out to me by the manufacturing manager:

We have complete flexibility in the functional aspect. We can take a skilled operator from a CNC machine and put him on any operation in the plant, and he will do it. That's stamping, steel stencilling, inspection, deburring. We have trained various people up in doing inspection functions. Welders do their own NDT inspection.

Demarcation between traditional tasks had been removed as a result of cellular work structures. For instance, previously the drilling operation had been a task normally performed by two operators, a skilled and an unskilled, but flexible working practices now meant that the skilled worker both marked out the work and completed the drilling function. Dick was the deputy convener, and had worked at Oil Tool Engineering for six years. He worked in Cell 3, where his work had changed:

I was on one particular machine, it was just an ordinary conventional NC lathe. Now I can work two machines in that cell. I can work a conventional NC lathe or I can move over to a 12B which is a larger conventional lathe.

One NC lathe operator outlined how greater flexibility had resulted in his processing more paperwork: 'I now have more paperwork to deal with; I have to check through the programs that we receive from the industrial engineers, to make sure there are no major faults.'

Semi-skilled operators had much less functional flexibility. They could not for example stand in for skilled workers or operate machines considered to be 'grade one'. The union had successfully protected the position of the skilled grade one work group, as the following comment from the manufacturing manager illustrates:

> If you are talking about restrictive practices, the skilled grade one would not allow a semi-skilled group three to do their job, because they are apprentice-trained. For example, if you had a group three semi-skilled fork-lift driver, they wouldn't take kindly to us training him up on a skilled grade one job and paying him that money, because they are very self-protective about their interests.

Thus the functional flexibility was largely confined to the skilled operators. This placed the semi-skilled in a vulnerable position in the event of any future redundancies in the plant. Dick stated that: 'There are a lot of the lower grades that work in the cell concerned; should a redundancy come in the future, they will be going'.

Flexibility was also achieved by using a large number of subcontractors: a total of sixty smaller firms, largely based in West Yorkshire and the North of England. The notion of the 'flexible firm' was illustrated by this comment of the plant manager:

> If we exceed our internal capacity, we will sub it outright now and I suspect it will be with great caution that we will increase the capacity internally. We will subcontract the peaks in production to avoid the recruitment and redundancy costs.

Since 1982 the stewards had an agreement with management that information on contractors would be disclosed on request. Many of the firms listed as contractors to Oil Tool Engineering were, according to the AEU District Secretary, non-union shops: 'They are all very small firms and my suspicion is there will be no trade union organization. They tend to be what I would call two-penny concerns'.[5]

The subcontracting of work only became an issue for the union when there was a dispute or at a time when workers were unable to obtain regular overtime. In principle the Union did not oppose the use of subcontractors. Joe, the AEU convener, put it like this:

> When we are working regular overtime nobody gives a damn what is going out. So we only monitor it when we see people on thirty-nine hours and machines standing idle. Then we need to find out from management what kind of work is going out, why it is going out, and why it can't be channelled back.

In discussions with the union, low machine performance rates were cited as the main justification by management for increasing the proportion of work contracted out, and according to Dick, the AEU deputy convenor, 'They say that the machine should be producing 80, 90 per cent, and all that's coming off is 50 per cent. So they say they can get better results outside. They are putting the blame back to us'. In effect it was spurious reasoning on the part of the management, to justify their policy of sub-contracting, since in all the discussions with production managers, it was pointed out that low machine utilization was an inherent characteristic of a cellular work system and should not be a critical factor in any appraisal exercise.

To summarize, the elimination of traditional job boundaries was evident and functional flexibility was prevalent among the grade one craft workers. At the other extreme semi-skilled workers were still allocated traditional semi-skilled tasks making their employment position vulnerable. These divisions were not so much dependent upon management choice, but on the union's traditional controls over details of work allocation within the plant.

Employment and Skills

In 1985 there was a major redundancy exercise at the plant. Employment fell from 664 to 450, a decrease of 32 per cent. The redundancies were not attributed to either new technology or cellular production methods. Fall in sales was cited as the cause of redundancies by the AEU convener: 'The only time jobs have been lost in ten years is when there was a slump in the industry'. Asked if new technology had resulted in job losses, the stewards thought that computerized manufacturing had in fact increased employment, especially among non-manual employees. As Joe expressed it, 'We have found there have been more people come in. Especially at the other side of the wall [white-collar workers]'. The appointment of an

Table 6.1   Results of cellular manufacturing system
at Oil Tool Engineering

	Britoil 5in. block-valve (days)		Shell 5in. block-valve (days)	
	Pre-cell	Cell	Pre-cell	Cell
Machining	106	18	98	35
Assembly	82	6	15	8
Total	188	24	113	43

information services manager was cited as an example of technology creating employment. But with the closure of the personnel department a precise breakdown of employment by occupation at the plant was not available to confirm the trend identified by industry data.

Cellular production can have an indirect impact on employment levels due to productivity improvements resulting from, inter alia, greater functional flexibility. The total number of days to machine and assemble a Britoil 5-inch Block-tree valve fell from one hundred and eighty-eight days to just twenty-four days as shown in Table 6.1. The dramatic productivity gains generated by cellular/JIT modes of production would reduce the need for direct labour and thus have a negative effect on long-term employment.

The major question of deskilling and shopfloor autonomy is, as stated previously, the control of programming. Management recognized that the division of tape generation and 'proving' between the production engineering department and the operators in the cells was becoming increasingly artificial and unnecessary. The new generation of 'user-friendly' CNC machines, of which the firm had sixteen, made it feasible to program at source. Moreover, the division was in conflict with their stated policy of utilizing operators' traditional skills and encouraging self-reliance – being 'their own expert' within the cellular work group. Future control over programming by operators would require the acquisition of knowledge through training. Indeed programming had already started to be included in the apprenticeship training syllabus and, according to the manager and AEU stewards programming at source, was currently being 'reviewed'.

The manufacturing manager's rationale for a separate programming function in the plant and future strategy was that:

In a traditional environment it may be better to have a separate programming department. But in the future programming will be done at source. We aim to incorporate programming at shopfloor level, with support from management support services. With NC you can't program on the shopfloor, but we have sixteen CNC machines which can be programmed at source.

The precise effects of CNC technology on operator skills depended upon the nature of the technology and existing working arrangements. In a small-batch environment it is common for skilled operators to have a considerable degree of discretion and control. Batstone et al. recognize that the exact implications of CNC technology on skills depends upon the nature of the machine tools 1987:155). Where NC technology may have prevented the diffusion of tape generation on the shopfloor, the newer CNC machines provide scope for programming at source. When the simpler 'menu-type' CNC machines are introduced into a factory which has no separate programming function (e.g. Balance Tools, Engrave), or when there is no clear management policy (e.g. Precision), new conceptual skills can be added to the operators' traditional craft skills.

At Oil Tool Engineering the extent of operators' programming skills varied a good deal. Some of the NC and CNC machine operators who had attended night-school for programming training, and did verify and edit the tapes on certain block functions. These tended to be the younger operators who clearly recognized the value of such training for their future employment and earnings. But the majority continued only to 'prove' the tapes; to quote Dick again, 'they will adjust, but if it's anything major, they won't'. The obstacle to operator programming was the non-manual union MSF (TASS). The control of programming held the key to skill enhancement, as far as the manufacturing manager was concerned:

Well it depends on what the operator involvement is with the CNC machine. Now CNC machines give you the opportunity to edit the actual tape on the machine. You have got to ask yourself, is that an operator's function, or is it an industrial engineering support function? If a CNC operator prepares and edits his own tape, and then runs the machine, then I would say that's very skilful. If someone else prepares it for him, and he just checks it, then in my opinion it is taking a lot of the skill out of the job. And to me that is not the best way to go . . . it de-motivates the operator; he gets bored.

In response to a questionnaire, none of the operators reported that CNC technology had reduced their skills, although when it comes to assessing operators' estimation of skills, much depends on their understanding of the term 'skill'. Secondly, most respondents considered that their skills had been enhanced by the CNC technology. Finally, some of the respondents reported that their skills had increased as a result of the cellular system. Operator comments provide an insight into workers' perception of change:

Physically, when the machine is set up, I have less to do. But actually getting to that stage requires more skill than a manual machine. People tend to think that working on a CNC machine tool is so straightforward, just load the program and watch it go. What they don't realize is that the program the operator receives is just a rough draft of what it should be. That is, if it was used on the component the job would probably turn out as scrap. The operator has the responsibility of making the program correct, while also cutting metal. – NC turner (age 37).

Setting up still requires the skill element, but on batch work using a CNC machine, work can be mundane and boring. – Turret Setter Operator (age 40).

Programming the machine. The movement from numerically controlled machines to computer numerically controlled machines has put the skill back in the craftsman's hands. – CNC Turret Setter Operator (age 45).

More skill programming and editing tapes, giving greater control over your job. – Test Equipment Inspector (age 48).

Programming, there is more skill. – Turner (age 38).

There is another aspect to operator skill and that is management choice. Two alternatives are available to management: direct control or responsible autonomy. They can employ relatively unskilled labour or skilled labour to operate CNC machines. It has already been noted that skilled operators may be employed for their diagnostic skills and as an insurance against the machine 'crashing'. In small-batch manufacturing frequent tool and program changes are more easily undertaken by adopting a skill enhancement strategy – a further recognition of the limits of direct control. In addition management may choose to employ skilled workers on CNC machines for commercial reasons. Customers may expect high-technology components to be produced by a skilled and experienced workforce. A skill enhancement strategy becomes a selling asset, as well as a justification for charging a higher price for the component. The plant manager made this point:

> It's possible to employ relatively unskilled operators to use machines and still get high tolerance levels. But you have got to be careful saying this to the customer. The customer may say: 'Why do you have such a large value-added when you are using employees with only two or three years' experience? We could go elsewhere'. Oil Tool manufacturers high-technology; we sell our experience to the customer.

The critical factor in judging whether operator skills are destroyed or enhanced is dependent upon the operator's involvement in programming. This in turn is dependent upon batch-size, the nature of the machines, existing working practices, and management choice. This case is an example of small-batch production; NC and CNC machines were operated by skilled workers all of whom were involved to varying degrees in verifying and amending tapes. Shopfloor involvement in programming was due to the management adopting Japanese manufacturing principles.

EMPLOYEE RELATIONS STRATEGY

In deciding to embark upon a transformation of production it was necessary to change attitudes, to 'knock down a lot of cultural barriers', and to gain a considerable degree of active cooperation from the shopfloor workers. Part of the firm's 'Japanization' programme, the Quality Education School and Zero-Defect Day have already been discussed. In addition to this programme of indoctrination, there was a discernible difference in the style of industrial relations management since the appointment of the new American plant manager, Bill Dorfmann. The well-known human resource management practice of team briefings was introduced, as were exercises in direct workforce communications. The Plant Manager explained the new approach: 'The unions, that's the biggest challenge, I guess. We have a closed shop here, and we have tried to communicate with everybody in the shop on a real personal basis'.

The shop stewards were deeply suspicious of management's motives. They believed that the workplace meetings were designed to undermine the union's authority. An example of direct workforce communication took place in February 1987, when there was a half-day stoppage. In part, it was ostensibly due to the introduction of control charts in a couple of areas in the workshop, but the stoppage also reflected workers' concern about the adoption of Japanese-style methods and the absence of a pay rise for 1987. The plant manager addressed the whole workforce to explain the need for the changes; after the meeting the workers voted to return to work and there was no opposition to the changes. The shop stewards' negotiating committee had been by-passed, and the stewards felt that their authority had been eroded. 'They are trying to talk direct to the workforce, rather than through the members' stewards' committee', pointed out the AEU convener, recalling the meeting to me: 'It was a very emotional situation, John. Bill Dorfmann told the shopfloor in no uncertain terms that all these changes had to come in . . . for the benefit of ourselves and the company . . . So at the end of the meeting, believe it or not, he got a bloody standing ovation. I was disgusted'.

Bill Dorfmann gradually worked his way round the factory, spending ten minutes with everybody on their duck-board, recalled Dick, the deputy convener.

Since the meeting there had been complaints from the shopfloor about the new working practices, but the stewards constantly reminded their members that they had agreed to the changes:

At each meeting this year . . . I've made them bloody aware of it . . . What people are saying is: 'There are all the changes taking place and we're getting nothing for them.' I have to remind them, 'Bill Dorfmann mentioned all these changes, even about your boots [workers were in future to be issued with one free pair of boots a year instead of two pairs]. What happened at the end of it? You gave him a bloody standing ovation. When you give somebody that, you are approving of what he is saying.' It shuts them up.

There was evidence that management's attempts to communicate directly with the workers was having a negative impact on employee relations. The plant manager had recently requested another shop-floor meeting and asked the convener to arrange it. There was much hostility to the meeting and the fact that a personal letter was sent direct to each worker's home. When the decision was taken to take industrial action in February 1988, that exercise was abandoned. Joe explained:

> All I heard from the shopfloor was 'Tell him to get stuffed. We don't want to know. If he's got anything to say, get it to the Committee on the table, it's up to them . . . Tell him to send another letter. Tell him to address it to all our wives this time. Bring the wives in on the negotiations'. There is a very strong attitude at the moment.

The plant manager, with his American experience of labour relations, found it difficult to comprehend the traditional craft workers' loyalty to the union. As he confided:

> There is still a tradition in this country, unfortunately, that says that if you are a skilled man in a trade union, your first allegiance really is to your union representative and your second allegiance is to your company. We have a lot of people with twenty and twenty-five years' service in the shop . . . however, if it comes to an issue that is indicated to our workforce as a union versus management issue, I have no doubt that everybody will side with the union.

UNION INFLUENCE AND ORGANIZATION

The AEU shop stewards' collective organization in the plant was referred to as the 'Committee'. The stewards' Committee was involved in negotiations and consultation on a wide range of issues, including levels of performance, sales, and a variety of labour regulation issues. The Committee did not play a formal role in the introduction of new technology and cellular configurations. A new technology agreement for instance was not negotiated, neither was there agreement on any aspect of organizational change. Why the stewards played such a marginal role in the process of change needs to be examined; however, this section first looks at the way the union shaped the general pattern of labour regulation.

Pay and conditions were negotiated annually at plant level, and although the workforce had agreed to receive no pay rise in 1987, over the years the union in the plant had considerable influence over the wage side of the wage-effort contract. Wage rates at Oil Tool Engineering were the highest in the district. In addition, the stewards had successfully persuaded the personnel manager, when the first NC and later CNC machines came in, that no operators using the machines would receive a differential rate. Thus all grade one operators, irrespective of whether they used NC or CNC, received the same rate of pay. This principle was important to establish, foster and maintain a united approach to management. The union had allies among the management for this union objective; giving additional payments to CNC operators precludes functional flexibility because operators are reluctant to move off the higher-paying machine. Also, the union was involved in the allocation of machines. NC and CNC machines could only be operated by grade one apprentice-trained operatives, and union pressure meant that only skilled operators could be fully flexible, moving from machine to machine, or, to a lesser function.

'We have no restrictive practices on a group one man coming down and doing any lesser job. So a group one man would, come down and do a semi-skilled and an unskilled function. All skilled men in that grade are flexible, we put them anywhere where they have the expertise to do that job,' maintained the manufacturing manager.

'We don't have anything written down . . . If a machine becomes vacant, and its a grade one machine, then they don't recruit anybody but a grade one man for that job. *We won't allow it anyway*,' [my emphasis] was the convener's opinion.

Team leaders were not allowed to operate the machine tools. In addition, the union had exercised some control over the recruitment of young workers on the shopfloor. No trainee from the Youth Training Scheme (YTS), for example, was allowed onto the shopfloor. Also, the stewards' committee exerted some influence on apprentice training. An apprentice committee monitored the progress of trainees and assessed their training needs. Management considered the stewards' contribution to be useful, but as the convener remarked, 'We have quite a lot of influence, but the management wants it also. If management were against it, our influence would be less'. The stewards and most of the men replying to my questionnaire considered that the union had been effective in safeguarding the general aspects of the employment. The AEU convener told me:

John, if there wasn't a union here, it could be really evil. What they want to do and what they would like to do, they just can't do it. They would love to be able to crack the whip, and say, 'Look, your production is only 99 per cent, lets see it a 100 per cent, or you're on your way out!'

Despite the adverse economic climate, the stewards were able to maintain significant control over work organization and in particular work allocation in the newly-established cellular work structures. However, what was significant about union influence on the pattern of labour regulation at Oil Tool Engineering was that it primarily protected the structural supports of the privileged skilled worker within the plant.

The AEU had been less successful however in influencing the general direction of technical and organizational change within the plant. The Union played no role in the choice of new machine tools. Neither did it influence the pace or direction towards cellular configurations. As the AEU convenor recognized, 'No, I don't think we've been successful at all in controlling the introduction of the cell system. We've had very little input into it'. The marginal role the union played in the process of change was explained by the incremental way the changes were introduced. NC technology was introduced into the plant in the late 1970s and the stewards saw its introduction as a continuous and necessary process. Indeed such was the evolutionary nature of technical change, and degree of technological inevitability, that the convener claimed 'there has been no new technology coming in since I've been the convener'. When the first spool cell was established in 1983, it was not negotiated with the union. There was no opposition to the first cell and consequently when the cellular system was expanded, management considered it unnecessary to consult the union about the changes. As Joe recalled, 'There were talks about talks, but there was no opposition at all to it. For the simple reason they didn't bother asking about the first cell, so they didn't bother asking about creating further cells'.

Management were able to pacify those workers affected by the first change to cellular working by promises of additional overtime. The acceptance of new working practices by the workers was explained to me by the deputy convener: 'They blinded them with figures . . . they conned them with bags of overtime and plenty of work'.

The absence of union involvement in the introduction of cellular methods was interpreted differently by senior management. Management believed that the stewards wanted to distance themselves from the process so that the union would not he incorporated into management control procedures. Secondly, the management explained the absence of union participation by citing stewards' fear that new work structures would lead to redundancies. In the plant manager's words,

> We tried to involve them . . . But there were two reactions. First, they didn't want to be too closely identified with it, because they didn't want to appear to be doing management's bidding. The second thing was, they were concerned that this was just a ploy to have more redundancies . . . The trade unions are real uncomfortable with anything that involves a breakdown in the confrontation experience. It means they have to operate in a kind of new setting.

A relatively weak bargaining position and union organization were important factors explaining the negligible role played by the stewards at Servo Engineering. In the case of Oil Tool Engineering, skilled workers dominated the stewards' committee were in a relatively strong bargaining position and, using Batstone et al. (1987) criteria, had a sophisticated organization. It is to the nature of workplace AEU organization that we now turn.

Union Organization

The AEU had 260 members at the plant; it was 100 per cent membership, with a post-entry closed shop. Almost three-quarters of the members were grade one, the rest were semi-skilled and unskilled grade two, three, and five. There was one EETPU member. The pattern of union membership and shop steward organization at Oil Tool is compared to that at Servo Engineering in Table 6.2.

Based on the stated criteria of union organization, the contrast between the two firms is impressive. In the first quarter of 1988 management had attempted to reduce the number of stewards at Oil Tool: 'They are trying to knock the stewards' committee down from fifteen to six, because we don't have as many people to represent,' said Joe. Whereas at Servo Engineering there were gaps in steward representation, at Oil Tool no such gaps existed. In 1988, all the steward positions were filled, with an average of 1:17. None of the stewards at Servo Engineering had undertaken any shop-steward training, whereas all those at Oil Tool Engineering had attended

Table 6.2   Union membership and steward organization at Oil Tool and
Servo Engineering, 1988

	Servo	*Oil Tool*
Union density (manual)	57%	100%
Check-off	No	Yes
Closed shop	No	Yes
Steward constituencies	9	15
Stewards elected	4	15
Steward density	1:50	1:17
Full-time steward	No	Yes
Senior stewards of 2 or more	No	Yes
Regular stewards meetings	No	Yes

Source: Steward interviews.

basic TUC steward training courses. The convener and deputy convener had also attended more advanced TUC and union weekend courses.

The stewards' committee met regularly every month, in working hours. There was a sub-committee which met more regularly and was involved in the more detailed negotiations with management; this included the convener, deputy convener, minutes secretary, and senior night-shift steward. The members of the sub-committee were an influential group of stewards and could be considered a 'quasi-elite' (Batstone et al, 1977). They were also the most critical opponents of the cellular system and management innovations, a point not missed by the plant manager:

> Out of our group of stewards . . . there are probably five who understand what we are trying to do but who resolutely resist it. They see it as an erosion of power . . . And it's that group who unfortunately are the leadership right now, and probably will be for a while, because the hardliners are the guys that a lot of people still stick by.

Intra-union organization is depicted in Figure 6.3

Regular stewards' meetings, full-time convener, stewards' bulletins and leaflets indicated a relatively high degree of intra-union organization. The crucial question is given this level of union sophistication, why did the AEU have so little influence over organizational change and the 'Japanization' of much of the manufacturing methods? First,

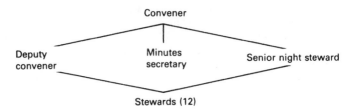

FIGURE 6.3   Intra-union organization at Oil Tool Engineering

despite having a high level of union organization, the stewards' committee had not developed a common strategy on CNC technology or cellular/JIT innovations. Joe confessed that, 'we haven't got a policy on new technology. We haven't got a policy on the cell system'.

Partly, the lack of any union strategy was due to membership acquiescence in the early stages when the first cell was established, but also there was no evidence that the stewards had attempted to formulate a policy that would begin to challenge management's proposed work structures. While union control was significant in shaping the detailed aspects of job redesign and labour regulation, in a small-batch, high-technology environment, the need to win commitment and active co-operation from a largely skilled workforce made management more susceptible to the union's demands. Thus when Batstone et al. assert that 'the high degree of sophistication of the AUEW was an important factor explaining the considerable range of union influence' (1987:155), they overstate the significance of union organization.

Second, with a sophisticated workplace union structure, but no broader perspective on management innovations, the stewards found it difficult to exert any influence on events once the first cell had been accepted by one group of their members: 'How it sneaked in I don't know. But once something is in and gets going, and there's no opposition to it, it's very hard to arrest it', the AEU convener told me.

Third, a particular work group's power is also a function of product market influences and the external labour market. Between 1982 and 1985 sales for the company's products fell by 25 per cent, and in 1986 the plant made an operating loss for the first time ever, of almost £6 million. In the same year there were redundancies at the plant, and overall total employment at the factory fell by 32 per cent between

1985 and 1987. The immediate catalyst to workers' acquiescence in Japanese methods and flexible working practices was the recession in Oil Tool's product market.

This chapter has focused upon the introduction of Japanese-style cellular and JIT methodology in a small-batch, unionized environment. The case is an example of how key aspects of Japanese manufacturing philosophy were applied to an engineering firm to reduce costs, improve quality standards and enhance control. It is interesting to juxtapose the previous case of Servo Engineering with Oil Tool Engineering, since both represent a logical response by the agents of capital to similar market conditions and quality improvement standards. Both firms were about the same size in terms of numbers employed. Both cases had invested in new CNC technology and cellular/JIT production. In both cases the plant was part of a group of companies, and the corporate headquarters were in the United States. In both cases contextual change rather than issues of labour control was the primary factor determining management's decision to introduce technical and organizational changes. The workforce in both plants was organized by the AEU. In other respects, the two cases are entirely different. The first case was involved in large-batch production, and the second in small-batch. Workplace unionism was weak in the first case, but relatively strong in the second. In the first case, management applied a direct control strategy and used CNC machine tools and microelectronic three-dimensional measuring instruments to deskill the workforce. In the second case, management adopted a responsible autonomy strategy and embarked upon an extensive 'education' programme and training to improve quality, to promote self-inspection, and produce more skilled and flexible craftsmen. In the first case management disciplined setter-operators if they amended programs. In contrast, in the second case, shopfloor involvement was encouraged by the management as part of their responsible autonomy strategy to create a totally flexible, cooperative, and skilled workforce with less direct hierarchical forms of control. Finally, it has been stressed that workplace union power depends upon a multiplicity of factors; workplace union organization *per se* is necessary, but insufficient, if workers are to challenge managerial prerogative, and exert some influence over their working lives.

7 The Packaging Company: Work Groups and the Polyvalent Worker

In 1985 Flowpak Engineering was in the forefront in cellular technology . . . the crest of the wave is here now.
Engineering consultant, June 1988

The preceding chapters investigated how aspects of the Japanese manufacturing paradigm have been imitated in both large and small-batch jobbing engineering. The next case-study features the introduction of Japanese manufacturing principles in a firm characterized by small-batch production and a high union density. The research on this case took place during a period between February 1987 and May 1988. A comprehensive report outlining the firm's deficiencies as perceived by eminent engineering consultants was made available, and is drawn upon in the study.[1] The depth of the case-study data permits a close analysis of some aspects of the capitalist labour process in the mid-1980s, together with an evaluation of management labour strategies, patterns of labour utilization, and its regulation in the manufacturing sector.

After discussing the company profile, the second section examines the changes in the manufacturing system and job design. In the third section the context of change and management's motives are discussed. The fourth section of this chapter examines the consequence of these management innovations for the workers in terms of job security, skills and shopfloor autonomy as perceived by the interviewees. Management strategy and union organization and influence over the process of change is then considered in section five. As in the investigation of other cases, where relevant, secondary evidence is quoted to validate the points raised by the interviewees.

COMPANY PROFILE

Flowpak Engineering is a company with a £14m turnover engineering automatic packaging machinery to the food, drinks, and pharmaceutical industries. The company employs about 350 workers. Flowpak Engineering produced the world's first packaging machine in 1885, and in 1985 produced the first microprocessor-controlled machine. Flowpak was structured on 1 January 1967 when it merged with three other packaging companies. In March 1987 the company was taken over by the UK-based food and drink machinery multinational AQC. Within the first nine months of the takeover the corporate management restructured the company through a programme of plant closures and redundancies.

At the West Yorkshire plant, prior to 1985, there were six levels of management control. The consultants considered this a hindrance to the decision-making process that encouraged a philosophy of barriers and demarcation: 'There is a "handing over" of problems at the "border post" between two parts of the organization, rather than an integrated approach'.[2] The consultants' report recommended that management control should be exercised through four levels: corporate director; factory manager; operations manager; working cell leader, and also recommended a new management appointment, which the consultants considered important if the firm was to adopt a just-in-time production philosophy. The report referred to the persons employed in the firm's purchasing department as 'order placers', lacking the necessary level of expertise to link purchasing with the work of manufacturing engineers; in other words to implement just-in-time methods. So the 'order placers' were replaced by a new purchasing manager, a graduate. Following the takeover by AQC the personnel department was trimmed and the 'Personnel Director' lost his title and became Company Personnel Manager for the West Yorkshire factory. The management structure at Flowpak is shown in Figure 7.1.

In the area of personnel management, there are prima-facie grounds for believing that line managers were taking greater responsibility for the 'people-management' of the business, and the personnel manager was seeking a closer identification with general management.[3]

A defining characteristic of multi-divisional companies is the existence of mechanisms by which corporate head office exercises control over its subsidiaries (Williams, 1975). Part of the questionnaire was

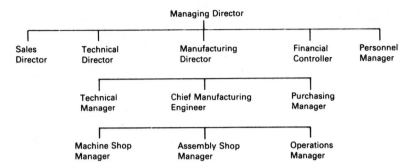

FIGURE 7.1   Management structure at Flowpak Engineering

aimed at identifying the extent of corporate office involvement in industrial relations matters. When first interviewed in February 1987, the personnel manager indicated that local management had 'complete discretion for manual and non-manual pay and redundancies'. But twelve months later it became evident that since the takeover, parameters on pay were outside the domain of local management. Richard Johnston, the company personnel manager, who had been with Flowpak Engineering for over twenty years, gave an insight into corporate office involvement:

> Our pay bargaining is now monitored rather more closely from the outside than it was. Previously we would have a management meeting. I would then do the negotiating. If at the end of the day I had to go two or three per cent more than we intended, that would be it . . . Now, if I want to go outside the budget I have to get permission from head office.

If we follow Kinnie's definition and include 'key operating decisions such as limits on wage offers', as a strategic industrial decision (1985:19), then since the takeover of Flowpak by AQC, there has been more corporate office involvement in strategic industrial decisions. This accords with the findings of a number of writers who have suggested that corporate managers secure control over subsidiaries by monitoring various key business indicators (e.g. Sisson and Scullion, 1985; Purcell and Gray, 1986; Edwards, 1987; Marginson et al., 1988).

THE PROCESS OF CHANGE

The Pre-Cellular System and Job Design

Prior to 1985, the machine shop at the plant followed a conventional layout. Groups of similar machine tools, lathes, milling machines, grinding machines and drills were located around the factory. Some of the characteristics of this type of structure such as incomplete components queuing at different workstations, long lead-times and traditional craft demarcation have already been described in earlier chapters. But the following comments from a machine operator give an insight into how the system worked:

> They would give you a raw bit of material. You would do your turning, then you would put it on the floor. A labourer would pick it up and put it in the stores. Then the miller would mill it, put it down on the floor again. It would go back to the stores again. The labourer touched it six times.
>
> Tim, skilled turner (age 25).

Skilled machine operators occupied a strategic position in this type of small-batch production. Operators interpreted engineering drawings, set up the machine tools, and monitored the machines' performance. NC and CNC operators also proved the programs generated by the white-collar tape programmers off the shopfloor. Generally a skilled operator would remain on one machine, for instance a lathe or a milling machine, permanently. There was no flexibility in terms of machinists performing tasks classified as 'semi-skilled', or machinists being transferred to the fitting shop to do assembly work. Semi-skilled tasks such as drilling or deburring would be done by a semi-skilled operator. Lifting and the ferrying of components around the factory, and cleaning, were undertaken by labourers.

The Cellular System and Job Redesign

Work was transformed by the introduction of seven cells in the machine shop and five in assembly. In the machine shop there were two turning cells, small and medium diameter; three cubic cells manufacturing large frames medium and small arms, plates and brackets. The cells were organized round a 'family' of parts of similar shape and dimension. Stores for material, cutting and painting constituted a cell. Finally, one cell produced 'crimp jaws': the machines in this cell were more specialized and here there was just one operator. The other cells had between six and ten operators. The machining cells could carry out all of the processes to complete the component, including deburring, plus extra hand-drilling and tapping, if necessary, in the cell, in order not to pass the problem to assembly, and inspection.

A variety of machine tools: milling, drilling, key-seating and grooving machines were located in each cell in order to complete a particular component. This means that some machines might be under-utilized, only being used maybe once in a week or even a month to complete a particular operation. The large amount of time some machine tools were not utilized was a characteristic of cellular production acknowledged by managers and workers alike, who have a working knowledge of the system. Thus Sayer is quite wrong when he asserts that: 'JIT . . . generates economies by reducing the amount of machinery which are at any time inactive' (1986:56).

Each cell was semi-autonomous within the factory: they were referred to as 'mini-businesses'. Cells could 'subcontract' to other cells to perform special operations; for example, heat treatment or grinding, and each was totally accountable for their equipment, cleaning and lubricating it. If the machines did require repairing the work was 'subcontracted' to the maintenance department. Further, the cell was accountable for their tools and fixtures. They had a tool budget and would be 'charged' by the finance department for what they bought. Special tools could be 'hired' from the tool store and charged to the cell. Nigel Conner, the manufacturing director, elaborated: 'The tool budget is divided amongst the cells and they decide what to buy within their allocated budgets. Where it doesn't matter who makes the decision . . . let them [the shopfloor] do it.'

This aspect of cell autonomy had caused friction between the cell leaders and the manufacturing engineers. The following remarks from one manufacturing engineer give insight into the friction:

Manufacturing engineers have recommended tools to be bought; the cell leader has said: 'I don't think we need that'. A job comes down a couple of weeks later: no tools to do the job. Likewise, the cell have suggested that we buy something, engineers have warned them against it . . . and it's been useless.

The machine shop had few sophisticated CNC machine tools. The consultants in 1985 had commented that there were 'too many older machine tools . . . no application of modern modular tooling concepts'. This was still the case in 1988. In 1985 the plant had seventy-two machine tools, with just three NC and six CNC machine tools.

The assembly cells were organized around the final product. Each assembly cell had a group of workers who had the skills to build the machine from supplied parts to final test. The assembly cells, also, were viewed as 'mini-businesses'. The management had created an internal market; the cells 'bought' their components from the machining cells, who effectively were their subcontractors. If the machining operations had not been completed, for instance, the component was not deburred, or if the quality was poor, the assembly cells had 'the right to refuse delivery'.

Division of Labour and Flexibility

Our philosophy is flexibility and quality control within the cell.
Manufacturing engineer, October 1987

The one man, one machine principle has gone completely out of the door.
AEU convener, March, 1987

Fragmentation of tasks and the division of mental and manual labour occupies a pivotal place in the deskilling debate. In contrast to the two earlier case-studies, the division of labour in the cells was less hierarchical at Flowpak Engineering, as shown in Table 7.1, and there were fewer supervisory and manual grades. The vertical hierarchy of control in the machine shop, via workshop manager, foreman and charge-hand was contracted at Flowpak by the elimination of the lower management positions of foremen and charge-hands. The cells served to reduce the need for direct control because the teams took on a degree of autonomy. This accords with Sayer's (1986) interpretation of the effect of just-in-time. The removal of supervisors and quality control inspectors flatten hierarchies within factories. Again, it must be stressed that it is not JIT techniques that flatten management hierarchies, but the incorporation of lower management coordinating tasks, and quality control functions within the cellular work structure.

The cell leader undertook a range of functions which were previously the responsibility of the foremen or works manager. If one classifies a traditional foreman 100 per cent, and an old-style works manager 200

Table 7.1   Division of labour within the machine cells at Servo, Oil Tool and Flowpak, 1988

Grades	Servo	Oil Tool	Flowpak
Supervisory			
	CS	STL	CL
	PC	TL	
	CH		
Manual			
	Setter	Skilled	Skilled
	Setter-operator	Semi-skilled(2)	Labourer
	Operator	Semi-skilled(3)	
	Labourer	Labourer	

Key: CS Cell supervisor   CL Cell leader
     PC Product coordinator   STL Senior team leader
     CH Charge-hand   TL Team leader

per cent, then the cell leader would be 130 per cent. All the cell leaders in the machine shop were appointed from the manual workers, and they remained in the manual workers' union, the AEU. This is in contrast to the other cases studied, where the cell supervisors and team leaders were either in the staff section of MSF or non-unionized. At Flowpak the cell leader typically was responsible for his cell's output and quality. This involved allocation of work: liaison with production control for delivery dates required: detailed discussions with manufacturing engineers concerning equipment, tooling, and programs; and liaison with finance personnel concerning the costs of his cell, for example, work-in progress costs, overhead costs and direct labour costs. The cell leader also had responsibility for direct supervision of the cell members and was given first-line disciplinary powers. The cell leader reported directly to the machine shop manager. In concept his role was described in an Ingersoll Engineers' discussion paper as: 'A mini business manager acting as a subcontractor to assembly, with Production Control being the "order placer".'

Tim, one of the machine-shop cell leaders described his role to me:

Mainly it's a turning cell, so I tend to move people off turning occasionally onto other machines in order to get the part through. It also involves looking after the tooling budget. I order my own stuff in that area . . . I'm in charge of quality. There is not much discipline required in the cell.

And some of his training:

> We had two or three-day man-management courses at Doncaster
> . . . There was simulated role-playing . . . you were a manager and
> you had to discipline someone . . . it was a bit embarrassing . . . I
> was dealing with people who had been charge-hands who had
> experience and it didn't go too well.

There were only two manual grades below cell leader: 'skilled
machinists' and 'labourer'. Traditional job boundaries among the
skilled machinists had been abolished and substantial horizontal and
vertical flexibility existed in the machining and assembly cells. Unlike
Oil Tool, semi-skilled grades did not exist, furnishing evidence of a
polarization of skills within the engineering industry. Functional
flexibility applied only to skilled workers. The four labourers working
on the shopfloor did not operate any machinery; their tasks were
confined to sweeping and lifting.

In theory, a skilled manual worker could be asked to operate any
machine tool on the shopfloor. In practice this did not happen,
because many of the operators had little experience of the newer
CNC machine tools. Apart from the recent additions, all the operators were employed as 'engineering craftsmen' and were expected to
operate any machine tool. The personnel director, Richard Johnston,
explained the concept of flexibility and its limitations:

> If you take the machine cell, you've got theoretically absolute
> flexibility within the cells. Having said that, that's just a bit of a
> pipe dream. For instance, we are introducing CNC machine tools.
> Some are good at it, some aren't. But the point is we have a very
> flexible attitude.

The following remarks from key personnel reveal the extent of
functional flexibility among the machine operators:

> Within the cells the majority of machine operators can manoeuvre
> between tasks. They manage their own flexibility.
>
> Manufacturing Director

> I was talking to a feller yesterday, he had worked forty-nine
> different machines. That's good. That's flexibility.
>
> Manufacturing Engineer

Flexibility . . . everybody has got to learn roughly every machine . . . Most people want to. It breaks the day up, they're not as bored as they have been in the past.

Cell Leader.

To explicate the concept of 'flexible attitude' some of the machine operators were asked to describe their understanding of flexibility and how it had changed their work. They put it like this:

We do varied amounts of work in our cell, drilling, milling. Its up to the cell leader. So, wherever he needs us, we go.

Malcolm (age 26).

Before the cell system was introduced, I was on small turning for three months. Whereas now . . . I can be anywhere in the day. Yesterday, I was on the big planer-miller, then on the milling machine, then back on the planer-miller. I might be on the grinder this afternoon. You never know what's going to crop up.

Jim, AEU Shop Steward (age 43).

We don't train turners and millers now. We train general machinists.

Albert, AEU convener (age 56).

The firm would normally subcontract 20 per cent of its production, but during a peak period the figure could increase to 30 per cent. But the aggregate figure does not reveal the qualitative change in the type of work being subcontracted out. More significantly, subcontracting had grown because of changes in product design. General machine work had not increased since there was generally spare capacity in the machine shop, but it was the machining of new material, like plastic and stainless steel fabrication, that was contracted out.

Subcontracting gave the firm greater flexibility in product design. To illustrate the point: when the firm had a foundry section there was a tendency to design a machine with a cast-iron 'chair'. The closure of the foundry and the general development of subcontracting meant that product design was not restricted to in-house production constraints. Wickens has described the close relationship between Japan manufacturers and their suppliers: 'he will have built up a long-term relationship with a single supplier' (1987:61–2). This aspect of Japanese management was apparent at Flowpak. More information was disclosed to the suppliers about future demand to facilitate planning and investment in the contract firms. The suppliers were also invited to comment and make an input at the design stage. The change in relationship, an important ingredient in the just-in-time philosophy, is expressed by the following quotations from two key managers:

> I like to think that they are working more with us, rather than for us . . . We like to keep them fully informed, make them aware as to why we want their particular parts in. So we like to think we are working a little more as a team now.
>
> Purchasing Manager.

> We involve our suppliers in the design of our machines in order to save costs. For example, in fabrication, the supplier will advise us against a curved edge, when a straight edge is equally as good and easier and cheaper to do.
>
> Manufacturing Director.

Subcontracting within the factory, between the cells, was understood by the workers and shop stewards to be a essential feature of the cell system, and accepted. Albert Smith, the convener, said that 'the cell system demands subcontracting'. Every fortnight Albert met with management to discuss projected workloads, identify the peaks in production, and the work to be contracted out. The shop stewards' attitude to subcontracting raises two points. External contracting was seen by them as a way of protecting the 'core' workforce and avoiding periodic redundancies. Also, it provides an example of a management giving union representatives a functional role in the production process. Among the drawing-office workers the issue of subcontracting was more contentious. Indeed, in March 1987 it was at the centre of a dispute. The case of Flowpak reveals that the shift away from direct employment towards contract work, a form of numerical flexibility (Nichol, 1986), is not confined to manual occupations. Subcontracting and subsequent changes in the capital–labour relation can equally apply to non-manual, professional engineering groups.

Total Quality Control (TQC)

> *Quality is of absolute importance. It must be a 'religion' and become a way of life. Quality should be 'bought off' by the assembly area from the machine shop.*
>
> Ingersoll Engineers, (consultants) 1985

Another significant aspect of functional flexibility visible at the plant was direct operatives inspecting their own work. Self-inspection and the absorption of 'quality inspectors' into the cells is another key element of Japanese-style manufacturing methods advocated by the consultants in 1985. It was pointed out to the senior management that a major failure of the orthodox system was that it promoted the habit of 'handing over your little bit of the job to the next man . . . and absolving [yourself] of the responsibility for its completion'. The cell was given responsibility for their own quality control. Inspection was part of the production process, not something carried out by a separate quality control department.

The principles of just-in-time to minimize buffer stocks and total-quality-control to achieve zero defects are closely related. The manufacturing process is more sensitive to operators' error, the smaller the buffer. Moreover, the adoption of these two principles enables management to identify the source of the error and to take appropriate corrective action. The machine shop manager explained the success of self-inspection in these terms:

> The inspectors spent a lot of the time justifying their position. But we didn't go to the root of the problem. Before, we would machine twenty components, and five would go into the scrap bin; this was an accepted pattern. Self-inspection and JIT forced us to look at the reasons why it's scrap.

The requirement for operators to inspect their own work, together with mutual disciplinary pressures may lead to an intensification of work. A manufacturing engineer gives an insight into the potential danger of intensifying work and stress:

> We leave the quality of the finished part to the cell concerned, and so it's easy to see if they are going to get their *knuckles rapped* [my emphasis] at the end of the day. Therefore, they don't like to make mistakes. We tend not to have too many.

While there appear to be a growing number of avant-garde engineering consultants preaching the virtues of Japanese-style manufacturing methods, the more negative aspects of possible chronic stress-related illness resulting from work intensity, has received little, if any, attention.

Restructuring of Rewards

A serious impediment to developing workers' behavioural skills of cooperation and problem-solving is a wage structure based upon individualized bonus payments. The firm's payment-by-results system was a serious obstacle to labour flexibility and management's attempts to nurture an ideology of 'team-work'. The importance of a flat-rate wage system was seen by Richard Johnston, the personnel director, as follows:

> I wouldn't say it's essential, but it's very, very desirable. We went for the simplest wage structure we could. There is no such thing as a good payments' system, there is only a series of bad ones. The trick is to choose the least bad one.

A flat-rate system obviates rivalry between internal divisions of labour, encourages communication between workers and behavioural skills of cooperation, and Richard Johnston described its benefits: 'As soon as people realized that there was no personal, peculiar advantage in hiding bits of knowledge, being inflexible, hogging the good jobs, and sticking to their machine and all that . . . it was like suddenly turning the key.'

Flowpak management rejected the idea of an incentive scheme based upon the cells, on the grounds that it would simply have been a modified version of the old piece-work scheme with its inherent problems of differential earnings. Low and high earning cells would undermine the objective of flexibility.

A STRATEGY TO SURVIVE

> *They [UK customers] frequently expressed sadness that Flowpak had 'lost its way' or allowed foreign competitors to 'walk all over them'.*
> Marketing Consultant, 1985.

> *Looks like Alfred Herbert to us in the years preceding closure.*
> Ingersoll Engineers, 1985

Flowpak's senior management's adoption of new manufacturing practices can to be explained in terms of the external perception of the firm in general, as exemplified by the above quotations; and the firm's relative decline in business performance in terms of profitability and market share in particular. Until the early 1980s the firm had been profitable. However, as was the case for many manufacturing companies, the recession in 1980/81 resulted in the firm incurring operating losses. Between 1980 and 1983 it had an operating loss of £9 million. In response to falling profits, the new senior management team initiated three major surveys of the firm's business operations – marketing, manufacturing, and industrial relations – using outside consultants, between 1984 and 1985. An 'image survey' among nineteen typical UK customers showed, on the one hand, that the company was perceived in the market place as a high quality supplier. However, like many other British companies, it was also seen as a company that had 'lost its way'. Compared to its European competitors the firm was considered to be inflexible. There was a reluctance to amend its packaging machinery specifications to suit the customers' unique requirements. The design area had a general philosophy of selling packaging machines rather than providing 'total solutions to customer packaging problems'.

In the areas of manufacturing and industrial relations senior management believed that 'control was missing' and they were simply 'fire fighting'. There are two elements to manufacturing control: production and assembly. Production control was based on a complex paperwork system which was recognized to be inappropriate. For example, the issue of a main batch and unit batches of a product could involve the issue of 'over 10 miles of paperwork'.[4]

Labour costs were an important factor influencing management strategy. Richard Johnston, the personnel manager, made the point forthrightly: 'what we needed to do was cheapen production and get it there faster'. Production was to be 'cheapened' in two ways. Firstly, the company's total labour costs were to be reduced by large-scale redundancies. Secondly, unit labour costs were to be reduced by introducing additional CNC machine tools and adopting new cellular and JIT manufacturing techniques. The technical and organizational changes in production methods were forecast to increase productivity by at least 20 per cent. In addition, management wanted to exert greater control over labour costs by rationalizing the company's payment system. Labour costs, therefore, were a central consideration in management's strategy for the companys' survival and the restoration of profitability.

The formation of the cells would decrease unit labour costs by reducing control requirements: lead times; inventory and work-in-progress; and enabling greater flexibility of labour. For instance, the twenty people allocated to the role of direct labour control, the supervisors, were reduced to six, and those six 'cell leaders' were productive within the cell.

Third, investment in microprocessor-based technology in the machine shop, production control and design office was considered an essential prerequisite to both increasing productivity and regaining control over the manufacturing process. The investigators found that the machine tools at Flowpak were outdated: 'too many older machine tools have been retained with the consequent proliferation of manufacturing methods and their controls. A computer aided design (CAD) and computer aided manufacture (CAM) system, using a Manufacturing Requirements Planning software package, was advocated to control production and reduce lead times, work-in-progress, and inventory. In addition, radical changes in product design were suggested, to reduce the total costs of manufacture. The application of microelectronics would require considerably fewer components than electro-mechanical packaging systems. This was to have significant implications for machinists, a point explored later. Prior to 1985, the Company operated a payment by results (PBR) system. The Donovan Commission considered payment by results to be a major problem for British industrial relations, creating inequitable wage structures, a 'confrontational' style of management–labour relations, and obstacles to more efficient working practices. Furthermore, it was argued that piecework bargaining weakened the wage/effort relationship because earnings were determined largely by the stewards' bargaining skill and workers' collective power, rather than by individual effort. Measured daywork (MDW), defined as a situation in which 'the pay of the employee is fixed on the understanding that he will maintain a specific level of performance, but the pay does not fluctuate in the short term with his actual performance' (Clegg, 1979:145), was recommended as a means of regaining control over the manufacturing labour process, and removing the perceived obstacles caused by payment-by-results (Cliff, 1970).

Flowpak's payment system, with its individualized bonus scheme based on piecework bargaining, was identified by senior management as problematic and in need of reform. The incentive payment system was seen to be too costly, creating time standards that were '20 per cent loose overall'. Unit labour costs could be reduced by the introduction of CNC technology and cellular/JIT methods. This accords with the findings of a study into the brewing industry by Davies. She found that the reduction of labour costs per unit of output was 'the most important reason for the introduction of microtechnology' (1986:134). In addition, it typically created a 'confrontational' relationship between management and workers. There was 'a tendency to screw the last farthing out of any possible agreement', recalled

Richard Johnston, the personnel manager. The AEU convener gave an additional insight into the divisive nature of payment-by-result systems:

> Piece-work schemes? It was the biggest cut-throat system ever introduced . . . Because although it motivated, it always created; 'Well let him get on with it, he gets more money than me'. So you had 10 per cent of the top earners, they were good; and we had 90 per cent who couldn't careless.

All these problems were sufficient to suggest to management the need for change. In addition, however, there was a worry that the individualized payment-by-results system was no longer an 'incentive' for workers to improve their effort levels. Flowpak's senior management were presented with a number of options. Their final choice was a rationalization process involving the closure of two other plants in the North of England and the installation of a computer system around a cellular configuration which was considered 'vital to regain control'.[5] As was the case at Oil Tool Engineering, senior management at Flowpak transformed the labour process and aimed to exert greater control and integration to survive economically and restore; profitability.

The main focus in this section has been cellular technology but, before considering the impacts of these changes, we should discuss other trends regarding CAD technology, product design and computer integrated manufacture (CIM) which ran parallel to the changes in the firm's manufacturing system.

The installation of CAD at Flowpak Engineering in 1983 was a substantial capital investment. Excluding training costs, the system cost £0.75m and the Company received a DTI grant of £60 000. The consultants considered the CAD system appropriate for the company's immediate needs, but found that there was: 'Little understanding of the overall-need for Computer Aided Manufacture (CAM), and the preparation of part programmes for machine tools'. Ingersoll Engineers, (1985:26)

This accords with Senker's study of UK engineering firms: 'few recognized its significance as a strategic step towards CAD/CAM' (Senker, 1985:228).

Simplifying the design of a machine and substituting electro-mechanical components for a micro-chip has far-reaching implications for engineering manual workers. The design function can cheapen production by the introduction of designs which involve simpler manufacturing processes, and by eliminating certain types of work altogether. Further, changes in design can affect not only how the product is manufactured, but where; by the introduction of new designs the amount of subcontract work can increase.

Conventional packaging machines involved the use of castings, bearings and chains; a large number of individual parts were bolted or screwed together. Microprocessors can automatically guide packaging machinery through a sequence of actions. Control of volumes, flows, weights and sequences are the types of operation performed by microelectronics. The incorporation of microprocessor control systems in the new 666 model considerably reduced the use of gears, cams, levers and castings within the machine design. Table 7.2 contrasts the number of selected mechanical components in the new 666 model and a more traditional machine, the 333.

Table 7.2   Changes in product design: mechanical components

Model	Gears	Cams	Bearing	Castings	Chains	Total
333	2	5	50	20	7	84
666	2	4	24	0	1	31

Source: Purchasing Department.

The incorporation of microprocessors and greater use of plastics in the new range of machines reduced manufacturing costs, caused changes in the production process and determined where components were made, either in-house, or subcontracted out. The switch from castings resulted in the closure of the foundry section in the factory and a total reliance on contractors to supply fabricated components. The substitution of metal components for plastic also meant that the proportion of 'bought-in' components in the new 666 models increased. The actual ratio between the parts manufactured on site and those externally purshased must, it was estimated, have increased from about 80:20 to 70:30. Flowpak Engineering was becoming an assembler rather than a manufacturer of packaging machines. The purchasing manager was in a key position to substantiate such a hypothesis:

I am confident in saying that it has increased . . . . well the electrical and electronic side is quite a bulk. So for that reason alone, I would be fairly safe in saying that the amount of purchased items in any machine is greater than it was two or three years ago.

The engineering consultants had maintained that the pre-cellular system of production control was grossly inefficient and a liability to the survival of the company. A new system to integrate design and manufacturing was a key recommendation. It was considered an urgent priority to link the operations control system with the existing CAD system, supplemented by computer aided manufacture software for part programme preparation. Without such systems it was felt that 'the proper control of the business will not be possible'. Essentially, the 'complex paperwork system' of production control was replaced by an IBM MAAPIC production and inventory control package which supplied print-outs for the machining and assembly cells. The machine shop and assembly managers received a computer print-out identifying work in priority order together with data on the required components, and materials. Thus priorities, instead of being decided by the machine shop manager, are now determined by a computer print-out, the 'Work-to-List'.

To sum up this section: it was evident that management had introduced successfully an integrated computer control system in the plant with the objective of enhancing control and integrating the manufacturing processes. This does of course raise further questions of the system as a means of monitoring workers' performance, and this aspect of control is examined in the next section.

THE TRANSFORMATION OF WORK: THE POLYVALENT WORKER?

This section will give more detailed attention to the implications of both cellular work structures and microtechnology for labour. The employment effects of Japanese-style production methods are first considered. To examine the questions of general deskilling, routinization of jobs and control, the tasks of machine operators are discussed. Table 7.3 shows employment losses at Flowpak Engineering between 1980 and 1985.

Employment in Flowpak Engineering fell from 649 to 317, a decrease of 51 per cent over the 1980–85 period. The reduction in skilled manual is well above the national and regional trends. Between 1980 and 1985 the number of semi-skilled workers fell from seventy-two to

Table 7.3 Employment by occupation at Flowpak, 1980–85

Occupational category (1)	Number 1980 (2)	1985 (3)	Percentage change 1980–85 (4)
Managerial staff	26	27	+4
Draughtsmen	25	19	−24
Technicians	87	72	−17
Clerical	173	78	−55
Supervisors	20	6	−70
Craftsmen	246	87	−65
Operatives	72	28	−61
Total	649	317	−51

Source: Questionnaire return from Personnel Manager.

twenty-eight, a reduction of 61 per cent. By 1987 the total number of semi-skilled workers had fallen to just seven, again reinforcing the view that the semi-skilled workers are most vulnerable to the encroachment of cellular work structures.

The substantial fall in employment was largely the result of the recession and the rationalization exercise. The managers interviewed attributed the reduction in the workforce to 'market factors'. This view was also shared by the stewards, but in addition, they blamed the fall in sales, and subsequent redundancies, on management's failure to invest in new machines in the 1970s when the company was profitable. Tony, a TASS steward, stated: 'They made a lot of money through the seventies . . . there was quite a bit of design work went on, but none of the machine designs seem to take off. We ended up in the early eighties with an out-of-date product range'.

Employment losses were affected by new technology and productivity-enhancing cellular production but, as pointed out in Chapter 4, isolating the employment effects of new technology and cellular and JIT methods is, in practice, enormously difficult. At Flowpak staff reductions occurred when the computerized production and inventory control system was installed. In the only reference by an interviewee to the question of technological unemployment, the personnel manager pointed out that the stores office had 'disappeared since the computer was installed'. As was the case of Oil Tool Engineering, new technology also led to new senior appointments in non-manual occupations. Several new managerial positions in the area of CAD operations, and purchasing to 'improve the level and quality of information within the business', were created in the period 1986–87.

Productivity-enhancing cellular production can have a negative effect on employment, *ceteris paribus*. Functional flexibility involving operators using a range of machine tools, the adoption of total quality control and the elimination of first-level supervisory staff increase productivity substantially, resulting in negative employment effects in both the direct and indirect workforce (Sayer, 1986; Turnbull, 1988). As far as Flowpak was concerned, the consultant's report made it perfectly clear that the objective of machining and assembly cells was 'the elimination of inefficiences normally associated with direct labour control'.

Cellular technology attempts to extract productivity improvements from the labour force by promoting functional flexibility, thereby increasing the rate of throughput in the factory. There was a general agreement among interviewees at Flowpak that cellular technology had increased the rate of throughput. Richard Johnston, the personnel manager, put it like this:

> Productivity figures need treating with a little caution. Undoubtedly what has improved is the throughput. Vastly. The average component going through the machine shop goes through four or five times faster than it used to. – February, 1988

A similar view was expressed by Albert, AEU convener:

> The average component was prepared and completed in twenty-one days before the introduction of the cell system; now the average is three days. – March, 1988

And Tim, a cell leader, added the following comment on productivity:

> Our lead-time is three days from when it enters the cell to getting it finished. Going back to the old system, it was about seven weeks.

The information provides evidence of improved productivity arising from technical and organizational changes. This assessment is consistent with the experience of a UK manufacturer operating JIT techniques, when over a twelve-month period 'productivity increased by 25 per cent and unit costs of production fell by 11 per cent'

(Turnbull, 1988:9). The net result of these changes in the labour process is a reduced demand for labour.

Changes in Manual Skills

At Flowpak Engineering the restructuring of shopfloor work increased the cluster of tasks performed by the machine operators. Within each cell craft machinists were expected to operate all the machine tools located in the cell. Task variety was also extended because of the reciprocal concept of total quality control; operators inspected and tested their own work. The reason given for the need to employ skilled labour was that, in spite of some rationalization in product design, typically orders were for small batches of diverse components. As one manufacturing engineer informed me: 'We have tremendous variety of component types not very conducive to very fully automated cells'. The diversity of skilled tasks involving the use of both conventional and NC and CNC machine tools for small batches precluded the use of semi-skilled operators.

In a small-batch environment skill acquisition was achieved through job flexibility and extra on-the-job training. The successful exploitation of cellular technology demanded that operators became proficient at a wider range of machining operations to achieve the necessary 'U-shape' flow of production and enhanced productivity. Job redesign increased the knowledge required to operate the configuration of machine tools. Those cells with CNC lathes and machining centres required new tape 'proving', and diagnostic skills. A manufacturing engineer elaborates: 'We have operators working the conventional machines, when they are not working the CNC, so very much are they keeping up their level of skill'. In total the operators in Cell 4 performed four processes: turning, using either conventional or CNC lathes; milling; drilling and grinding. In Cell 2, which produced component parts of medium cubic families, was situated a CNC Cincinnati machining centre. This machine performed a range of milling operations and also drilling and tapping functions. To fully exploit the technology the operators had to learn to conceptualize all the functions and perform the operations in the most appropriate sequences to avoid re-setting the cutting tools after certain operations.

Each cell has been described as a 'mini-business', with work being 'contracted' to other cells within the factory, and cells 'hiring' special tools or equipment. To avoid queuing for the machines within the cell, and to minimize contracting and hiring costs, additional planning skills were needed by the cell members. It was put to me like this by one of the manufacturing engineers:

> The idea is, a day's planning is sorted out the night before so that the jobs, the planning, the tools, everything comes down on the trolley in the cell at once. So it's a whole new way of thinking . . . It's hard on the older generation.

Thus, Japanese work structures had increased the range of machining tasks and involved additional planning and coordinating tasks. A prerequisite for cellular technology is the development of what Sayer refers to as 'behavioural skills of cooperativeness and self-discipline'. To fully exploit labour power, to cultivate workers' problem-solving skills requires a more involved and cooperative workforce than the more orthodox manufacturing systems. One manufacturing engineer held that 'Our philosophy of flexibility within the cell, is trying to motivate the cell to work as a team to improve productivity'.

The removal of individualized bonus payments, and twice weekly 'team' meetings were designed to act as a conduit for transmitting information to the workforce and fostering collective problem-solving skills. One of the cell leaders described the meetings: 'Generally we just talk between ourselves and if we are falling behind I'll ask them why'.

In terms of skilled manual engineering workers, discretion plays a vital role in skill determination. Without discretion work is 'rule-bound' and involves little mental conceptual content (Jacques, 1961). The case provided examples of both reduced and enhanced discretion. The use of the computerized production inventory and control system (CPICS) for scheduling and prioritizing work had usurped the traditional role of the foreman. The work-to-list determined the order of priority so that the cell had 'little control over production'. However, operators had some discretion over job assignments within the parameters set by the CPICS. They were able to alter the sequence of work by grouping similar components together, to obviate the need for resetting the machine. Moreover, the extent of operators' responsibilities for machining the component parts and the maintenance of quality standards is indicative of operator discretion. The fact that the cell leader did not supervise operators' work closely adds support to this view. It will be recalled that the cell members had limited discretion over tooling.

Although operator discretion was considerably curtailed by a set tool budget and a philosophy that limited choice, the point should not be lost, that compared to conventional engineering practice, operator discretion and autonomy was enhanced through the process of job redesign. Discretion was also increased after cells were given responsibility for making fixtures. As Albert put it: 'Now if you want a fixture, you've to make it. We have no tool-room making fixtures. Your cell makes the fixture. You design it yourself, and you make it yourself'.

The manufacture of fixtures was made easier by the process of standardization and radical changes in product design. By standardizing many of the components, the need for new fixtures was minimized.

Operator discretion was relatively limited, in the sense of control over machining methods and use of resources, but in contrast to a more conventional work structure, cellular technology, with related practices, offered a wider range of tasks and enhanced operator discretion and shopfloor autonomy. Comments from operators give an additional insight into the effects of Japanese-style manufacturing practices:

> The cell system has increased skill by an enormous percentage, an enormous percentage. Because it's made people that always milled for twenty years, now they can turn, now they can bore . . . and now they are emerging as being general machinists. Most of us have the ability now to go on machines we only stared at before.
>
> Albert, grinder; AEU convener (age 56).

> You get more variety and you get more skills.
>
> Malcolm, machine operator (age 26).

> Well I think most people are more skilled in a variety of machines. It's an increase in skill over a wider scope.
>
> Patrick, machine operator (age 56).

The concept of alienation is an objective state although it has subjective implications. If a lathe operator's work is fragmented and there is no scope for discretion, s/he cannot achieve their potential self-realization. A contented lathe operator is no less alienated in this sense than a dissatisfied and bored one. Thus, an apparent absence of alienation is not necessarily reflected in perceived psychological benefits of job satisfaction. However, one operator referred to increased job satisfaction and reflected obliquely on the concept of 'self-actualization' arising from the new work structure:

> Its more interesting . . . You are using your skills you have been taught. This is where the interest comes in, because you might get a piece of steel, or a casting, and you might complete it yourself. And you have done milling, boring, drilling, and it's a finished component when it leaves you. You can actually stamp your name on it.
>
> Jim, machine operator; AEU shop steward (age 43).

Table 7.4 shows the answers of shop stewards and workers to the questions in relation to the work of manual workers affected by cellular modes of production. In all cases machine operators reported that the cellular system had increased their skills. This was consistent with the views of all the managers interviewed. Each gave a favourable effect on machinists' skills as a result of cellular methods. Interest and variety of work had been enhanced by the change according to the manual workers, including fitters.

Sayer (1986) and Turnbull (1988) have suggested that the elimination of waiting time arising from just-in-time techniques leads to an increase in work intensification. At Flowpak Engineering, increases in productivity followed from the intensification of work through reorganizing production into cellular configurations. The cellular system served to intensify the work process by increasing functional

Table 7.4   Stewards' and workers' accounts of the effects of cellular technology upon the work of machine operators

	Not at all	Decrease		Increase	
		Small	Large	Small	Large
Skill			2	1	3
Planning	3	2		1	
Discretion	3			1	2
Interest					6
Variety			1		5
Pace of work	5			1	
Mobility	2			1	3

flexibility and adding additional skills across the craft machinists. For instance, in Cell 4, skilled machinists operated both CNC and conventional machine tools. The machinist set up the two CNC lathes, and between the machining cycles, he operated a manual lathe.

However, the sense of work intensification was not perceived by work groups. Most of the respondents believed that cellular and JIT production methods had not led to an increase in work intensity. This apparent contradiction between theory and practice can be explained by two parallel developments. The introduction of Japanese-style practices was accompanied by the abolition of a payment-by-results award system in favour of a flat-rate system. Managers and workers recognized that once the individualized performance-related incentive bonus scheme was abolished the pace of work relaxed. Jim, a machine operator makes the point of forthrightly:

> Pace . . . it can be less. Under the old piece work scheme, you chase the clock and you think, 'Right I've made my bonus, I'm an hour in front now'. You go for a walk to the stores and have a natter; go to the toilet, so that's an hour's lost production. Whereas now, there is no time on jobs, so you go at an even pace.

Some insight into the question of work intensification is afforded by the responses from other workers to my question whether the cellular system had increased the pace of work:

> We've increased productivity by 20 per cent. But you didn't need anybody to create blood or sweat. The system . . . . is just working more efficiently.
>
> Albert, AEU convener.

> Before the pressure was on you to beat the clock all the time. Now the pressure has gone. Perhaps we don't individually work as hard, but we do get the work out faster.
>
> Patrick, Operator.

Management abolished the PBR system primarily to encourage flexibility, but they also recognized the limitations of mutual social control. Richard Johnston gives an additional, albeit expected, perspective to effects of cellular and JIT on the pace of work:

> I would like to see a bit more motivation. I think people enjoy their work, I wish some of our people would work a bit harder . . . This is one of the effects of getting rid of the bonus scheme. – February, 1988.

Cellular/JIT techniques embodies principles which offer management the opportunity to extract higher productivity from labour by work intensification. As there are no automatic 'impacts' stemming from technical change, so too with cellular technology, there are no self-acting impacts once introduced into a firm.

In earlier chapters the question whether managements have de-skilled manual engineering workers has centred on the disjunctures between programming and machining tasks. The responsibility for programming at Flowpak was the Manufacturing Engineering Department's which was established in 1986 to facilitate a closer working relationship between design activities and the machine shop. The manufacturing engineers, or MEs as they were referred to, had staff status and were members of TASS (MSF). Prior to 1986, programming was done by TASS members in what was then called the Planning Department. The NC and CNC machine tools were not considered 'user-friendly' and did not easily lend themselves to programming at source, according to the MEs. The 'proving' exercise to test the efficacy of the program generated by the MEs was completed by the skilled operators on the machine. Minor amendments to the specifications, such as, tool feed and speeds, were performed by the operator. With the introduction of CNC the task range had increased. Operators had to learn new skills: tape-editing, setting-up, and diagnostic skills to detect tool wear by changes in the level of noise. As Jones points out: 'operators must have sufficient machining experience to diagnose tool wear to "Prevent an expensive scrapping of tool, component or both"'. (Jones, 1983:195). These skills which required certain levels of mathematical competence, and an appreciation of the idiosyncracies of particular CNC machines, were acquired through a combination of off- and on-the-job training. The company had not yet adopted a 'skill fragmentation' strategy. A manufacturing engineer explained the importance of employing skilled operators on CNC machine tools:

> I don't think you can start employing semi-skilled or lower-skilled labour on CNC . . . The machining skills are obviously taken away from them. They have the input at the planning stage. They make sure the tapes are OK, they 'prove' the tape. Then they set it going. You can hear when a tool is about to break . . . there is a skill level in running it once its going.

The MEs appeared to justify their control over program generation for three reasons. First, the machines were relatively old and were unsuitable for manual data input (MDI), 'The controls are very old anyway, it [CNC] doesn't allow consecutive machining and programming . . . but we want to keep it off the shopfloor', insisted one manufacturing engineer. Secondly, it was not efficient in a small-batch production for operators to be writing their own programs. Terry, a manufacturing engineer, justified the separation of programming and machining in this way: 'When he's programming he's not working . . . You lose production when the guys start planning and programming'. Thirdly, it was suggested to me that there was a general deficiency in programming skills among the operators. To quote from a later interview: 'Off the record, we do have difficulty getting guys in as skilled as the fellows that were trained through our company'.

Wilkinson's research revealed friction between programmers and CNC operators on the shopfloor. The programmers were frequently referred to as 'office wallahs' whose 'lack of shopfloor experience' rendered their planning instructions highly suspect and subject to correction, increasing the workload of the operators and swelling the perceived importance of management's reliance on the CNC operators. At Flowpak there was some discord between the manufacturing engineers and the general machinists, but it was managed. There was no obvious friction over the control 'key' for instance. However, if you talked to the operators they did consider that MEs had little practical experience and they were 'never there when needed'; and the skilled manual workers grumbled that there was poor liaison between the ME department and the cells. Although it was 'official' policy that ME personnel should generate programs, the machine operators were beginning to encroach upon the role of the manufacturing engineer. The most proficient operators were becoming increasingly involved in more than simply 'proving' tapes generated by the MEs, they had begun to generate their own tapes for some of the CNC machines. The machine shop manager turned a blind-eye to the practice; indeed he considered programming at source, with qualifications, more conducive to efficiency. He told me that 'The Cincinnati machining centre is the most successful machine in the cellular structure because we don't rely on anybody else. Unofficially some operators are writing tapes . . . My experience . . . for small batches, its better to program on the shopfloor'.

The demarcation between the MEs and shopfloor operators did appear to follow a zero-sum pattern, with MSF member's loss becoming AEU member's gain. As the machine shop manager remarked: 'If we went too far along this road, the ME's tape function would become redundant. The only way is to get MEs on good jig and fixture work and progressing jobs through'. Simple amendments to programs were communicated back to the ME department; more complex amendments tended to be a joint exercise involving the operator and the ME. The programming functions, either writing or proving tapes, further increased the range of tasks performed by the shopfloor operators and their discretion in the metal-cutting process.

On the one hand, the restructuring of work at Flowpak involved an intensification of management control; on the other, the cells produced a relaxation of direct control. Control was a blend of coercive-autonomy. The relaxation of management controls is a condition and consequence of cellular work structures. The need for functional flexibility, cooperation and the building of a 'team' approach to work and problem-solving, make close supervision, 'low-trust' management–workers relations inappropriate. The Japanese-style system resulted in vertical role integration, with the cell leader taking over the coordinating, work allocation and first-line disciplinary tasks previously done by the foreman. Bureaucratic systems of control over shopfloor workers gave way to more informal and self-organizing forms of control. Each cell member was expected to contribute equally to the cell's targets, and members were under scrutiny from their workmates. Individual workers felt that they had a moral obligation to 'put a full day in'. Jim's comments provided an insight into this form of self-organized control:

> I think it's a matter of conscience. A person who, as I say, under the old scheme might go away for an hour, now he will think twice: Are they going to think they are carrying me because I've been away? . . . Because you are a close-knit community in the cell system. You get little niggly remarks: 'Where have you been all morning?' That sort of thing, and it gradually works its way in psychologically.

Most importantly, perhaps, the shop stewards and AEU convener became involved in this process of control and they gave oral warnings to members whom they or the cell leader considered not to be 'pulling their weight'. One cell leader told me that if he had any disciplinary problems he usually went to see the union convener.

Asked about discipline within the cell, the AEU convener vividly described how cell members 'teach self-discipline'; if a worker was considered to be 'slacking', the cell 'kicks his bottom'. This *prima-facie* case of union incorporation is further examined later.

At a more collective level there was an intensification of management control over the work process. Cellular/JIT techniques and new-technology were introduced to 'regain control' over the labour process. The computer system was used to monitor and evaluate workers' performance and set the parameters for shopfloor autonomy. The need for some means of monitoring was accepted by both management and the union. The personnel manager maintained that 'CNC/CAM . . . offers better control. The ability to control is important', and according to the AEU convener, 'If we have a slacker, it's not only necessary for the cell to find him, it's necessary for management to know him'.

Labour process commentators have highlighted the potential of microtechnology for monitoring workers. But these studies show that new technology complements rather than replaces the traditional role of the line manager in the machine shop.

INDUSTRIAL RELATIONS STRATEGY

The critical question that emerges out of this case-study is how management gain the commitment and co-operation for the technical and organizational changes from the shop stewards and workers? It seems that two processes were important. There was a clear ideological process designed to win over workers and legitimize management actions. In addition, management exploited the fear of unemployment to achieve their objectives. Furthermore, as already indicated, the managers won over the shop stewards by incorporating them into certain aspects of the management structure.

There was a general consensus amongst managers and shop stewards alike, that the new senior management had introduced initiatives to increase worker involvement and generally projected what industrial relations theorists would describe as human resource management. Interviewees spoke about management being 'more casual', it had 'opened up', become 'more informal' and provided 'lots more information'. Formal consultative meetings were less important for the manual workers. Informal 'chats' between the

personnel manager and the AEU shop stewards had replaced formal
consultative committee meetings. Richard Johnston, the personnel
manager, gives an insight into the changes:

> Previously we had very formal joint consultations. We have
> stopped that too. The only thing that's at all formal is when
> occasionally we have to negotiate something like an annual wage
> deal . . . What we do now is, we get them in and have a chat. We
> don't keep minutes.

The relative shift in the bargaining power towards management in
the 1980s had precipitated an approach to labour relations which
avoided formal industrial relations procedures and relied increasingly
upon various forms of 'employee participation'. Richard Johnston
described the approach:

> Ten or twelve years ago I got very much involved in employee
> participation. It floundered because the managers weren't con-
> vinced. Their hearts weren't in it. So when we introduced the cell
> system we didn't use the word participation. We said look: once a
> week get your people in the cell and talk to them about what they
> are supposed to be doing during the week. Don't have people
> taking notes. It's informal and it's very important that you do it.

The technical director gave additional insight into the changes in
management style when he said, 'We started talking to our employees'.
Too often surveys conducted by industrial relationists rely solely on
managers' accounts of events and changes. But in this case, the shop
stewards' and workers' accounts of the changes show a striking
similarity to the managers' responses:

> The new directors, personnel department, they have opened up.
>   Tony, TASS Representative.

> The us and you attitude has gone completely. There is no such
> thing . . . Totally flexible industrial relations! They provide lots
> more information.
>   Albert, AEU Convener.

> They are a lot more casual. They try to be very open.
>   Jim, AEU shop steward.

> People actually know who the managing director is now . . . He is
> actually trying to communicate.
>   Tim, cell leader.

Disclosure of company information was just one aspect of an industrial relations strategy aimed at substantially modifying the pure cash nexus, and moving towards a relaxation of direct controls. Management also attempted to achieve their goals through worker commitment and cooperation. Unlike Oil Tool Engineering, there were no slogans exhorting the shopfloor workers to 'beat the competition', but there were extensive 'awareness' sessions organized for the line managers and workforce to convince them of the need for fundamental change. A 'discussion system', involving groups of workers drawn from different sections of the factory, was established. Group discussions were held with the intention of building the values of team work to modify traditional habits, and workers' consciousness, and because such parallels can be drawn with Japanese capitalists' methods of control. Regular cell briefings were part of the ideological process to convince the workforce of the need for an increase in work intensity, flexibility and commitment.

The use of external consultants and what may be referred to as the 'Japanese factor', helped to persuade the shop stewards and the workers that it was imperative to introduce the technical and organizational changes advocated by senior management. Hiring external engineering consultants had the effect of legitimizing management's proposals in the eyes of the workforce. To quote Richard Johnston, 'We were very much helped by the consultants because it was well known that Ingersoll were good at this sort of thing. And what we were trying to do was respectable. And I think there was tacit support from the union officials'.

Describing cellular and just-in-time production methods as being Japanese, while attributing that country's manufacturing success to such techniques, may serve to shape workers' attitudes to the necessity for change (Graham, 1988:74).

Trade union representatives' and workers' acceptance of the changes in work organization was conditioned further by economic coercion. Several writers have associated changes in workers' attitude and behaviour to developments in the political economy of British capitalism since the 1980/81 recession. Managers responding to an Incomes Data Services (IDS) survey in 1984, said that 'the weakening of the trade unions' bargaining power has been a crucial element in their ability to bring about greater craft flexibility than before'. Blyton and Hill's survey of managers in the engineering industry found that the recession had 'engendered a search for more efficient and cost-effective production, with surviving workforces being required to accept a greater degree of job flexibility' (1985:74). Unemployment and Government's economic policies also facilitated the changes at Lucas Electrical: 'the developments described at LE have been facilitated, or at least reinforced, by the political and economic policies of the Thatcher Government' (Turnbull, 1986: 202). There is no doubt that in the case of Flowpak Engineering, management played the 'dole card' to facilitate the transformation of work at the plant; as Richard Johnston put it to me, 'we really told them [shop stewards] that unless we changed ourselves very radically we were going to go down the Swanee. We based the whole thing if you like on fear, to be honest'.

Within the context of a recession, and more specifically the fall in the demand for packaging machinery, management were able to exploit their enhanced bargaining position to regain control over the labour process. This was partly achieved through plant closures and redundancies, and by convincing the surviving workforce of the need for radical change. In this management were greatly assisted by the attitude and actions of the shop stewards in the plant.

Some radical writers have written upon the probable efficacy of the Donovan Commission's reform as far as shop steward incorporation is concerned. It is claimed by these writers that managers have successfully moderated the behaviour of shop stewards by incorporating them into the management decision-making process (Hyman, 1979; Terry, 1978; Lane, 1982). If through information disclosure and 'discussion' groups workers and their representatives develop an awareness and appreciation of plant viability, then there is potential for workplace trade unionism to become an additional tool for management (Batstone, 1984:234).

The manual shop stewards at Flowpak appeared to develop a managerialist perspective on many issues. In particular, the persuasive influence of the AEU stewards was an important factor in management gaining support for their plans to adopt Japanese-style production methods. Asked how important it was to get the support of the stewards for the changes. Richard Johnston said: 'It was absolutely vital. There was no way you could have done it without'. The AEU convener referred to having to 'sell' the new working methods to his members, and management recognized the importance of shopfloor meetings which were organized by the stewards. It was a 'fifty–fifty' effort, with both management and shop stewards transmitting information down to the shopfloor. Some union members expressed dismay that the cell leaders would continue to operate the machines. It is common practice that foremen do not operate the machines. This was the case with 'team leaders' at Oil Tool Engineering. However, the shop stewards at Flowpak argued the case that the cell leader was simply playing the traditional role of charge-hand, and as such could operate the machines.

The stewards, particularly the convener, assisted the process of functional flexibility and the elimination of job boundaries by encouraging the operators to 'have a go' and try the different machine tools. The convener also had developed a new awareness of the factory's economic viability. Albert espoused what one would describe as a managerialist perspective:

> Working with management requires education . It doesn't require the old shop steward where he threw his cap down and said: 'I want another half-crown a week, and I'm not interested how to give it me'. No. Now you have got to understand what the hell all that means. . . . In my meetings with members, I've got to make them realise that this Company is them. Because I told them it will do none of them any good to stand in a dole queue with the managing director and say: 'By God, we showed you, didn't we?' Because we are still in the dole queue. So I've tried in my last few years to help people realize that this is their company.

The views of the convener were also shared by other senior stewards, and possibly display the potency of the ideology of 'new realism'.

Finally, union incorporation was most clearly apparent in the way manual stewards played a managerial role by exerting control 'over' rather than 'for' their members. The convener would reprimand cell members for 'slacking' or 'soldiering'. The convener believed that it was necessary for the cell and management to identify dilatory workers by computerized monitoring. If an operator consistently failed to meet production targets, he would be approached by both the cell leader and shop steward and asked why. Albert put it like this:

> The shop steward and the cell leader have a talk to the man. 'What's your problem, flower? You know, ten hours to do that – come on? It's not on. You know it, we know it. What's happening?' If that has no effect, then it becomes the convener's and the manager's job.

It was also recognized by the management that the manual shop stewards were acting as an agency of control over the membership (Hyman, 1979); to quote Richard Johnston again, 'The shop stewards chase us to chase the chaps, to make sure that we are pressing them hard.'

The tendency for the manual shop stewards to adopt a managerialist perspective did not escape the attention of AEU stewards from Oil Tool Engineering who visited the plant to investigate the cellular system. Joe Greenwood, the AEU convener from Oil Tool makes the point forthrightly:

> Flowpak? What we have seen of it up there, the union, or the convener, seems to be absolutely integrated into the cell system. We came across two fellers who were talking, and as we were walking out he said; 'Bloody hell, them two are going to have to pull their finger out.' This is the union convener! I just couldn't believe my ears. He's not a union convener – he's part of management! No wonder they don't need any supervisors up there.

It is not easy to discern the relative influence of the plant convener on the process of technical change. Certainly he appeared to be politically out-of-step with the stewards from Oil Tool and also the AEU District Committee. However, cooperating with management and identifying with their company's problems and successes is currently advocated by some sections of the AEU's national leadership. Addressing an ACAS conference, Gavin Laird, general secretary of the engineering union (AEU), declared that today, 'realism means a commitment to working with management, whom trade unionists should regard as partners, not opponents'.[6] If Gavin Laird's statement reflects the AEU's official position, then the convener at Flowpak would appear to be actively pursuing his union's policy of 'realism'. On the other hand, the AEU convener was in a pre-eminent position in the steward hierarchy to encourage and 'lubricate' the process of change.

Cellular production methods require high-trust labour – management relations, and steward incorporation is one way of spiking the collective strength of labour. What should be stressed is that the manual stewards accepted in principle the need to increase work intensity, although in contrast to the previous regime when the payment by results (PBR) system operated, work intensity appeared to relax. Also they became increasingly prepared to cooperate with management. Batstone (1984) suggested that in most cases managers have not attempted to dismantle the institutional bases of workplace trade unionism. However, in this case one may conclude that the shop stewards continued to enjoy a high profile in the plant, because they helped to achieve management's goals.

Pattern of Labour Regulation and Union Organization

Before 1985, the shop stewards had a high profile at Flowpak, negotiating times for the bonus scheme and resolving, disputes over payment or times. As the personnel manager recalled, they were 'always high profile within our business; usually based on conflict'. There were detailed meetings with the shop stewards about cellular production and new technology. This process of consultation was considered important, first, because of the prominence of the AEU stewards in the factory. The AEU was the pacemaker, and the union had an experienced convener with a 'special role and status within the company'. Secondly, the majority of the workers were members of the AEU; to succeed, the managers had to win the commitment and cooperation of the shopfloor workers. During a period of radical change the last thing management wanted was a confrontation with the manual unions; therefore, the union was involved almost from the time it was announced that outside consultants were to be brought in.

Despite being involved in the preliminary meetings there is no evidence that the shop stewards influenced the general nature of the changes. Part of the problem of assessing the degree of union influence is the change in management's style of conducting industrial relations. There was no written agreement covering the introduction of either cellular or CNC technology. As mentioned earlier, formal negotiations had tended to give way to informal 'chats'; and as Richard Johnston confessed: 'We have informal discussions before we have formal ones . . . In fact it's sometimes difficult to know where the informal discussions end and the formal discussions begin.'

The general decline in importance of written agreements was confirmed by the convener: 'Management and unions do what's good for each other all the time. Why do we need a bit of paper? I trust them implicitly and they trust me exactly the same'.

In contrast to other studies (e.g. Batstone et al, 1987), the manual shop stewards did not demand a new technology agreement. Managers and shop stewards explained the absence of such an agreement along the following lines. First, the incremental nature and extent of the technical change. Computer numerical controlled machine tools were first introduced into the factory in 1984, but the vast majority of the machine tools were conventional, and fairly old at that. Out of a total of approximately 112, less than 10 per cent were CNC. Secondly, the manual workers did not consider CNC 'significant'; new technology was seen by most operators as simply an extension of their repertoire of machining tasks. Thirdly, the CNC machine tools, and the computer for coordinating and integrating production and inventory, were not viewed as a threat to manual workers' jobs. To the shopfloor workers, the main threat to job security came from external competition and rationalization, and the investment in new technology was a demonstration of management's continued commitment to the plant. The convener believed investment in new technology was necessary because 'otherwise you don't go forward'. Fourthly, the stewards did not consider a new technology agreement was relevant or necessary to their industrial relations environment. As Albert explained it: 'No we didn't negotiate a new technology agreement because of, I suppose, trust. If I don't like the way they interpret something, we all get together and we sit down and thrash it out and we come out with a common view'.

What may appear to be a naive statement nonetheless illustrates an important point regarding the nature of joint regulation. Trade union influence should not be measured by the existence of written agreements *per se*, but by the ability of workers and their representatives successfully to challenge managerial prerogative. Although there is no evidence that the union affected the plans for job redesign or choice of CNC machine tools, the convener said that senior management canvassed his opinion before introducing new machine tools. Albert told me:

> If there is going to be any new machinery in here, they'll usually involve me, will management, to give them my pennyworth. I'm not saying they allow me to make the decision, but there again, they have to stand by their monetary decision, and I haven't.

It is of course possible for interviewees to exaggerate their own importance. Equally, it is important to differentiate between consultation and workplace bargaining to determine jointly agreed rules or investment choice. In this case, there seemed little evidence to suggest that the latter was common practice. However, in exchange for greater consultation and involvement in what could be seen as the formulation of management policy, management had gained commitment and cooperation from the workers and their representatives.

If the senior stewards adopted a managerialist perspective on some issues, it would be misleading to suppose that this resulted in a quiescent workforce. The manual stewards did not oppose, indeed they encouraged the elimination of traditional craft controls in the machining shop, but they did nonetheless shape the general pattern of labour regulation. On the question of remuneration, the rationalization process and the continued prospect of redundancy meant that the issue of enhanced payment for greater functional flexibility and wider responsibility were not raised by the stewards. The wage rates at Flowpak were some of the lowest in the District. But, unlike the operators cited by Wilkinson (1983), the skilled operators did not use their newly acquired skills to bargain for higher basic rates. However, the union did influence pay structures in other ways. It was, for instance, opposed to a differentiated rate for CNC operators. Thus, as was the case with Oil Tool, all skilled operators received the same wage rate irrespective of whether they used the CNC machines. If management had been tempted to resolve the skill shortages by paying a higher rate for CNC operators, there is little doubt that they would have experienced concerted opposition from the union. The stewards were also opposed to re-introducing a PBR scheme, favoured by some cell leaders and operators. But they did have support for this union objective from management, anxious to promote job flexibility. In this there are parallels with the case of Oil Tool Engineering.

In addition to this, craft status and privilege were defended. Only grade one apprentice-trained operators were allowed to use the machine tools. Horizontal flexibility existed within the machine shop, but vertical flexibility, involving unskilled work, was restricted by the union. The union objection was explained to me by Albert:

Once you've finished your component, you've got to stamp it, it's got to have a part number on and they wanted a skilled man to stamp it. I said no. We ought to have at least one semi-skilled man in each cell to do this trimming, stamping, fetching, carrying. They agreed. They recruited two or three more semi-skilled men, and now they do that.

In the same vein management's aim of creating a 'generic' engineering craftsman capable of performing two hitherto separately defined trades – machinists performing fitting tasks, and fitters doing electrical work – was thwarted by opposition from the EETPU. The fitters and the electricians were in different unions, the AEU and the EETPU, but fitters were already doing electrians' work; management, however, did not wish to 'advertise it, and draw attention to it'. It was felt by the management that more progress on functional flexibility could be achieved unofficially, in a gradual process, rather than by attempting to confront directly the issue of job demarcation, as was explained by Richard Johnston:

> In due course we shall have fitters-electricians, it will be one job. At the moment it's a line we are somewhat reluctant to cross . . . I think the big obstacle there is the union, the EETPU. We do know if we were to tackle this head-on and we drew attention to ourselves, we would have a rather distracting battle, and we would rather get on with things we can do something about.

In small-batch engineering job flexibility tends to involve skilled machinists operating a range of machine tools and doing functions which traditionally have been completed by semi-skilled operators, such as radial-arm drilling and deburring. Flexibility did not extend to semi-skilled operatives encroaching upon work traditionally undertaken by craft workers. The AEU full-time district secretary outlined the Union's position:

> You tend to find that skilled men do functions these days which traditionally have been semi-skilled. The pressure has come from management. Our members have been willing to do it as a means of achieving some more money. What we do try to keep a strict control of is the semi-skilled guy coming into the skilled sphere.

Finally, it can be seen that by replacing the foreman with a cell leader, the cellular system changed the social organization of work. This resulted in a clear conflict of roles between the management's concept of the cell leader as a 'mini business manager' and group membership of the same cell and craft union: unlike the cell supervisors at Servo and team leaders at Oil Tool, cell leaders at Flowpak worked alongside other manual workers on the machines, and were members of the same craft union. Japanese management–labour relations can take oppressive forms because of peer-group pressures. The cells serve to generate self-organized forms of control; each member is expected to contribute equally to the group's perceived implicit contract. In the event of a worker 'slacking', the cell leader, members of the cell and the shop steward reprimanded the worker. To quote Albert, 'Any slackers in the cell are quickly told 'I don't get a penny more than you, therefore if you're doing nowt, I've got to do more'. The cell leader . . . all the men in stand around him in a circle'.

When the cells were established the union insisted that the cell leader should not have the authority to discipline workers. As Albert put it, 'His position would be intolerable in a cell if he had disciplinary power, because he has to work with them, and you can't work with and against'.

The traditional shop-steward role of representing members was eliminated, and in the first disciplinary stage at least, the steward actually participated in the process of moral coercion, thereby intensifying social control. However, the Union's insistence that cell leaders should not formally have managerial disciplinary power increased the propensity of management to invoke formal disciplinary procedures. Between September 1987 and February 1988, approximately twenty written warnings, mainly on time-keeping, but some on workers' performance, were issued. Prior to the introduction of the cellular system, the average was about two or three a year. Two reasons were given for the increased use of the disciplinary procedure. First, the economic motive had lessened with the abolition of the PBR system; the workers had to be 'chased more'. Secondly, the union put pressure on the management to use the formal disciplinary procedures of oral and written warnings to avoid the cell leader becoming involved in disciplining fellow union members. Richard Johnston contended that, 'There is a need to crack the whip occasionally with recalcitrant people over time-keeping. And we have had a certain amount of pressure from the union to do it that way . . . They don't want the cell leader involved in disciplining.'

Paradoxically, union intervention in the disciplinary process intensified self-organized forms of control in the cells and simultaneously encouraged the formalization of management's disciplinary procedure. Where management increases worker and steward involvement and this builds worker commitment and cooperation, it does not necessarily mean that workers forego all their controls (Batstone, 1984), but at the root of those controls is craft self-interest. As at Oil

Table 7.5   Union membership and steward organization at Flowpak,
Oil Tool and Servo Engineering, 1988

	Servo	Oil Tool	Flowpak
Union density (manual)	57%	100%	100%
Check-off	No	Yes	Yes
Closed shop	No	Yes	Yes
Steward constituencies	9	15	6
Stewards elected	4	15	6
Steward density	1:50	1:17	1:23
Full-time steward	No	Yes	No
Senior stewards of 2 or more	No	Yes	Yes
Regular stewards meetings	No	Yes	Yes

Source: Steward interviews.

Tool, skilled workers at Flowpak occupied most of the stewards'
positions in the plant, and it is to union organization that this section
now turns.

The manual workers were organized by three trade unions: the
AEU, EETPU and the TGWU. Of the vast majority of the shopfloor
workers, 142 were in the AEU, with just five electricians in the
EETPU and seven semi-skilled workers in the general union. Table
7.5 shows the pattern of union organization at Flowpak and the other
two detailed case-studies. The union profile of Flowpak is remarkably similar to that of Oil Tool. Apart from a higher steward density,
the only major difference between the two plant is the absence of a
full-time convener. The union convener at Flowpak did nonetheless
spend an average of sixteen to twenty-four hours a week on union
duties and related activities. He also had his own office where union
committee meetings were held. The stewards' committee regularly
met every two weeks in works hours. On the shopfloor there was 100
per cent membership of the AEU under a post-entry closed shop
agreement.

The manual stewards did not meet the non-manual TASS stewards: 'No we never meet TASS; I can't solve their problems, they
can't solve mine', maintained Albert, who had been the union
convener in the factory for over thirteen years, and had attended
TUC day-release courses. He described himself as a 'right-winger',
and considered the AEU District Committee meetings whose members were 'not in touch with reality', 'an absolute waste of time'.
There had been a relatively high turnover of shop stewards, and

Albert tended to dominate the stewards' committee. He explained the nature of his leadership as exerting 'tight control over other stewards. I have had a fair turnover of stewards . . . you can imagine after thirteen and a half years you've got a lot of truth in, haven't you. So you've got to lead rather than be led'. The longevity of his reign as convener helped to ensure the compliance of other stewards.

Within the factory there was a relatively high degree of intra-union organization, but it is difficult to assess to what extent workplace union organization affected union influence on management decision-making. As was found in the other case studies, the stewards' committee had not formulated a strategy either on CNC or cellular technology. The decision to introduce cellular methods was presented as a *fait accompli* and, given the state of the product and labour markets, it is not surprising that union influence appeared to be marginal. The use of external consultants was an important factor explaining union acceptance of the changes. The manufacturing strategy advocated by the consultants legitimized management's plans and actions in the eyes of the workers and their representatives. However, once the cellular system was introduced, the union had a fair degree of influence on detailed aspects of the labour process.

This chapter has provided a detailed account of the introduction of new technology and Japanese manufacturing and labour practices, a decision which was propelled by disquiet at control over the production process and wage structure in the context of an unfavourable external 'image' and squeezed profit margins. The need to regain control over the production process was the most important reason for introducing a computerized control system and cellular work structures. And contrary to some earlier studies (e.g. Jones, 1983:191), labour costs were a significant factor influencing the decision-making process; so was the antagonistic nature of industrial relations in the plant resulting from the wage system. The elimination of traditional job boundaries among skilled machinists had been achieved. However, the degree of functional flexibility should be seen in perspective. The notion of a multi-skilled craftsman, performing both machining and fitting, or machining and labouring, had not been achieved although clearly it was a long-term objective. Management still encountered union opposition to creating a polyvalent manual engineer. Nevertheless, the fact that the firm was not on a 'greenfield' site with all the associated advantages in terms of labour malleability and 'new style' agreements, and in a industry with a high union density, task flexibility achieved in the cellular system gave management considerable scope in labour utilization and integration.

The case-study data provide additional evidence of the complex nature of management strategies regarding manual skills and control over the labour process. Some of the predicted 'impacts' of cellular and JIT techniques had not materialized. This is not to say, however, that these methods have not the potential for negative effects on labour's skills. Flowpak is an example of a successful adoption of Japanese-style management practices on a 'concrete' site, rather than the more publicized 'greenfield' sites. The case-study data have further highlighted the choice that exists between using CNC technology and Japanese-style methods as means of deskilling machine operators, or using manufacturing innovations to enhance skills. In a small-batch, unionized environment the cellular system is capable of reversing the process of general deskilling and routinization of engineering work. As such it is capable of creating an application of technology which is a viable alternative to the deskilling scenario. This of course does not imply an altruistic policy on the part of British management. A skill enhancement policy provides managers with greater flexibility of deployment, thereby maximizing the full potential of cellular work-structures in terms of productivity and profitability.

8 Conclusions

The previous four chapters have provided a detailed and contextualized analysis of major changes in the organization of work caused primarily by Japanese-style manufacturing methods. The conclusion aims to bring together the principal findings from the case-study chapters and relate them to the labour process and industrial relations themes posed at the outset of the book. The conclusion is organized into four sections. The sections focus on the identified themes: the adoption of Japanese management, job content and skills, job control and management strategy. The chapter ends by considering some of the implications for industrial relations practitioners of the findings discussed. However, before considering the themes and implications, it would be useful to summarize the observed adoption of Japanese-type production management practices.

DIFFUSION OF JAPANESE MANAGEMENT

The main conclusions from this empirical study are that a transformation of work based on the Japanese-type manufacturing paradigm is evident among non-exceptional UK manufacturing companies. The important point is that by focusing on non-exceptional organizations, the findings suggest that the transfer of Japanese production concepts into the UK economy is wider than hitherto accepted. Of the six firms selected for more detailed study, three had introduced cellular and just-in-time methods in the mid-1980s. The findings accord with earlier commentators who have claimed that the Japanization of British industry is now beyond question (Turnbull, 1988; Oliver and Wilkinson, 1988). The cellular system is an adaptation of 'group technology', which attempted to influence job design in the 1960s and 1970s, but according to Littler and Salaman, only spread to 10 per cent of batch engineering firms and remained 'the gospel peddled by a few avant-garde consultants' (1984:90). The limited diffusion of group technology was caused by the 'information burden'; also there were 'too many variables and too much unpredictability' (ibid., 1984:87). The findings have shown that in the 1980s, the obstacles to group technology described by Littler and Salaman have largely been eliminated by the development of sophisticated microcomputerized systems.

There are many variations of cellular/JIT methods in practice; in the three firms introducing the Japanese manufacturing paradigm, there were three idiosyncratic modes of application. At Servo Engineering, the eight cells contained both machining and assembly operations, and produced a finished product. Each cell functioned as a 'mini factory' within a factory. In contrast, Oil Tool's management had designed a different system with selective cells operating in parallel with a conventional machine tool configuration. The mode of application was different again at Flowpak Engineering; each cell functioned as a 'mini factory', but there were separate machining and assembly cells, forming an internal market with complex arrangement of 'subcontracting' between cells. Moreover, the evidence from the three case studies suggests that the effects of cellular/JIT, in terms of job content, job control and pace of change are more profound than the familiar labour process analysis of NC and CNC technology.

Sayer (1986) stated that labour process theorists had paid little attention to changes in the social organization of manufacturing. By providing a detailed account and evaluation of the diffusion and implications of cellular work structures and just-in-time, both in large and small-batch production and in established 'concrete', as opposed to 'greenfield' sites, outside the automobile and electronic industries, this book goes some way towards compensating for this neglect and deficiency in previous labour process research and interpretation. It also provides an antidote to generalized speculation about the 'implications for labour' of the just-in-time system.

JOB CONTENT AND SKILLS

For most critics on the political left, Japanization has very limited potential to enhance workers' skills. But, using a two-dimensional model of skill; technical competencies and autonomy, the findings from these cases show that Japanese production methods have the potential to enhance manual workers' skills. An important qualification should, however, be made. Increases in operators' skills and shopfloor autonomy were only apparent in those manufacturing environments characterized by 'one-off' or small-batch, high added-value products. In this type of manufacturing environment all the managers when faced with a choice between a skills fragmentation and skill enhancement strategy, chose the latter for operational reasons. It was generally felt by managers that skilled operators were best able to coax the best performance out of their CNC machines, and had the necessary diagnostic skills to prevent expensive 'crashes' and damage to the machines.

The implications of Japanese-type production techniques and CNC technology on workers' skills and shopfloor power were seen to be diverse, depending upon such factors as batch size, product constraints, machine innovation, plant size, internal organizational structure, and the custom and practice of the shopfloor. For example, the multifarious skill deployment patterns were strongly associated with batch size. In the large-batch environment the critics of cellular and just-in-time methods have a much stronger case. At Servo Engineering, for example, there was evidence of progressive deskilling. The semiskilled CNC operator's task was limited to 'pushing buttons', and the skilled setters were prohibited from amending tapes without management's written approval. The rationale for this strategy was formally explained in terms of maintaining 'quality standards'. But during discussions it was evident that management policy was also tempered by a general mistrust of operators working an individualized bonus scheme: 'Without that system you would have people altering programs willy nilly . . . Getting round the bonus . . . and everything that goes with it', was the way it was put by one cell leader.

If the dominant paradigm for production was based on progressive deskilling at Servo Engineering, this tended not to be apparent at Flowpak and Oil Tool Engineering. In small-batch environments, all the managers preferred their CNC operators to be skilled with machining experience on conventional machines. At Flowpak, although it was official policy that manufacturing engineers generated programs, the more proficient operators were beginning to encroach upon the role of the MEs. The management turned a blind eye to this practice because it enabled the machines to be run more efficiently.

The extent of operators' programming skills was found to vary a good deal both between and within firms. At Oil Tool and Flowpak, for instance, the operators writing short programs and proving and editing the tapes generated by production engineers, were typically the younger operators. These workers recognized that increased functional flexibility in the internal division of labour was a means of augmenting their skills and increasing their marketability in the external labour market. Thus, when Hyman argues that 'increased flexibility . . . reduces the general marketability of the worker's skill' (1988:53), he over-simplifies the notion of functional flexibility and neglects to locate his analysis in different modes of production and internal labour markets. The outcomes of change in new work-patterns were the consequence of managerial choice and negotiation. In terms of CNC and operators' skills, parallels can be drawn between the small-batch engineering establishments of Flowpak and Oil Tool, and those of 'Odessy Engineering' and 'Illyad Engineering' (Wilson and Buchanan, 1988).

In the two cases where a Japanese-type manufacturing system was installed in small-batch environments, the variety of skills performed by the craft operators increased, as did autonomy. However, as many critics of job enrichment schemes have noted, a greater range of tasks does not necessarily imply increased skills or greater shopfloor auton-omy. The effects of 1970s-style job redesign are succinctly expressed in a well-known statement from a chemical worker: 'You move from one boring, dirty, monotonous job to another boring, dirty, mono-tonous job . . . you're supposed to come out of it all 'enriched'. But I never feel 'enriched' – I just feel knackered' (Nichols and Beynon, 1977:16).

For the purposes of this research the significance of task variety in the assessment of engineering manual craft skills depended upon the nature of the tasks, and the discretion afforded to workers as to how, and when, those tasks were performed. At Oil Tool Engineering operators were encouraged to be self-reliant, and learn new inspec-tion and quality-control tasks. Similarly, at Flowpak Engineering, the successful exploitation of Japanese-type manufacturing management demanded that operators became proficient at a wider range of machining operations. In terms of knowledge, the effects of cellular work structures increased the knowledge required to operate the configuration of machine tools, both conventional and CNC. In those cells with CNC lathes and machining centres, the CNC operators may have experienced a downgrading of their psychomotor machining skills, but they had to learn new programming and diagnostic skills. The CNC operators had to learn new kinds of cognitive skills in software writing in order to conceptualize all the machining functions and perform the operations in the most cost-effective way. A cellular work-structure had increased the range of tasks on both conventional and CNC machines, and involved additional planning and coordinat-ing tasks.

Enlarging shopfloor workers' job profiles and giving them some measure of 'responsible autonomy' has however, nothing, to do with altruism. At Flowpak and Oil Tool Engineering, the managers required not merely the passive compliance of the craft workers, but the active enlistment of workers' ingenuity. initiative and cooperation. The fact that manufacturing involves more than technical hardware, is a social process, is recognized by writers such as Abernathy et al. They argue that:

> Building a truly competitive organization also requires active enlistment of the best efforts of workers, especially line workers. Their skills, commitment, and enthusiasm are the means by which strategic goals get translated into practice.
>
> (1983:125)

Much of the evidence warning of deskilling and work intensification is based on data acquired by looking through a consultant's lens, rather than a manager's or worker's lens, or actual observation of the labour process. Further, the newer debates on flexible specialization and Japanization have tended to focus on large-batch production – usually motor vehicle manufacturing. Few commentators have observed the effects of Japanese style manufacturing techniques in a small-batch, 'concrete' and unionized organization. This is not to say however, that such techniques have not potential negative implications for labour.

Inside the academic milieu, the just-in-time manufacturing philosophy has received considerable attention. However, it has been suggested here that there is substantial ambiguity regarding the precise meaning of the terms 'cellular' and 'just-in-time' production among academics. The literature and interpretations of both the generic significance of the Japanese production paradigm and its implications for labour, have polarized around two schools of thought: the 'flexible specialization' thesis based on an upskilling model, and the 'degradation of work' thesis associated with Braverman's deskilling model (Wood, 1989).

Writers such as Abernathy et al., 1983; Piore and Sabel, 1984; Tolliday and Zeitlin, 1986; and Whipp and Clark, 1986, have introduced an optimistic tenor into the academic literature. The contention of these authors is that a more 'flexible' system, incorporating techniques such as just-in-time, represents a new phase in capitalist relations of production, and has the potential of liberating workers from dull repetitive work associated with 'Fordism'. Moreover, where Fordism prescribed for the separation of conception and execution, it is argued that the flexible specialization model calls for a reversal of task specialization, and therefore has the potential to increase skills. Whipp and Clark share Abernathy's view of developments in the motor vehicle industry. Given the prospects of greater 'consumer choice', operators' cognitive skills will be enhanced when each new vehicle is 'treated both as part of a large batch and also as a unique product' (1986:208).

Others take a less sanguine view of Japanese-style manufacturing techniques, seeing them as a method of eliminating imperfections in the Fordist model and a form of 'flexible Taylorism' (Sayer, 1986; Turnbull, 1988; Hyman, 1988; Thompson, 1989; Tomaney, 1990). Turnbull has argued that cellular/JIT production does not beneficently lead to any 'significant reskilling or skill enhancement' (1988:9–12), and Hyman asserts that 'flexibility . . . entails intensified segmentation within the workforce, between the relatively sheltered and disadvantaged, and the vulnerable and oppressed' (1988:56).

The evidence from these case-studies suggest that neither of these contradictory interpretations of Japanese-type manufacturing are correct. Writers such as William Abernathy are over-optimistic in applying their analysis and interpretation of just-in-time to mass standardized production. What he and other optimists tend to forget is that skill involves more than simply an enlargement of tasks undertaken by assembly-line workers. Moreover, flexible specialization theorists have rediscovered technological determinism, believing that flexible working will automatically have progressive implications for labour. The pessimists have focused their attention exclusively on volume production in general, and the automobile and electrical industries in particular.

This book has presented a more nuanced, middle position, arguing that the generic significance of Japanese-type cellular work structures on manual workers' skills is indeterminate, and the direction of change is not a simple one of upskilling or deskilling. Skills are shaped and determined by social choice and negotiation and a complex configuration of opportunities and constraints, inter alia: batch size, the nature of the product, markets, and trade union organization and influence. In short, when Japanese production management concepts are introduced in small-batch production, management are much less likely to choose a job deskilling strategy. However, this proposition needs to be heavily qualified. If cellular/just-in-time methods with new generations of CNC machine tools in small-batch manunacturing, offer the prospect of upskilling operators, then these should not be automatically generalized to large-batch production or other industries. The effects of parallel changes in volume production, as demonstrated by the case of Servo Engineering, are likely to be different depending upon choice by key decision-makers and the political process associated with technological change. It does mean, however, that a universal deskilling thesis associated with the Japanese production paradigm is difficult to sustain because of a complex assortment of countervailing determinants in capitalist production.

CONTROL AND MANAGEMENT STRATEGY

In terms of managerial control, three findings from the study are worth emphasizing: the potential of microtechnology to monitor operator performance, management relinquished control to enhance control, and the importance of managerial ideology. First, microtechnology can be and was used extensively by managements to measure and monitor operators' productivity, and quality and such information was used as input to a variety of management decisions from payment, through appraisal and training, to dismissal. Six out of the twelve case-studies reported that the new technology enabled a more detailed monitoring of job elements and worker performance. Managers used CAD/CAM systems to monitor production and eliminate human variability and the control over operators was considered to be 'not very important'. However, the larger the plant in terms of full-time employees, the greater the attraction of electronic monitoring of workers' performance.

Second, the new work arrangements illustrated the paradox of both enhanced shopfloor autonomy and managerial control. At Flowpak and Oil Tool Engineering, on the one hand, examples of increased freedom and discretion were given to the cells; operators had discretion in scheduling the work and job assignments within the parameters set by the central computer. On the other hand, the computerized production and inventory control (CPIC) system, by providing regular 'work-to-list' to determine work priorities, data on operator performance, and information on the flow of material, heightened control by senior management over the entire labour process. Increased shopfloor autonomy is, therefore, contingent upon the installation of computerized information systems designed to improve the flow of information on all aspects of the production process to senior management. The utilization of the CPIC system alongside the cellular work configuration suggests that management control can best be conceptualised by the term: computer-controlled autonomy, an adaptation of a term used by Dankbaar (1988).

Third, the findings from Flowpak and Oil Tool highlighted the importance of managerial ideology to achieve worker compliance. Bendix has defined managerial ideologies as:

> All ideas which are espoused by or for those who exercise authority in economic enterprises and which seek to explain and justify that authority. (1956:2)

The function of such ideologies is to interpret the facts of authority so as to neutralize or eliminate the conflict between management and subordinates, thereby making authority more effective, argues Bendix. Further, it is held that the prime function of ideology is not so much to encourage workers to see their role and the firm in terms favourable to management, but 'to establish the framework within which discussions of what is fair, reasonable, possible at work occurs' (Littler and Salaman, 1984:65). In practice management labour strategy tends to be a combination of consent and economic coercion. The blend varies depending upon workers' position in the productive hierarchy, usually relatively more consent towards the top, more economic coercion at the bottom of the hierarchy (Fox, 1985:66).

In those factories where Japanese-type manufacturing techniques were implanted, management attempted to inculcate attitude of cooperation and engender 'team' identities directed towards managerial goals. This process involved induction and 'education' programmes, workers signing a 'quality pledge', and poster campaigns; the object was to generate worker-commitment to the new work arrangements. The rationale behind the programme can be found in the assumption that a committed workforce will be more flexible, cooperative, and self-disciplined, and more productive.

Burawoy (1979) and Knights and Collinson (1985), have given accounts of how workers in self-organized workgroups create a 'culture' that reproduces the conditions of the workers' own subordination. Moreover, workers achieve high quality-standards despite the relaxation of management control and the fact that 'the internal policing of these standards is much more effective than any controls that management might apply directly to the shopfloor' (ibid., 1985:204). In the case of Flowpak, just as at Allied (1979) and Slavs (1985), evidence was provided of what Burawoy calls the 'coercive culture system'. The cellular system enabled management to reduce direct supervisory costs and maintain production standards, by relying on an internally generated shopfloor system based on an oppressive form of peer-group pressure. To put it another way, the cellular system had the effect of diverting any conflict over pace of work and production standards from management to the shopfloor.

One other point is worth emphasizing. When interpreting and evaluating managerial strategies and actions towards labour at the point of production, attention needs to be devoted to analysing other 'contingencies' such as the organization of internal and external labour markets and the dynamics of product markets (Wilkinson, 1983; Thompson, 1983, 1989; Clark et al. 1988; Kelly, 1985; Child, 1985; Whipp and Clark, 1986; McLoughlin and Clark, 1988).

The redesign of work, in a heightened competitive environment, is seen to be driven less by intent to control and discipline labour than, for example, the importance of quality and delivery schedules (Knights and Willmott, 1990). In their account of the pattern of innovatory change within Austin-Rover, Whipp and Clark maintain that the interaction of capital, management and labour has a significant impact on the choices of new work structures and their implementation. They are critical of some writers in the Braverman tradition who by concentrating on the capitalist profit system and the problems of accumulation, tend to ascribe to employers 'an almost unfettered power to design and organize their chosen forms of the labour power' (1986:13). Whipp and Clark's perspective on issues of change and governance is emphasizing management choice within constraint, rather than the regulation of the labour process *per se*. Adaptation to change at work does not simply occur 'automatically or by decree' (Whipp and Clark, 1986:213).

The findings from this small sample of cases suggests that in private sector manufacturing, 'strategic objectives' (Buchanan, 1982) were the principal stimuli to management decision-making and action. Faced with a contraction in the motor vehicle industry, the management at Servo introduced Japanese manufacturing methods and CNC technology for strategic and operational reasons, at a time of 'heightened importance of excellence in manufacturing' (Abernathy et al., 1983:9). Again, at Oil Tool, senior management let it be known that a Japanese-type manufacturing system was introduced, not so much to enhance management's control and to subordinate labour, but for strategic reasons. But clearly, outcomes of the strategic decision will affect how work is organized, and workers' autonomy and power.

Similarly, Flowpak's senior management faced a £9m loss between 1980 and 1983, and customer-orientated strategic objectives were behind the decision to transform the labour process. However, there were internal performance-orientated 'operational objectives' which clearly were related to the achievement of the strategic objectives, and impinged upon managerial choice. Flowpak's management wanted to improve productivity and reduce labour costs. The management also had 'operational objectives' designed to replace the antiquated paperwork system of control.

The findings suggest that labour regulation strategies are not the *raison d'être* for management's existence. The case-studies reveal the multiplicity of logic in play and complexity of social control processes acting simultaneously at various levels within capitalist relations of production. In the case of Flowpak, the redundancy strategy which was formulated at corporate level tempered workers' actions and guaranteed compliance and cooperation. At plant level, the new technology integrated the manufacturing system and provided senior management with spontaneous information on key production variables. On the shopfloor the CPIC system and cellular work structures allowed management to 'regain control' and use control methods superior to any that management might apply directly to the shopfloor.

It can be argued that Harry Braverman's seminal work had the dual effect of renewing the study of the industrial workplace, but served to obscure and restrict our understanding of the capitalist labour process. The adoption of Braverman's analytical framework led many labour process theorists to neglect, what the Human Relations school of sociological study has always understood, the two interrelated aspects of the factory: its technical and its social organization. Production, moreover, involves more than hardware and a technical division of labour; it is a social process. Labour process theorists have tended to focus their research and theorizing only upon one aspect of change, technological change. This may be one reason why the labour process 'bandwagon has run into sand' (Storey, 1985).

MANAGING ORGANIZATIONAL CHANGE

This study did not set out to address policy issues for management or trade unions. Rather, it identifies changes in the organization of work and the management of the employment relationship, of which practitioners of labour relations will need to take cognizance when formulating policies for the 1990s. The implications of these changes for organizations and workers may now be addressed.

Management and Japanization

If managers are to adopt optimal policies, three findings from the study are worth considering. The impact of Japanese-style production management on the organization's effectiveness, the management of change, and labour-relations policies. In terms of post-Fordist British capitalism, this study has shown that fundamental changes in social relations and skill deployment can have a catalytic effect on quality and productivity, even in 'concrete' sites with relatively old plant and equipment, and with a heritage of adversarial industrial relations.

The challenge for managers is to design a manufacturing system that makes the most of productive people, rather than perpetuating the Fordist model of work based on narrow specialization with control directed from above. The most striking point about the findings from this study was that a system based on functional integration, and which assumed that shopfloor workers want to make decisions connected with their work, created a flexible and effective manufacturing operation. At Oil Tool and Flowpak, the throughput times for components were drastically reduced. For example at Oil Tool, the total number of days to machine and assemble a block-tree valve fell from 188 days to 24 days. In the mid 1980s productivity in British manufacturing was reported to be significantly up. The political left in Britain has been keen not to ascribe any success to the economics of Thatcherism, and argued that the productivity rises can be put down to closure of outmoded plant and work intensification (e.g. Jones, 1983b). The increases in productivity at the firms studied arose from changes in labour's performance and working practices. In the cases of Oil Tool and Flowpak, Japanese-type manufacturing techniques were the major factors explaining productivity gains, with new technology complementing the organizational changes. In other words the productivity gains were real.

As far as the management of change is concerned, the case-study data reveal four important points. The findings accord with earlier industrial relations studies that show that trade unions are not an obstacle to technological change, but also that shop stewards have become more sympathetic to management views and accepted the hegemony of managerial authority in recent years. Generally, the stewards saw the introduction of new technology as a continuous and necessary process.

The adoption of the trade unions' principal strategy instrument, the new technology agreement, was limited. In only three out of the twelve cases had management and unions negotiated a new technology agreement. The evidence shows that new technology agreements were more prevalent the larger the size of the establishment. At Servo, on the union side there was a sense of technological determinism, in that CNC technology was essential 'to keep people in work'. The AEU stewards did not seek to negotiate a new technology agreement at Flowpak. Against the incremental nature of the changes and the commonly held view among the manual workers that CNC was insignificant, the new technology simply represents an extension of their repertoire of machining skills. In addition, the stewards believed that new technology did not pose a threat to jobs.

Although the research concentrated on the developments taking place inside 'core' employment relationships, the trade unions in these establishments played a marginal role in the process of technological change. Formal consultation were more frequent in those larger establishments with a steward hierarchy and organization; none of the managers or stewards interviewed said that bargaining or consultation had taken place regarding investment strategy. Where the union did have an input was *after* the new equipment had been installed. Enhanced payment to operators using CNC machines was the most often cited area of union involvement and influence.

At Servo Engineering it was acknowledged by managers, stewards and workers that the union in the plant played an insignificant role in the process of change. The union had no influence regarding the choice of the machinery or the design of the cellular system: the technical division of labour was unilaterally determined by management. In the case of Oil Tool, labour was in a relatively strong bargaining position and had a sophisticated stewards' organization; but again, the union played no role in the choice of new machine tools or the pace and direction towards a cellular configuration. Early consultation with the AEU stewards was considered an important part of management's strategy of gaining acceptance for the changes at Flowpak. There is no evidence that the shop stewards influenced the general nature of the organizational forms. However, assessing the degree of union influence was problematic due to the shift from formal bargaining to an informal style of management–labour relations.

Although the unions did not influence management's investment strategy, once the new machines were installed, in all three cases studied in detail, the AEU exerted some influence over job redesign. Even at Servo, where union organization since the 1983 strike had collapsed, the union's insistence on maintaining traditional craft demarcation prevented management achieving functional flexibility in the tool room. At Oil Tool, industrial relations were rather more adversarial. The 'committee' had not negotiated a new technology agreement, but the AEU played a significant role in shaping work organization, including a common wage rate for CNC and non-CNC users, the manning of the machines, recruitment and training. Flowpak provided evidence of stewards accepting the hegemony of managerial authority, but as pointed out, the union still shaped the general pattern of labour regulation. However, the general impact of AEU bargaining and influence over the pattern of work organization at Oil Tool and Flowpak was to consolidate the position of the skilled members at the expense of the semi-skilled occupational groups.

A further aspect worth considering is the way the organization manages its main resource, people, and the labour-relations considerations in the formulation of policy, given the high dependency relations associated with Japanese manufacturing paradigm. A survey of UK-based manufacturing companies that had emulated Japanese-style manufacturing techniques found that the same companies did not appear to be using the concomitant human resource management policies: 'practices likely to be supportive of harmonious industrial relations were conspicuous primarily by their absence' (Oliver and Wilkinson, 1989:86). The evidence suggested that the human resource management and labour relations practices which 'fit' Japanese manufacturing practices frequently appear to be out of step with them. The apparent absence of a human resource management policy commensurate with Japanese-type work arrangements is particularly important for management. If it is perceived by workers that Japanese-style methods were implanted 'on the back' of a recession and a weakened trade union movement, it raises the question whether the changes have created a resentful workforce whose long-term commitment to the organization's goals is highly questionable. For management to implement a Japanese-type manufacturing strategy without stable labour relations can have a devastating impact on output and performance.

In 1988, for example, Ford Motor Company (UK) experienced its first national strike for a decade. The repercussions of the UK stoppage were felt within twenty-four hours in Ford's European plants and its suppliers. At Ford's plant in Genk, Belgium, 2000 workers were laid off the day after the start of the strike. The production of automobiles at Saarlouis and Cologne in Germany were also seriously affected by the UK strike (Simonian, 1988). The seriousness and speed of the repercussions of the strike illustrates the high inter-operational dependencies created by Japanese-type manufacturing methods (Wilkinson and Oliver, 1990). Again, in February 1990 the rapid domino effect of just-in-time production was demonstrated when three Ford assembly plants were closed, two in the UK and one in Belgium, following a strike by 1600 electricians and some maintenance craftsmen (Done, 1990). Senior management need to assess how far the changes in the management of people in the 1990s are adequate to satisfy the needs of a flexible, high-dependency manufacturing system, and to decide how seriously they want to embrace the philosophy of Japanese human resource management.

Trade Unions and Japanization

It is clear that Japanization will provide an immense challenge to European and North American trade unions throughout the 1990s, the effects on employment shaping the outcome of technological change, the intensity of work and associated stress, union organization, and bargaining power. Japanese manufacturing concepts and CNC technology had negative direct and indirect employment effects. Overall, employment in the sample of twelve workplaces declined from 6240 to 4198, a fall of 32 per cent. The aggregate figure disguises far greater falls in employment in some of the case-studies; one firm reported making more than half its workforce redundant – from 649 to 317, a fall of 51 per cent. Although it was possible to quantify the extent of employment changes and the impact on occupational engineering groups within the case-studies, isolating the independent direct effects of microprocessor technology and cellular manufacturing was problematic.

Two scenarios emerged in relation to technological and organizational change and employment. On the one hand, some organizations had undertaken large-scale investment in new technology over a short space of time, making the negative employment effects clearly apparent to union representatives and managers. New CNC technology was cited by two organizations, and one organization cited Japanese production methods as a reason for labour reductions. Technological unemployment was apparent at Servo following substantial investment in robotics and computerized production control. On the other hand, new technology was introduced in an incremental manner, making it difficult for union representatives and managers to isolate the direct employment impacts. In the interviews rarely did managers identify new technology as a prime cause for manpower reductions. At Oil Tool, the AEU convener when asked if a new technology agreement would have protected jobs, replied 'there hasn't been that much technology coming into the place anyway'. However, touring the plant it was apparent that new machines had been installed during the 1980s, but in a piecemeal way which did not lead to any trauma in working arrangements. Stewards and managers attributed job losses to the recession in the oil extraction industry. There may of course be an industrial relations motive for minimizing the technology factor. If workers believe that new technology is the prime reason for job contraction, rather than external factors outside their sphere of influence, there may be resistance to technology from workers.

The productivity gains extracted by cellular/JIT modes of production would, *ceteris paribus*, reduce the demand for direct labour in the 'core' firm. In addition, higher productivity would reduce the need for subcontracting and therefore adversely affect employment in the 'peripheral' supplier firms. In the case of Flowpak, the level of subcontracting of general machining work was substantially reduced, and this would have had a negative employment effect in the organizations which had previously completed machining work under contract.

Direct and indirect unemployment clearly arose from technological change. However, this empirical study did leave some questions on the employment displacement effects unanswered. For instance, the problem of disentangling the independent direct effects of Japanese-type manufacturing techniques from the new technology. The fall in employment at Servo, Oil Tool and Flowpak Engineering was largely the result of the 1980–81 recession and falling market share. Also, the research did not identify the indirect employment effects of the changes in those factories which had previously undertaken contract work. Finally, the study did not estimate how many redundancies would have resulted from higher costs and loss of competitiveness, if the changes had *not* taken place.

So far, union representatives in the United Kingdom have found it difficult to challenge managerial prerogative on the question of choice of new technology and Japanese-style work organization. In particular, without a union strategy, the incremental nature of technical diffusion proved difficult to combat. As one steward said, 'it just crept in. It isn't a clear-cut thing'. The stewards had given little consideration to the changes at Servo. In the case of Oil Tool there was a relatively high degree of intra-union organization, yet the stewards committee had not developed a common strategy on either CNC technology or Japanese manufacturing methods. This absence of a strategy was explained in terms of membership acquiescence in the early stages of the transfer to cellular/JIT methods, the lack of any broader perspective on management innovation and the threat of redundancy caused by the recession in the oil extraction industry.

Burawoy, in *Manufacturing Consent*, describes how the Allied Corporation gained compliance by protecting its 'technical core' from the uncertainties of and contingencies of the recession. The company was able to do this by 'externalizing certain costs' because of its monopoly position. As Burawoy argued, 'The insulation of the technical core is more easily accomplished by large corporations, which have the power to externalize costs by raising the prices of their products' (1979:133).

In the 1980s, management at Flowpak experienced intense European competition and therefore they were in no position to isolate their workforce from the market. Unlike the situation at Allied, Flowpak provides evidence of worker-compliance through threats of redundancy and economic coercion. And therefore fear was an important ingredient of a successful corporate strategy.

Kelly (1985), Ramsay, (1985), Sayer (1986), Turnbull, (1988) and Tomaney (1990), plausibly argue that functional flexibility, reductions in buffer stocks, and total-quality-control are a sophisticated form of labour intensification and therefore have largely negative implications for workers. In theory, Japanese production management aims to maximize capital's side of the wage–effort exchange (Thompson, 1989). In practice, however, this managerial goal is dependent on the way the workforce responds and attempts to control the outcome. At Servo, it was evident that the new standard times set were less generous, 'tighter' than pre-cellular structures and there was evidence of work intensification. At Flowpak and Oil Tool Engineering, increases in productivity did result from flexible cellular work structures. A sense of work intensification, however, was not perceived by the work groups. This apparent conflict between theory and practice can be explained by two parallel developments. The adoption of Japanese-type practices was accompanied by the abolition of a payment-by-results award system in favour of a flat-rate wage system. Management abolished the PBR system to encourage flexibility; respondents indicated that once the individual performance-related scheme was abolished the pace of work relaxed. In general, Japanese-style work configurations enabled management to rationalize production without necessarily increasing labour intensification. Obviously, cellular/just-in-time work structures embody principles which offer management the opportunity to extract higher productivity from labour by work intensification. Equally, however, as there are no automatic 'impacts' stemming from new technology, so too with Japanese-type practices: there are no self-acting impacts once introduced into the organization.

Japanization is associated with non-unionism or collaborative enterprise unions. While there was evidence that shop stewards accepted the hegemony of managerial authority, especially at Flowpak Engineering, there is no evidence that Japanization has damaged workplace union organization or undermined the position and authority of shop stewards. At Servo Engineering, union organization was weak but this had more to do with the outcome of the 1983 strike than Japanese work methods. It seems more likely that managements have been attempting to use a variety of techniques to win workers and steward cooperation (Batstone, 1984). Further, the diffusion of Japanese labour management concepts coinciding with a shift of bargaining power towards management does not confirm that destroying workplace unionism was an express, or implicit, objective of management in introducing the practices (Marchington, 1989).

However, observers have warned that the current fashion for human resource management practices closely identified with Japanization, such as individual performance appraisal, direct communications, and unitary ideology could potentially weaken workplace trade unionism by shifting the identification of workers away from a group union-identity towards an individual company-identification (Oliver and Wilkinson, 1988). Japanization is likely to damage workplace trade unionism in some contexts, but not in others

(Piore and Sabel, 1984). The judgement must be an empirical one. In other words, the ability of Japanese work systems to destroy union organization is contingent upon the context in which it is utilized. The crucial question is, to what extent are the unions aware of the strategic and control issues surrounding the Japanization discourse, its potential to intensify the exploitation of the most vulnerable workgroups, and foster among the relatively advantaged and sheltered 'core' groups, an 'enterprise consciousness', thereby undermining trade union 'collective consciousnes'?

A further issue for workers and their trade unions is the new bargaining opportunities presented by the Japanese manufacturing paradigm. There are at least two contrasting views here. It has been argued that whereas the productivity bargaining of the 1960s heightened the role of the workplace union representative, Japanese-style production methods in the 1980s did not offer equivalent scope for the extension of bargaining (Linn, 1986). Other have argued that the shift towards more flexible work structures could serve to enhance the power capacity of workers (Kelly, 1988; Oliver and Wilkinson, 1988). Japanese-style production techniques are a high-dependency manufacturing strategy. Moreover, the Japanese configuration of working arrangements requires management to give their subordinates a relative degree of autonomy, and a manufacturing philosophy that aims to minimize or achieve zero inventory makes production inherently vulnerable to stoppages. After a decade of restrictive trade union legislation and an economic climate unfavourable to militant trade unionism, the strike at Ford (UK) in 1988 brought home to workers and managers alike, the dependency and bargaining power unwittingly afforded by Japanese-style manufacturing systems. As Wilkinson and Oliver argue, Ford Motor Company's combination of Europe-wide integrated manufacturing and Japanese-style manufacturing practices 'inadvertently provided a significant shift of power to labour . . . Ironically, it was Japanese-style production integration which gave workers the ability to hit Ford so hard in their resistance to Japanese work practices' (1990:19). Of course, whether such new-form capitalist production methods enhance the power capacity of workers or not, in reality, the relative power capacity of organized labour is also dependent on wider changes in the political economy of European capitalism.

Finally, it is a misconception to assume that flexibility across a range of what were previously demarcated skills necessarily diminishes workers' bargaining power. Japanese-style manufacturing requires extensive cooperation from workers, is inherently vulnerable and is contestable. The fact that Ford workers were willing to exploit, and had the union organization to make them highly capable of exploiting the just-in-time system is a further reminder that production is a social process and concessions can be extracted through collective bargaining. A major question facing trade unions is how far can they seek involvement and influence in the 'partnership organization', without losing their independence? The evidence from these case-studies is relevant here. Where Japanese production methods were implanted shop stewards coexisted with cell leaders, management did not seek to impose a 'new realist' agreement with the union, and although there was evidence in one context of the union playing a collaborative role, in another the union did retain its independence from the company it organized in, and played a more traditional adversarial role despite the inimical economic and political climate, redundancies and threats of closure. Throughout their history trade unions have had to respond and adapt to new forms of capitalist production methods. The process of Japanization does pose serious threats to trade unions but it does not negate the *raison d'etre* of trade unionism; collective negotiation in order to maximize labour's side of the wage–effort exchange.

Notes

PREFACE

1. Confederation of Health Service Employees (1979), *How Will The Chip Affect You?*
2. Bratton, J. and Waddington, J. (1981), *New Technology and Employment*, London: Workers' Education Association.

CHAPTER 1: INTRODUCTION

1. Towers, B. (1982), Editorial: 'The economy, unemployment and industrial relations', *Industrial Relations Journal*, vol. 13, no. 4, p. 7. See also Sparrow, P. (1986), 'The erosion of employment in the UK; the need for a new response', *New Technology, Work and Employment*, vol. 1, no. 2 p. 101.
2. See, for example, Towers, B. (1983), Editorial: 'The IRJ in 1983', *Industrial Relations Journal*, vol. 14, no. 1, p. 7; Kinnie, N.J. (1985), 'Changing management strategies in industrial relations', *Industrial Relations Journal*, vol. 16, no. 4 p. 23; Brown, W. (1986), 'The Changing Role of Trade Unions in the Management of Labour', *British Journal of Industrial Relations*, vol. XXIV, no. 2, p. 164.
3. Torode, J. (1984), 'In search of the elusive "new worker"', *The Guardian*, 12 April.

CHAPTER 2: PERSPECTIVE ON JAPANIZATION

1. Groom, B. (1984), 'Flexibility: A *Cause Célèbre* of the 1980s', *Financial Times*, 25 June, and cited in Nicols, T., (1986), *The British Worker Question: A New Look at Workers and Productivity in Manufacturing*, London: Routledge & Kegan Paul, p. 201.
2. Green, D. (1988), 'Just-in-time for Scottish Components', *Financial Times*, April, p. 33.

CHAPTER 3: TRADE UNIONS AND CHANGE AT WORK

1. Trades Union Congress, *Meeting the Challenge: First Report of the Special Review Body*, London: TUC (1988:5).
2. Labour Research Department, (1988) 'New wave union busting', *Labour Research*, vol. 77, no. 4 London: LRD.
3. See Leadbeater, C. (1987), 'Unions Go To Market', *Marxism Today* September.
4. Trades Union Congress, (1979) *Employment and Technology*, London: TUC.

5. Quoted in Trades Union Congress, (1965) *Automation and Technological Change*, London: TUC, p. 2.
6. For a review of these developments see Friedman, A. (1983), *Managerial Organizational and Industrial Relations, Implications of Advances in Data Processing and Information Technology: Survey of Research*, University of Bristol.
7. Ken Gill is now General Secretary of MSF following the merger of TASS and ASTMS in 1987.
8. Gill, K. 'Micro-Electronics and Employment'. Statement to AEUW Officials' Conference, Eastbourne, September 1978.
9. EETPU *An Ideal Technology Agreement for EETPU Stewards*, 1980, p. 1.
10. AUEW–TASS, *New technology: A Guide for Negotiators*, October 1978, p. 1.
11. EETPU, 1980, op. cit. p. 3.
12. AUEW-E, Letter from General Secretary John Boyd, to all District Secretaries, 11 February 1981.
13. An agreement between AUEW-E; GMB; TGWU; EETPU; NUSMWCH & DE and Lucas Electrical Ltd (Switchgear).
14. An agreement between TASS and Rolls Royce Ltd, Scotland.
15. Walton, W.: Presidential Address to the Yorkshire and Humberside Engineering and Shipbuilding Employers' Association, 14 December 1981.
16. Quoted by Huw Beynon (1983), 'False Hopes and Real Dilemmas: The Politics of the Collapse in British Manufacturing', *Critique*, no. 16, p. 7.

CHAPTER 4: PATTERNS OF CHANGE

1. Bratton, J. (1986), *The Effects of Microelectronic Technology on Industrial Relations: A Survey of Engineering in Leeds*. A report for Leeds City Council Industry and Employment Development Committee, February.
2. Quoted in LRD (1986), 'Flexibility', *Bargaining Report*, no. 56, November, p. 5.
3. ACAS (1985), *Annual Report*, and cited by LRD (1986), *Bargaining Report*, no. 51, May, p. 3.
4. Fanblade, Leeds, West Yorkshire.
5. Bratton, J. op. cit.
6. AEU Convener, Servo Engineering, see Chapter 5.
7. Bratton, J., op. cit.
8. Fanblade, Leeds, West Yorkshire.
9. Mining Power Ltd, Wakefield, West Yorkshire.
10. Flowpak Engineering, West Yorkshire.
11. Oil Tool Engineering, West Yorkshire.
12. Bratton, J., op. cit.
13. New technology agreement between Pumps Ltd (UK) and Shop Stewards Committee, 19 February 1987.

CHAPTER 5: THE COMPONENTS COMPANY: JAPANIZATION IN LARGE-BATCH PRODUCTION

1. Dwyer, J., (1988), 'Manufacturing software: CIM', *Financial Times*, 26 May.
2. Figures quoted in Fine, B. and Harris, L., 1985, p. 258.
3. Griffiths, J. (1988), 'Car parts makers face challenges', *Financial Times*, 16 February.
4. Dwyer, J. (1988), 'Manufacturing software: MRP II, A philosophy comes in from the cold', *Financial Times*, 26 May.
5. Hoyt, N. Wheeler, (1976), 'Punishment theory and industrial discipline', *Industrial Relations*, vol. 15, no. 2.
6. Letter to General Secretary, AUEW, from District Secretary, 10 February 1983.
7. *Socialist Worker*, 12 February 1983.

CHAPTER 6: THE DRILLING MACHINE COMPANY: JAPANIZATION IN SMALL-BATCH PRODUCTION

1. Dixon, M. (1987), 'Recruitment and personnel services, learning from the dinosaurs', *Financial Times* Survey, 16 July.
2. Oil Tool Engineering, *Annual Report*, 1987, p. 5.

CHAPTER 7: THE PACKAGING COMPANY: WORK GROUPS AND THE POLYVALENT WORKERS

1. Ingersoll Engineers, (1985), *Manufacturing Strategy for Flowpak: Final Report*, January.
2. Ibid. p. 32.
3. For a discussion of this trend in personnel management, see Dixon, M. (1987), 'Recruitment and personnel services, learning from the dinosaurs', *Financial Times* Survey, 16 July.
4. Ingersoll Engineers, op. cit., p. 8.
5. Ibid. p. 18.
6. See 'Laird urges cooperation with companies', *Financial Times*, 12 November 1987, p. 12.

Bibliography

ABERNATHY, W., CLARK, K., KANTROW, A. (1983), *Industrial Renaissance: Producing a Comparative Future for America*, New York: Basic Books.

ACAS, (1988), *Labour Flexibility in Britain: The 1987 ACAS Survey*, London: ACAS.

ACKROYD, S., et al. (1988), The Japanisation of British Industry', *Industrial Relations Journal*, vol. 19, no. 1.

ADAMS, R.J. (1989), 'North American industrial relations: divergent trends in Canada and the United States', *International Labour Review*, vol. 28, no. 1.

ALLEN, J.M. and CAMPBELL, M. (1976), *Employment Performance and the Structure of Industry in Leeds, 1948–73*, Leeds Polytechnic Discussion Paper, no. 3.

ALLEN, V.L. (1966), *Militant Trade Unionism*, London: Merlin.

ARMSTRONG, P. (1986), 'Management Control Strategies and Inter-Professional Competition: the Cases of Accountancy and Personnel Management', in D. Knights and H. Willmott (eds).

ARMSTRONG, P. (1988), 'Labour and Monopoly Capital', in R. Hyman and W. Streeck (eds).

ATKINSON, J. (1984), 'Manpower Strategies for Flexible Organizations', *Personnel Management*, August.

ATKINSON, J. (1985), 'The changing corporation', in D. Clutterbuck (ed.).

ATKINSON, J. and GREGORY, D. (1986), 'A Flexible Future: Britain's dual labour force', *Marxism Today*, vol. 30, no. 4.

AUEW, (1941), 'From craftsman to programmer? ', *AUEW Journal*, June.

AZIM, A.N., (1985), 'Differences and similarities between unions in Japan and North America', paper submitted to International Business Division, May.

BAIN, G.S. (ed.), (1983), *Industrial Relations in Britain*, Oxford: Blackwell.

BAIN, G.S. and Price, R. (1983), 'Union Growth: Dimterminants, and Density', in Bain, G.S.(ed.) (1983).

BALDAMUS, W. (1961), *Efficiency and Effort: an Analysis of Industrial Administration*, London: Tavistock.

BALDRY, C., Connolly, A. (1986), 'Drawing the line: computer-aided-design and the organization of the drawing office', *New Technology, Work and Employment*, vol. 1, no. 1.

BAMBER, G. (1980), 'Microchips and industrial relations', *Industrial Relations Journal*, vol. 11, no. 2.

BAMBER, G. and WILLMAN, P. (1983), 'Technological Change and Industrial Relations in Britain', *Bulletin of Comparative Labour Relations*, no. 112.

BAMBER, G. (1988), 'Technological Change and Unions', in R. Hyman and W. Streeck, (eds).

BARAN, B. (1988), 'Office Automation and Women's Work: The Technological Transformation of the Insurance Industry', in R.E. Pahl, (ed.).

BARRON, I. and CURNOW, R. (1979), *The Future with Microelectronics*, London: Pointer.

BASSETT, P. (1987) *Strike Free: New Industrial Relations in Britain*, London: Papermac.

BASSETT, P. (1988), 'Non-unionism's growing ranks', *Personnel Management*, March.

BATE, S.P. and MURPHY, A.J. (1981), 'Can Joint Consultation Become Employee Participation', *Journal of Management Studies*, vol. 18, no. 4.

BATSTONE, E. et al. (1977), *Shop Stewards in Action*, Oxford: Blackwell.

BATSTONE, E. (1984), *Working Order*, Oxford: Blackwell.

BATSTONE, E. and GOURLAY, S. et al. (1986), *Unions, Unemployment and Innovation*, Oxford: Blackwell.

BATSTONE, E. et al. (1987), *New Technology and the Process of Labour Regulation*, Oxford University Press.

BEAUMONT, P.B. (1987), *The Decline of Trade Union Organization*, London: Croom Helm.

BECKERMANN, G. and VAHRENKAMP, R. (1979), 'The Industrialisation of the Service Sector: the Case of Computer Aided Design (CAD)', in Rothwell, R. and Zegveld, W. (1979), *Technical Change and Employment*, London: Francis Pinter.

BEECHEY, V. (1983), 'The sexual division of labour and the labour process: a critical assessment of Braverman', in S. Wood (ed.), 1983.

BEECHEY, V. (1985), 'The Shape of the Workforce to Come'. *Marxism Today*, vol. 29, no. 8.

BELANGER, J. (1987), 'Job control after reform: a case study in British engineering', *Industrial Relations Journal*, vol. 18, no. 1.

BELL, D. (1973), *The Coming of Post Industrial Society*, New York: Basic Books.

BENDIX, R. (1956), *Work and Authority in Industry, Ideologies of Management in the Course of Industrialization*, New York: Wiley.

BEYNON, H. (1975), *Working for Fords*, Wakefield: EP Publishing.

BEYNON, H. (1983), 'False Hopes and Real Dilemmas: The Politics of the Collapse in British Manufacturing', *Critique*, 16.

BEYNON, H. (1987), 'Dealing with Icebergs: Organization, Production and Motivation in the 1990s', *Work, Employment and Society*, vol. 1, no. 2.

BIRD, D. (1990), 'Industrial Stoppages in 1989', *Employment Gazette*, July.

BLACK, J. and ACKERS, P. (1988), 'The Japanization of British Industry: A case study of quality circles in the carpet industry', *Employee Relations*, vol. 10, no. 6.

BLACKABY, F. (ed.) (1979), *De-industrialisation*, London: Heinemann.

BLACKBURN, P. et al. (1985); *Technology, Economic Growth and the Labour Process*, London: Macmillan.

BLACKLER, F. and BROWN, C. (1982), 'The law and job design: comments on recent Norwegian legislation', *Industrial Relations Journal*, vol. 13, no. 4.

BLAUNER, R. (1964), *Alienation and Freedom*, Chicago University Press.

BLOCK, R.N. (1988): 'American industrial relations in the 1980s:

transformation or evolution?', Paper presented at the conference on the Transformation of United States Industrial Relations, Purdue University, May, 1988, and quoted in Adams (1989).

BLYTON, P. and HILL, S. (1985), 'Research note: output and employment – a study of decision making in the engineering industry', *Industrial Relations Journal*, vol. 16, no. 2.

BOON, J. et al. (1981),'The Development of Operator Programmable NC Lathes', unpublished paper, UMIST.

BRADLEY, H. (1986), ' Technological Change, Management strategies and the development of gender-based job segregation in the labour process', in D. Knights and H. Willmott (eds).

BRADLEY, K. and HILL, S. (1983), 'After Japan: The Quality Circle Transplant and Productive Efficiency', *British Journal of Industrial Relations*, vol. XXI, no.3.

BRADY, T. (1984), *New Technology and Skills in British Industry*, Brighton: Falmer.

BRATTON, J. and WADDINGTON, J. (1981), *New Technology and Employment*, London: WEA.

BRATTON, J. (1989), 'Technical Change, Work and Management Strategies: The Case of the Engineering Industry in Leeds', unpublished PhD thesis, University of Manchester.

BRAVERMAN, H. (1974), *Labor and Monopoly Capital*, New York: Monthly Review Press.

BRAVERMAN, H. (1976), 'Two Comments', *Monthly Review*, vol. 28, no. 3.

BRIGGS, P. (1988), 'The Japanese at work: illusions of the ideal', *Industrial Relations Journal*, vol. 19, no. 1.

BRIGHT, D. et al. (1983), 'Industrial Relations of Recession', *Industrial Relations Journal*, vol. 14, no. 3.

Brighton Labour Process Group. (1977), 'The Capitalist Labour Process', *Capital and Class*, no. 1.

BROWN, W. (ed.) (1981), *The Changing Contours of British Industrial Relations*, Oxford: Blackwell.

BROWN, W. (1986), 'The Changing Role of Trade Unions in the Management of Labour', *British Journal of Industrial Relations*, vol. XXIV, no. 2.

BUCHANAN, D. and BODDY, D. (1983), *Organizations in the Computer Age: Technological Imperatives and Strategic Choice*, Aldershot: Gower.

BUCHANAN, D. and HUCZYNSKI, A. (1985), *Organizational Behaviour*, London: Prentice-Hall.

BUCHAN, D. (1989), 'Storm cloud gathers over the social character', *Financial Times*, 12 June, 1989, p. 18.

BURAWOY, M. (1978), 'Towards a Marxist Theory of the Labour Process: Braverman and Beyond', *Politics and Society*, vol. 8, no. 3/4.

BURAWOY, M. (1979), *Manufacturing Consent: Changes in the Labour Process under Monopoly Capitalism*, Chicago University Press.

BURAWOY, M. (1985), *The Politics of Production*, London: Verso.

BURBIDGE, J. (1982), 'Japanese Kanban System', *Production Management and Control*, January–February.

BURNES, B. (1988), 'New technology and job design: the case of CNC', *New technology, Work and Employment*, vol. 3, no. 2.

BURNS, A. et al. (1983), 'The miners and new technology', *Industrial Relations Journal*, vol. 14, no. 4.

BURROWS, G. (1986), *No-Strike Agreements and Pendulum Arbitration*, London: Institute of Personnel Management.

CAIRNCROSS, F. (1981), 'Where have all the jobs gone?', *The Guardian*, April, 6.

CAMPBELL, A. and CURRIE, W. (1987), *Skills and Strategies in Design Engineering*, Paper presented at 1987 Labour Process Conference, UMIST, April.

CAMPBELL, A. and WARNER, M. (1987), 'New Technology, innovation and training: a survey of British Firms', *New Technology, Work and Employment*, vol. 2, no. 2.

CHADWICK, M.G. (1983), 'The Recession and Industrial Relations: a Factory Approach', *Employee Relations*, vol. 5, no. 5.

CHARLTON, J.H. (1983), 'Employee Participation in the Public Sector: A Review', *Journal of General Management*, vol. 8, no. 3.

CHILD, J. (1972), 'Organizational structure, environment and performance: the role of strategic choice', *Sociology*, vol. 6, no. 1.

CHILD, J. (1985), 'Managerial strategies, new technology, and the labour process', in D. Knights, H. Willmott, and D. Collinson (eds).

CLARK, J. et al. (1984), 'Industrial Relations, new technology and division within the workforce', *Industrial Relations Journal*, vol. 15, no. 3.

CLAYDON, T. (1989). 'Union de-recognition in Britain in the 1980s', *British Journal of Industrial Relations*, vol. XXVII, no. 2.

CLEGG, H. (1976), *Trade Unionism under Collective Bargaining*, Oxford: Blackwell.

CLEGG, H. (1979), *The Changing System of Industrial Relations in Great Britain*, Oxford: Blackwell.

CLIFFE, T. (1970), *The Employers' Offensive*, London: Pluto.

CLUTTERBUCK, D. (ed.) (1985), *New Patterns of Work*, Aldershot, Gower.

COATES, D. and HILLARD, J. (1986), *The Economic Decline of Modern Britain: The Debate Between Left and Right*, Brighton, Wheatsheaf Books.

COCKBURN, C. (1983), 'Caught in the Wheels', *Marxism Today*, vol. 27, no. 11.

COLLINSON, D. and KNIGHTS, D. (1986), 'Men Only: Theories and Practices of Job Segregation in Insurance', in D. Knights and H. Willmott (eds).

Conference Socialist Economists, Microelectronics Group, (1980), *Microelectronics, Capitalist Technology and the Working Class*, London: CSE Books.

COOLEY, M. (1980) (Revised edition 1987), *Architect or Bee?*, Slough/London: Langley Technical Services/Hogarth Press.

CORIAT, B. (1980), 'The restructuring of the assembly line: A new Economy of time and control', *Capital and Class*, no. 11.

COSTELLO, N. et al., (1989), *Beyond the Casino Economy*, London: Verso.

Counter Information Services, (1979), *Report on New Technology*, London: CIS.

Coventry Workshop, (1979), *Crisis in Engineering: Machine Tool Workers Fight for Jobs*, London: Institute for Workers' Control.

COWLING, K. (1981), 'Can the British car industry survive?', *Marxism Today*, vol. 25, no. 8.

COWLING, K. (1982), 'The heartland of depression', *Marxism Today*, vol. 25, no. 12.

CROSS, M. (1985), *Towards the Flexible Craftsman*, London: Technical Change Centre.

CROSS, M. (1988), 'Changes in working practices in UK manufacturing, 1981–88', *IRRR*, 415, May.

CROWTHER, S. and GARRAHAN, P. (1987), 'Invitation to Sunderland: Corporate power and the Local Economy', Paper presented to the conference on the Japanisation of British Industry, UWIST, Cardiff.

CROUCH, C. (1979), *The Politics of Industrial Relations*, Glasgow: Fontana.

CROUCH, C. (1982), *Trade Unions: the Logic of Collective Action*, Glasgow: Fontana.

DANIEL, W.W. and MILLWARD, N. (1983), *Workplace Industrial Relations in Britain*, London: Heinemann.

DANIEL, W.W. (1987), *Workplace Industrial Relations and Technical Change*, London: Frances Pinter.

DANKBAAR, B. (1988), 'New production concepts, management strategies and the quality of work', *Work, Employment and Society*, vol. 2, no. 1.

DAVIES, A. (1984), 'Manpower matters: change by agreement?', *Journal of General Management*, vol. 19, no. 4.

DAVIES, A. (1986), *Industrial Relations and New Technoloqy*, London: Croom Helm.

DEATON. D. (1985), 'Management style and large-scale survey evidence', *Industrial Relations Journal*, vol. 16, no. 2.

DICKENS, P. and SAVAGE, M. (1988), 'The Japanisation of British industry? Instances from a high growth area.' *Industrial Relations Journal*, vol. 19, no. 1.

DICKSON, D. (1974), *Alternative Technology and the Politics of Technological Change*, Glasgow: Fontana/Collins.

DISNEY, R. (1990), 'Explanations of the decline in trade union density in Britain: an appraisal', *British Journal of Industrial Relations*, Vol. 28, no. 2.

DODGSON, M. and MARTIN, R. (1987), 'Trade union policies on new technology: facing the challenge of the 1980s', *New Technology, Work and Employment*, vol. 2, no. 1.

DOERINGER, P.B. and PIORE, M.J. (1971), *Internal Labour Markets and Manpower Analysis*, Lexington, Mass.: Heath.

DONE, K. (1990), 'Electricians throw a spanner in the works', *Financial Times*, 6 February.

DONOVAN, (1968), *Royal Commission on Trade Unions and Employers' Association, Report*, Cmnd. 3623, London: HMSO.

EATON, A.E. and VOOS, P.B. (1989), 'Unions and contemporary innovations in work organization, compensation, and employee participation', Queen's Papers in Industrial Relations, Queen's University at Kingston, Canada.

EDWARDS, P.K. and SCULLION, H. (1982), 'The local organization of a national dispute: the British 1979 engineering strike', *Industrial Relations Journal*, vol. 13, no. 1.

EDWARDS, P.K. (1984), *The Management of Productivity: A Preliminary Report of a Survey of Large Manufacturing Establishments*, Warwick: Discussion Paper, IRRU.

EDWARDS, P.K. (1985), *Managing Labour Relations Through the Recession*, University of Warwick, IRRU.

EDWARDS, P.K. (1987), *Managing the Factory*, Oxford: Blackwell.

EDWARDS, P.K. and SISSON, K. (1989), 'Industrial Relations in the UK: change in the 1980s'. An ESRC Research Briefing.

EDWARDS, R. (1979), *Contested Terrain: The Transformation of the Workplace in the Twentieth Century*, London: Heinemann.

ELGER, T. (1979), 'Valorisation and "Deskilling": A Critique of Braverman', *Capital and Class*, no. 7.

EFILWC, (1985), *The Role of the Parties Concerned in the Introduction of New Technology*, Dublin: European Foundation for the Improvement of Living and Working Conditions.

EITB, (1985), *Sector Profile: The Engineering Industry, Trends in its Manpower and Training*, Watford: Engineering Industry Training Board.

EITB, (1986), *Regional Profile: Trends in Engineering Manpower and Training in Yorkshire and Humberside*, Watford: Engineering Industry Training Board.

EITB, (1989), *Making More of CAD*, Stockport: Engineering Industry Training Board.

Employment Gazette, (1989), 'Membership of trade unions in 1987', May.

Employment Gazette, (1990), 'Union density and workforce composition', August.

ESLAND, G. and SALAMAN, G. (eds) (1980), *The politics of Work and Occupations*, Milton Keynes: Open University Press.

ETUI, (1996), *Flexibility of Working Time in Western Europe*, Brussels: European Trade Union Institute.

FINE, B. and HARRIS, L. (1985), *The Peculiarities of the British Economy*, London: Lawrence & Wishart.

FLOUD, R. (1976), *The British Machine Tool Industry, 1850–1914*, Cambridge University Press.

FORESTER, T. (1980), *The Microelectronics Revolution*, Oxford: Blackwell.

FRANCIS, A. and WILLMAN, P. (1980), 'Microprocessors: Impact and Response', *Personnel Management*, Spring.

FRANCIS, A. et al. (1982), 'The Impact of Information Technology at Work: The Case of CAD-CAM and MIS in Engineering Plants', in Bannon, L., Barry, U., and Holst, O. (eds) *Information Technoloqy: Impact on a Way of Life*, Dublin: Tycooly International.

FOX, A. (1974), *Beyond Contract: Work, Power and Trust Relations*, London: Faber.

FOX, A. (1985), *Man Mismanagement*, (2nd edn), London: Hutchinson.

FREEMAN, R. and PELLETIER, J. (1990), 'The impact of industrial relations legislation on British union density', *British Journal of Industrial Relations*, vol. 28, no. 2.

FRIEDMAN, A. (1977), *Industry and Labour, Class Struggle at Work and Monopoly Capitalism*, London: Macmillan.

FRIEDMAN, A. (1983), *Managerial, Organizational and Industrial Relations Implications of Advances in Data Processing and Information Technology*, SSRC Paper.

FRIEDMAN, A. (1986), 'Developing the managerial strategies approach to the labour process', *Capital and Class*, no. 30.

FRIEDMAN, A. (1987), 'Specialist labour in Japan: computer skilled staff and the subcontracting system', *British Journal of Industrial Relations*, vol. XXV, no. 3.

FRYER, (1981) *Sunday Times*, 3 May.

GARRAHAN, P. (1986), 'Nissan in the north east of England', *Capital and Class*, no. 27.

GATTIKER, U.E. (1990), *Technology Management in Organizations*, London: Sage.

GERSHUNY, J. (1985), 'New technology: what new jobs?', *Industrial Relations Journal*, vol. 16, no. 3.

GENNARD, J. and DUNN, S. (1983), 'The impact of new technology on the structure and organization of craft unions in the printing industry', *British Journal of Industrial Relations*, vol. XXI, no. 1.

GENNARD, J. et al. (1989), 'Trade union discipline and non-strikers', *Industrial Relations Journal*, vol. 20, no. 1.

GIDDENS, A. and MACKENZIE, G. (eds) (1982), *Social Class and the Division of Labour*, Cambridge University Press.

GILES, E. and STARKEY, K. (1988), 'The Japanisation of Xerox', *New Technology, Work and Employment*, vol. 3, no. 2.

GILL, C. (1984), *New Technology: its Effect on Work Organization*, Paper for the EIASM Workshop on industrial Relations, Brussels, November.

GILL, C. (1985), *Work, Unemployment and the New Technology*, Cambridge: Polity Press.

GILL, C. (1987), 'Editorial: the NTWE in 1987', *New Technology, Work and Employment*, vol. 2, no. 1.

GODDARD, R. (1987). 'Waves of change at Seacroft', *Packaging Week*, April.

GOODLAD, J. (1982), 'Employee participation: alpha or omega?', *Management Accounting*, February.

GOODRICH, C. (1975), *The Frontier of Control*, London: Pluto.

GORDON, D.D. (1988), *Japanese Management in America and Britain*, Aldershot: Avebury.

GOSPEL, H. and LITTLER, C.R. (eds) (1983), *Managerial Strategies and Industrial Relations*, London: Heinemann.

GOSS, D. (1987), 'Instant Print: technology and capitalist control', *Capital and Class*, no. 31.

GOSS, D. (1988), 'Diversity, complexity and technological change: an empirical study of general printing', *Sociology*, vol. 22, no. 3.

GRAHAM, I. (1988), 'Japanisation as mytholoqy', *Industrial Relations Journal*, vol. 19, no. 1.

GREEN, F. (1989) (ed.), *The Restructuring of the UK Economy*, Brighton: Harvester Wheatsheaf.

GREEN, K., Coombs, R., and Holroyd, K. (1980), *The Effects of Microelectronic Technologies on Employment Prospects: A Case Study of Tameside*, Aldershot: Gower.

GRIFFITHS, A. and WALL, S. (1989), *Applied Economics*, (3rd edn), London: Longman.

GUEST, D.E. (1986), 'Workers' participation and personnel policy in the UK: some case studies', *International Labour Review*, vol. 125, no. 6.

GUEST, D.E. (1987), 'Human resource management and industrial relations', *Journal of Management Studies*, vol. 24, no. 5.

HAGUE, R. (1989), 'Japanising Geordie-Land?', *Employee Relations*, vol. 11, no. 2.

HAKIM, C. (1987), 'Trends in the flexible workforce', *Employment Gazette*, November.

HALL, S. and JACQUES, M. (1989), *New Times*, London: Lawrence & Wishart.

HARRIS, L. (1988), 'The UK economy at a crossroads', in *The Economy in Question*, J. Allen and D. Massey (eds) London: Sage.

HARTMANN, G., NICHOLAS, I., SORGE, A. and WARNER, M. (1983), 'Computerised machine tools manpower consequences and skill utilisation: a study of British and West German manufacturing firms', *British Journal of Industrial Relations*, vol. XXI, no. 2.

HELLER, F. (1987), 'The technological imperative and the quality of employment', *New Technology, Work and Employment*, vol. 2, no. 1.

HILL, S. (1981), *Competition and Control at Work*, London: Heinemann.

HINES, C. and SEARLE, G. (1979), *Automatic Unemployment*, London: Earth Resources Research.

HINTON, J. (1973), *The First Shop Stewards Movement*, London: Allen & Unwin.

HOBSBAWM, E.J. (1964), *Labouring Men*, London: Weidenfeld & Nicolson.

HYMAN, R.(1972), *Strikes*, London: Fontana/Collins.

HYMAN, R. (1979), 'The politics of workplace trade unionism', *Capital and Class*, no. 8.

HYMAN, R. (1980), 'Trade unions, control and resistance', in G. Esland and G. Salaman (eds).

HYMAN, R. (1987), 'Trade unions and the law: papering over the cracks?', *Capital and Class*, no. 31.

HYMAN, R. (1988), 'Flexible specialization: miracle or myth?', in R. Hyman and W. Streeck (eds).

HYMAN, R. and STREECK, W. (eds) (1988), *New Technology and Industrial Relations*, Oxford: Blackwell.

IDS (1982), 'CAD: Agreements and Pay', Study 276, London: Incomes Data Services.

IDS (1983), 'Draughtsmen and CAD', Study 302, London: Incomes Data Services.

IDS (1983), 'Temporary Workers', Study 295, London: Incomes Data Services.

IDS (1984), 'Craft Flexibility', Study 322, London: Incomes Data Services.

IDS (1985), 'CAD and Draughtsmen', Study 347, London: Incomes Data Services.

IDS (1986), 'Flexibility at Work', Study 360, London: Incomes Data Services.

IDS (1988), 'Team Tactics', Study 419, London: Incomes Data Services.

IDS (1988), 'Flexibility Working', Study 407, London: Incomes Data Services.

IDS (1990), 'Flexibility in the 1990s', Study 454, London: Incomes Data Services.

IMAI, M. (1986), *Kaizen: The Key to Japan's Competitive Success*, New York: Random House Business Division.

Ingersoll Engineers Ltd (1990), *Competitive Manufacturing: The Quiet Revolution*.

IRRR, (1984), Industrial Relations Review and Report, 'Merit Pay for Manual Workers', No. 319, May.

IRRR, (1989a), 'Decentralised Bargaining in Practice', no. 440, 23 May.

IRRR, (1989b), 'Decentralised Bargaining in Practice', no. 454, 19 December.

IRRR, (1990), 'Developments in European Collective Bargaining: 1', no. 460, March.

JACKSON, M.P. (1987), *Strikes*, Brighton: Wheatsheaf.

JAQUES, E.(1961), *Equitable Payment*, London: Wiley.

JAIN, H.C. (1990), 'Human resource management in selected Japanese firms, their foreign subsidiaries and locally owned counterparts', *International Labour Review*, vol. 129, no. 1.

JEFFERYS, J.B. (1946), *The Story of the Engineers 1800–1945*, London: Lawrence & Wishart.

JEFFERYS, S. (1986), *Management and Managed: Fifty Years of Crisis at Chrysler*, Cambridge: CUP.

JENKINS, C. and SHERMAN, B. (1979), *The Collapse of Work*, London: Eyre Methuen.

JENKINS, C. and SHERMAN, B. (1981), *The Leisure Shock*, London: Eyre Methuen.

JONES, B. (1983), 'Destruction or Redistribution of Engineering Skills: the Case of Numerical Control', in S. Wood (ed.).

JONES, B. and SCOTT, P. (1987), 'Flexible manufacturing systems in Britain and the USA', *New Technology, Work and Employment, vol. 2, no. 1.*

JONES, D.T. (1983b), 'Productivity and the Thatcher experiment', *Socialist Economic Review*, London: Merlin.

JURGENS, U. (1989), 'The transfer of Japanese management concepts in the international automobile industry', in S. Wood (ed), (1989), *The Transformation of Work?*, London: Unwin Hyman.

KATZ, H. (1988), 'Policy Debates over Work Reorganization in North American Unions', in Hyman and Streeck (eds).

KELLY, F.E. and CLEGG, C.W. (ed.), (1982) *Autonomy and Control of the Workplace*, London: Croom Helm.

KELLY, J. (1978), 'Understanding Taylorism: some comments', *British Journal of Sociology*, vol. 29, no. 2.

KELLY, J. (1982), 'Useless Work and Useless Toil', *Marxism Today*, vol. 26, no. 8.

KELLY, J. (1985), 'Management's Redesign of Work: Labour Process, Labour Markets and Product Markets', in D. Knights et al. (eds).

KELLY, J. et al. (1987), 'Symposium: British Workplace Industrial Relations 1980–84', *British Journal of Industrial Relations*, vol. XXV, no. 2.

KELLY, J. (1988), *Trade Unions and Socialist Politics*, London: Verso.

KELLY, J. and BAILEY, R. (1989), 'Research note: British trade union membership, density and decline in the 1980s', *Industrial Relations Journal*, vol. 20, no. 1, Spring.

KELLY, J. and RICHARDSON, R. (1989), 'Annual Review Article 1988', *British Jornal of Industrial Relations*, vol. XXVII, no. 1.

KEYS, J.B. and MILLER, T.R. (1984), 'The Japanese management theory jungle', *Academy of Management Review*, 9.

KINNIE, N.J. (1985), 'Changing management strategies in industrial relations'', *Industrial Relations Journal*, vol. 16, no. 4.

KINNIE, N.J. (1987), 'Bargaining within the enterprise: centralized or decentralized?', *Journal of Management Studies*, vol. 24, no. 5.

KNIGHTS, D., WILLMOTT, H. and COLLINSON, D. (eds) (1985), *Job Redesign Critical Perspectives on the Labour Process*, Aldershot: Gower.

KNIGHTS, D. and COLLINSON, D. (1985), 'Redesigning work on the shopfloor: a question of control or consent?', in D. Knights et al. (eds).

KNIGHTS, D. and WILLMOTT, H. (ed.) (1986a), *Managing the Labour Process*, Aldershot: Gower.

KNIGHTS, D. and WILLMOTT, H. (eds) (1986b), *Gender and the Labour Process*, Aldershot: Gower.

KNIGHTS, D. and WILLMOTT, H. (eds) (1988), *New Technology and the Labour Process*, London: Macmillan.

KNIGHTS, D. and WILLMOTT, H. (eds) (1990), *Labour Process Theory*, London: Macmillan.

KOCHAN, T.A. et al. (1986), *The Transformation of American Industrial Relations*, New York: Basic Books.

KONO, T. (1984), *Strategy and Structure of Japanese Enterprise*, London: Macmillan.

KUSTERER, K.C. (1978), *Know-How on the Job*, Boulder, Colo.: Westview.

KUWAHARA, Y. (1987), 'Japanese Industrial Relations', in G. Bamber and R. Lansbury (eds), *International and Comparative Industrial Relations*, London: Allen & Unwin.

LRD (1982), 'Survey of New Technology', *Bargaining Report*, no. 22, London: Labour Research Department.

LRD (1986), 'Flexibility', *Bargaining Report*, no. 56, London: Labour Research Department.

LAFLAMME, G. et al. (1989), *Flexibility and Labour Markets in Canada and the United States*, Research Series: Department of Industrial Relations, Laval University, Quebec, Canada.

LANE, T. (1974), *The Union Makes Us Strong*, London: Arrow Books.

LANE, T. (1982), 'The unions: caught on the ebb tide', *Marxism Today*, vol. 26, no. 9.

LASH, S. and URRY, J. (1987), *The End of Organized Capitalism*, Cambridge: Polity.

LEADBEATER, C. (1986), 'The State of the Movement', *Marxism Today*, vol. 30, no. 9.

LEADBEATER, C. (1989), 'Fighting over restructuring', *Financial Times*, 25 April.

LEE, D.J. (1981), 'Skill, Craft and Class: a theoretical Critique and a Critical Case', *Sociology*, vol. 15, no. 1.

LEEDS TRADES COUNCIL, (1981), *Industry and Employment in Leeds 1981*, Leeds Trades Council/TUCRIC.

LEGGE, K. (1989), 'Human Resource Management: A Critical Analysis', in J. Storey (ed.).

LEVIDOW, L. and YOUNG, B. (eds) (1981), *Science, Technology and the Labour Process: Marxist Studies Volume I*, London: CSE Books.

LEVIDOW, L. and YOUNG, B. (eds) (1985), *Science, Technology and the Labour Process Marxist Studies Volume 2*, London: Free Association Books.

LEWIS, P. (1989), 'Employee participation in a Japanese-owned British electronics factory: reality or symbolism?', *Employee Relations*, vol. 11, no. 1.

LEWIS, R. (ed.) (1986), *Labour Law in Britain*, Oxford: Blackwell.

LINN, I. (1986), *Single Union Deals: A Case Study of the Norsk-Hydro*, Northern College/TGWU Region 10, Barnsley: Northern College.

LINTNER, V.G. et al. (1987), 'Trade unions and technological change in the UK mechanical engineering industry', *British Journal of Industrial Relations*, vol. XXV, no. 1.

LITTLER, C.R. (1978), 'Understanding Taylorism', *British Journal of Sociology*, vol. 29, no. 2.

LITTLER, C.R. (1982), *The Development of the Labour Process in Capitalist Societies*, London: Heinemann.

LITTLER, C.R. and SALAMAN, G. (1982), 'Bravermania and beyond: recent theories of the labour process', *Sociology*, vol. 16, no. 2.

LITTLER, C.R. and SALAMAN, G. (1984), *Class at Work: The Design, Allocation and Control of Jobs*, London: Batsford.

LITTLER, C.R. (1985), 'Taylorism, Fordism and Job Design' in D. Knights et al. (eds).

LONG, P. (1986), *Performance Appraisal Revisited*, London: Institute of Personnel Management.

LOWSTEDT, J. (1988), 'Prejudices and wishful thinking about computer aided design', *New Technology, Work and Employment*, vol. 3, no. 1.

MACINNES, J. (1987), *Thatcherism at Work Industrial Relations and Economic Change*, Milton Keynes: Open University Press.

MANWARING, T. (1981), 'The Trade Union Response to New Technology', *Industrial Relations Journal*, vol. 12, no. 4.

MARCHINGTON, M. (1980), 'Problems with Participation at Work', *Personnel Review*, Summer.

MARCHINGTON, M. (1987), 'A review and critique of research on devel-

234 Bibliography

opments in joint consultation', *British Journal of Industrial Relations*, vol. XXV, no. 3.

MARCHINGTON, M. (1986), 'Editorial note', *Employee Relations*, vol. 18, no. 5.

MARCHINGTON, M. (1989), 'Problems with team briefings in practice', *Employee Relations*, vol. 11, no. 4.

MARGINSON, P. (1988), 'What do corporate offices really do?', *British Journal of Industrial Relations*, vol. XXVI, no. 2.

MARGLIN, S.A. (1974), 'What Do Bosses Do? The Origins and Functions of Hierarchy in Capitalist Production', *Review of Radical Political Economy*, vol. 6, no. 2.

MARSH, A. (1965), *Industrial Relations in Engineering*, Oxford: Pergamon.

MARSH, R. (1987), 'Foreword' in P. Wickens.

MARSTRAND, P. (ed.) (1984), *New Technology and the Future of Work and Skills*, London: Pinter.

MARTIN, R. (1981), *New Technology and Industrial Relations in Fleet Street*, Oxford University Press.

MARX, K. (1970), *Capital*, Volume I, London: Lawrence Wishart.

MASSEY, D. and MEEGAN, R. (1982), *The Anatomy of Job Loss*, London: Methuen.

MASSEY, D. (1988), 'What's happening to UK manufacturing?', in J. Allen and D. Massey (eds), (1988).

MCGUFFIE, C. (1985), *Working in Metal*, London: Merlin.

MCKENDRICK, E. (1988), 'The rights of trade union members: Part I of the Employment Act 1980', *Industrial Law Journal*, vol. 17, no. 3.

MCKENNA, S. (1988), 'Japanisation and Recent Developments in Britain', *Employee Relations*, vol. 10, no. 4.

MCLOUGHLIN, I. and CLARK, J. (1988), *Technological Change at Work*, Milton Keynes: Open University Press.

MEYER, P.B. (1986), 'General Motors' Saturn Plant: A quantum leap in technology and its implications for labour', *Capital and Class*, no. 30.

MILLWARD, N. and STEVENS, M. (1986), *British Workplace Industrial Relations 1980–1984*, Aldershot: Gower.

MOORE, R. and LEVIE, H. (1981), *The Impact of New Technology on Trade Union Organization*, Study 11, Oxford: Ruskin College.

MORE, C. (1980), *Skill and the English Working Class, 1870–1914*, London: Croom Helm.

MORE, C. (1982), 'Skill and the survival of apprenticeship', in S. Wood (ed.).

MORISHIMA, M. (1982), *Why Has Japan Succeeded? Western Technology and the Japanese Ethos*, Cambridge: CUP.

MORRIS, J. (1988), 'The who, why, and where of Japanese manufacturing investment in the UK', *Industrial Relations Journal*, vol. 19, no. 1.

MORTIMER, J.E. (1970), *Trade Unions and Technological Change*, Oxford: OUP.

MOWDAY, R. et al. (1982), *Employee–Organization Linkages: The Psychology of Commitment, Absenteeism and Turnover*, London: Academic.

MSC (1982), *MSC Training Studies Report of a Survey of Electronic Occupations in England and Wales*, Sheffield: Manpower Services Commission.

MSC (1984), *New Technology and the Demands for Skills*, Sheffield, Manpower Services Commission.

MSC (1985), *The Impact of New Technology on Skills in Manufacturing and Services*, Sheffield: Manpower Services Commission.

MUELLER, W.S. et al. (1986), 'Pluralist beliefs about new technology within a manufacturing organization', *New Technology, Work and Employment*, vol. 1, no. 2.

MURRAY, R. (1985), 'Benetton Britain: the new economic order', *Marxism Today*, vol. 29, no. 11.

MURRAY, R. (1988), 'Life after Henry (Ford)', *Marxism Today*, vol. 32, no. 10.

MUSSON, A.E. and ROBINSON, E. (1969), *Science and Technology in the Industrial Revolution*, Manchester University Press.

NEDC (1985), *Changing Working Patterns and Practices*, London: National Economic Development Council.

NEWTON, K. (1981), 'Simple analytics of the employment impact of technological change', *Prometheus*, vol. 2, no. 2.

NEWTON, K. and LECKIE, N. (1987), 'Employment effects of technical change', *New Technology, Work and Employment*, vol. 2, no. 2.

NICHOLS, T. and BEYNON, H. (1977), *Living With Capitalism: Class Relations and the Modern Factory*, London: Routledge & Kegan Paul.

NICHOLS, T. (1980), 'Management ideology and practice', in G. Esland and G. Salaman (eds).

NICHOLS, T. (1980), *Capital and Labour*, Glasgow: Fontana.

NICHOLS, T. (1986), *The British Worker Question: A New Look at Workers and Productivity in Manufacturing*, London: Routledge & Kegan Paul.

NOBLE, D.F. (1977), *America by Design: Science, Technology and the Rise of Corporate Capitalism*, New York: Alfred Knopf.

NOBLE, D.F. (1979), 'Social choice in machine design: the case of the automatically controlled machine tools', in A. Zimbalist (ed.).

NORA, S. and MINE, A. (1980), *The Computerization of Society*, Cambridge, Mass.: MIT Press.

NORTHCOTT, J. and Rogers, P. (1982), *Microelectronics in Industry: What's Happening in Britain*, Report no. 603, London: Policy Studies Institute.

NORTHCOTT, J. and ROGERS, P. (1984), *Microelectronics in British Industry: The Pattern of Change*, London: Policy Studies Institute.

OECD (1970), *NC Machine Tools*, Organization for Economic Cooperation and Development .

O'HIGGINS, P. (1986), 'International standards and British labour law', in R. Lewis (ed.) (1986).

OI, W. (1962), 'Labour as a quasi-fixed factor', in J.E. King (ed.) (1980), *Readings in Labour Economics*, Oxford University Press.

OKUBAYASHI, K. (1989), 'The Japanese industrial relations system', *Journal of General Management*, vol. 14, no. 3.

OLIVER, J.M. and TURTON, J.R. (1982), 'Is there a shortage of skilled labour?', *British Journal of Industrial Relations*, vol. XX, no. 2.

OLIVER, N. and WILKINSON, B. (1988), *The Japanization of British Industry*, Oxford: Blackwell.

OLIVER, N. and WILKINSON, B. (1989), 'Japanese manufacturing techniques and personnel and industrial relations practice in Britain: evidence
and implications', *British Journal of Industrial Relations*, vol. XXVII,
no. 1.

ORAM, R. (1990), 'How Boeing is struggling to re-tool itself', *Financial
Times*, 21 February.

OUCHI, W. (1981), *Theory Z: How American Business Can Meet the
Japanese Challenge*, Boston: Addison-Wesley.

PAHL, R.E. (ed.) (1988), *On Work: Historical, Comparative and Theoretical Approaches*, Oxford: Blackwell.

PASCALE, R.T. and ATHOS, A.G. (1986), *The Art of Japanese Management*, Harmondsworth: Penguin.

PENN, R. (1983), 'Skilled manual workers in the labour process,
1856–1964', in S. Wood (ed.).

PENN, R. and SCATTERGOOD, H. (1985), 'Deskilling or enskilling?: an
empirical investigation of recent theories of the labour process', *British
Journal of Sociology*, vol. XXXVI, no. 4.

PENN, R. and SIMPSON, R. (1986), 'The development of skilled work in
the British coalmining industry, 1870–1985', *Industrial Relations Journal*,
vol. 17, no. 4.

PERKINS, G. (1986), *Employee Communications in the Public Sector*,
London: IPM.

PHILLIPS, B. and TAYLOR, A. (1980), 'Sex and skill: notes towards a
feminist economics', *Feminist Review*, no. 6.

PIERCY, N. (ed.) (1984), *The Management Implications of New Information Technology*, London: Croom Helm.

PIORE, M. and SABEL, C. (1984), *The Second Industrial Divide*, New
York: Basic Books.

POLLARD, S. (1965), *The Genesis of Modern Management*, London: Ar-
nold.

POLLERT, A. (1988), 'Dismantling flexibility', *Capital and Class*, no. 34.

POOLE, M. (1986), 'Profit-sharing and share ownership schemes in Britain', *Employee Relations*, vol. 8, no. 5.

PRICE, R. (1988), 'Information, consultation and the control of new technology', in R. Hyman and W. Streeck (eds).

PRYCE, V. and NICHOLSON, C. (1988), 'The problems and performance
of employee ownership firms', *Employment Gazette*, vol. 96, no. 6.

PURCELL, J. and SMITH, R. (eds) (1979), *The Control of Work*, London:
Macmillan.

PURCELL, J. (1982), 'Macho managers and the new industrial relations',
Employee Relations, vol. 4, no. 1.

PURCELL, J. and SISSON, K. (1983), 'Strategies and practice in the
management of industrial relations', in G. Bain (ed.).

PURCELL, J. and GRAY, A. (1986), 'Corporate personnel departments
and the management of industrial relations: two case studies in ambiguity',
Journal of Management Studies, vol. 23, no. 2.

PURCELL, J. and AHLSTRAND, B. (1989), 'Corporate strategy and the
management of employee relations in the multi-national divisional
company', *British Journal of Industrial Relations*, vol. XXVII, no. 3.

RAJAN, A. (1985), *Training and Recruitment Effects of Technical Change*, Aldershot: Gower.

RAMSEY, H. (1985), 'What is participation for? A critical evaluation of "labour process" analyses of job reform', in D. Knights, et al. (eds) (1985).

RANDELL, G. (1989), 'Employee Appraisal', in K. Sisson (ed.) (1989).

RHODES, E. and WIELD, D. (eds) (1985), *Implementing New Technologies: Choice, Decision and Change in Manufacturing*, Oxford: Blackwell.

RHODES, J. (1986), 'Regional dimensions of industrial decline', in R. Martin and B. Rowthorn (eds) *The Geography of Deindustrialization*, London: Macmillan.

RIMMER, W.G. (1955), 'Leeds and its industrial growth; engineering I: the 19th century', *Leeds Journal*, vol. 25, July/August.

RIMMER, W.G. (1955), 'Leeds and its industrial growth; engineering II: the 20th century', *Leeds Journal*, vol. 25, Sept/October.

ROBINS, K. and WEBSTER, F. (1982), 'New technology: a survey of trade union response in Britain', *Industrial Relations Journal*, vol. 13, no. 1.

ROLFE, H. (1986), 'Skill, deskilling and new technology in the non-manual labour process', *New Technology, Work and Employment*, vol. 1, no. 1.

ROLFE, H. (1990), 'In the name of progress? skill and attitudes towards technological change', *New Technology, Work and Employment*, vol. 5, no. 2.

ROSE, M. and JONES, B. (1985), 'Managerial strategy and trade union response in work organization schemes at establishment level', in D. Knights et al. (eds).

ROTHWELL, R. and ZEGVELD, W. (1979), *Technical Change and Employment*, London: Francis Pinter.

ROSENBROCK, H.H. (1985), 'Can human skill survive microelectronics', in E. Rhodes and D. Wield (eds).

RUSSELL, D., LANSBURY, R. and DAVIS, E.M. (eds) (1984), *Technology, Work and Industrial Relations*, London: Longman.

SADLER, P. (1970), 'Sociological aspects of skill', *British Journal of Industrial Relations*, vol. 8, no. 1.

SADLER, P. (1980), 'Welcome back to the "automation" debate', in T. Forester (ed.).

SALAMAN, G. (1979), *Work Organization Resistance and Control*, London: Longman.

SALAMAN, G. (1981), *Class and the Corporation*, Glasgow: Fontana.

SALAMAN, G. (1982), 'Managing the frontier of control', in A. Giddens and G. Mackenzie (eds).

SAUNDERS, C. (1978), *Engineering in Britain, West Germany and France: Some Statistical Comparisons*, University of Sussex: SERC.

SAYER, A. (1986), 'New developments in manufacturing: The just-in-time system', *Capital and Class*, no. 30.

SCARBOROUGH, H. (1984), 'Maintenance workers and new technology', *Industrial Relations Journal*, vol. 15, no. 4.

SCHONBERGER, R. (1982), *Japanese Manufacturing Techniques: Nine Hidden Lessons in Simplicity*, London: Collier Macmillan.

SCHONBERGER, R. (1986), World Class Manufacturing, London: Collier Macmillan.

SCHWARZ, B. (1977), 'On the monopoly capitalist degradation of work', *Dialectical Anthropology*, vol. 2, no. 2.

SENKER, P., HUGGETT, C., BELL, M. and SCIBERRAS, E. (1976), *Technological Change and Manpower in the UK Toolmaking Industry*, Watford: EITB.

SENKER, P. et al. (1983), *Learning to Use Microelectronics: a Review of Empirical Research on the Implications of Microelectronics for Work Organization, Skills and Industrial Relations*, Brighton: Science Policy Research Unit, University of Sussex.

SENKER, P. (1984), *Implications of Information Technology for Engineering Industry Skill Needs*, Brighton: SPRU.

SENKER, P. (1985), 'Implications of CAD/CAM for Management', in E. Rhodes and D. Wield (ed.).

SENKER, P. and BEESLEY, M. (1985), 'Computerised production and inventory control systems: some skill and employment implications', *Industrial Relations Journal*, vol. 16, no. 3.

SENKER, P. and BEESLEY, M. (1986), 'The need for skills in the factory of the future', *New Technology, Work and Employment*, vol. 1, no. 1.

SIMPSON, B. (1986), 'Trade Union Immunities', in R. Lewis (ed.) (1986).

SINGH, A. (1977), 'UK industry and world economy: a case of deindustrialization?', *Cambridge Journal of Economics*, vol. 1.

SISSON, K. and SCULLION, H. (1985), 'Putting the corporate personnel department in its place', *Personnel Management*, December.

SISSON, K. (1989), *Personnel Management in Britain*, Oxford: Blackwell.

SLEIGH, J. et al. (1979), *The Manpower Implications of Microelectronic Technology*, London: HMSO.

SMITH, D. (1988), 'The Japanese Example in South West Birmingham', *Industrial Relations Journal*, vol. 19, no. 1.

SMITH, R. (1979), 'The maximisation of control in industrial relations', in J. Purcell and R. Smith (eds).

SORGE, A. and STREECK, W. (1988), 'Industrial relations and technical change: the case for an extended perspective', in R. Hyman and W. Streeck (eds).

SPARROW, P. (1986), 'The erosion of employment in the UK; the need for a new response', *New Technology, Work and Employment*, vol. 1, no. 2.

STANDING, G. (1984), 'The notion of technological unemployment', *International Labour Review*, vol. 123, no. 2.

STARK, D. (1980), 'Class struggle and the transformation of the labour process', *Theory and Society*, no. 9.

STOREY, J. (1983), *Managerial Prerogative and the Question of Control*, London: Routledge & Kegan Paul.

STOREY, J. (1985), 'The means of management control', *Sociology*, vol. 19, no. 2

STOREY, J. (1986), 'The Phoney War? new office technology: organization and control', in D. Knights and H. Willmott (eds).

STOREY, J. (1988), 'The people-management dimension in current programmes of organizational change', *Employee Relations*, vol. 10, no. 6.

STOREY, J. (ed.) (1989), *New Perspectives on Human Resource Management*, London: Routledge & Kegan Paul.

SWORDS-ISHERWOOD, N. and SENKER, P. (1978), 'Automation in the engineering industry', *Labour Research*, November.

SWORDS-ISHERWOOD, N. and SENKER, P. (1980), *Microelectronics and the Engineering Industry-The Need for Skills*, London: Francis Pinter.

SZYSZCZAK, E. (1986), 'Employment protection and social security', in R. Lewis (ed.) (1986).

TAYLOR, A. (1989), *Trade Unions and Politics*, London: Macmillan.

TERRY, M. (1978), 'Shop stewards: the emergence of a lay elite? University of Warwick, IRRU Discussion Paper.

THOMPSON, P. (1981), 'Class, work and the labour process in marxism and sociology: a survey and evaluation', unpublished PhD thesis, Liverpool University.

THOMPSON, P. (1983), *The Nature of Work An Introduction to Debates on the Labour Process*, London: Macmillan.

THOMPSON, P. and BANNON, P. (1985), *Working the System: The Shopfloor and New Technology*, London, Pluto.

THOMPSON, P. (1988), '"Japanisation": threat or myth?', *International Labour Reports*, Issue 27–28, Summer.

THOMPSON, P. (1989), *The Nature of Work*, 2nd edn, London: Macmillan.

TOLLIDAY, S. and ZEITLIN, J. (eds) (1986), *The Automobile Industry and its Workers: Between Fordism and Flexibility*, Cambridge: Polity.

TOMANEY, J. (1990), 'The reality of workplace flexibility', *Capital and Class*, no. 40, Spring.

TOWERS, J. (1982), 'Editorial: The economy, unemployment and industrial relations', *Industrial Relations Journal*, vol. 13, no. 4.

TOWERS, B. (1987), 'New features-trends and developments in industrial relations. Managing labour flexibility', *Industrial Relations Journal*, vol. 18, no. 2.

TOWERS, B. (1989), 'Running the gauntlet: British trade unions under Thatcher, 1978–88', *Industrial and Labor Relations Review*, vol. 42, no. 2.

TOWNLEY, B. (1989), 'Employee communication programmes', in K. Sisson (ed.) (1989).

TREVOR, M. (1983), *Japan's Reluctant Multinations: Japanese Management at Home and Abroad*, London: Francis Pinter.

TREVOR, M. (1988), *Toshiba's New British Company*, London: Policy Studies Institute.

TUCRIC (1980), *The Impact of New Technology on the Working Lives of Women in West Yorkshire*, Leeds: Trade Union and Community Resource and Information Centre.

TUCRIC (1982), *New Technology and Women's Employment*, Leeds: Trade Union and Community Resource and Information.

TUC (1965), *Automation and Technological Change*, London: Trades Union Congress.

TUC (1979), *Employment and Technology*, London: TUC.

TUC (1981), 'Quality Circles', London: TUC, April.

TUC (1984), *Women and New Technology*, London: TUC.

TUC (1988), *Meeting the Challenge*, London: TUC, August.

TURNBULL, P. (1986), 'The Japanisation of British industrial relations at Lucas', *Industrial Relations Journal*, vol. 17, no. 3.

TURNBULL, P. (1988), 'The limits of Japanisation: "just-in-time", labour relations and the UK automotive industry', *New Technology, Work and Employment*, vol. 3, no. 1.

WABE, S. (1977), *Manpower Changes in the Engineering Industry*, Watford: EITB.

WADDINGTON, J. (1988), 'Business unionism and fragmentation within the TUC', *Capital and Class*, no. 36.

WALSH, K. (1987), 'Are disputes in decline? Evidence from UK industry', *Industrial Relations Journal*, vol. 18, no. 1.

WARNER, M. (1980), 'Different sides of the fence? A study of managerial and shop steward perceptions of employee influence', *Personnel Review*, vol. 12, no. 1.

WARNER, M. (ed.) (1984), *Microprocessors, Manpower and Society – A Comparative Cross-national Approach*, Aldershot: Gower.

WARNER, M. (1985), 'Microelectronics, technical change and industrialised economics: an overview', *Industrial Relations Journal*, vol. 16, no. 3.

WATSON, T. (1986), *Management, Organization and Employment Strategy*, London: Routledge & Kegan Paul.

WATSON, T. (1987), *Sociology, Work and Industry*, 2nd edn, London: Routledge & Kegan Paul.

WEDDERBURN, D. and CROMPTON, R. (1972), *Workers' Attitudes and Technology*, Cambridge: CUP.

WELLS, J. (1989), 'Uneven development and deindustrialization in the UK since 1979', in F. Green (ed.) (1989).

WEST, A.C. (1980), 'Introducing participation: an example from the British ports industry', *Journal of Occupational Psychology*, no. 53.

WHIPP, R. and CLARK, P. (1986), *Innovation and the Auto Industry*, London: Francis Pinter.

WHITEHILL, A., and TAKEZAWA, S. (1978), *The Other Worker*, Honolulu: East–West Center Press.

WICKENS, P. (1987), *The Road to Nissan*, London: Macmillan.

WIENER, R. (1976a), *The Economic Base of Leeds*, Leeds, WEA.

WIENER, R. (1976b), *The Engineering Industry in Leeds*, Leeds: WEA.

WIGHAM, E. (1973), *The Power to Manage*, London: Macmillan.

WILKINSON, B. (1983), *The Shopfloor Politics of New Technology*, London: Heinemann.

WILKINSON, B. and OLIVER, N. (1988), 'Editorial', *Industrial Relations Journal*, vol. 19, no. 1.

WILKINSON, B. and OLIVER, N. (1990), 'Obstacles to Japanisation: the case of Ford UK', *Employee Relations*, vol. 12, no. 1.

WILLIAMS, O.E. (1975), *Markets and Hierarchies*, New York: Free Press.

WILLIAMS, R. and MOSELEY, R. (1982), *Technology Agreements: Consensus, Control and Technical Change in the Workplace*, A paper presented to the EEC/FAST Conference, January.

WILLIAMS, R. and STEWARD, F. (1985), 'New technology agreements: an assessment', *Industrial Relations Journal*, vol. 16, no. 3.

WILLIAMS, V. (1984), 'Employment implications of new technology', *Employment Gazette*, May.

WILLMAN, P. (1980), 'Leadership and trade union principles', *Industrial Relations Journal*, vol. 11, no. 4.

WILLMAN, P. (1986), *Technological Change, Collective Bargaining and Industrial Efficiency*, Oxford: Clarendon.

WILSON, F.M. (1988), 'Computer Numerical Control and constraints', in Knights, D. and Willmott, H. (eds), *New Technology and the Labour Process*, London: Macmillan.

WILSON, F.M. and BUCHANAN, D.A. (1988), 'The effects of new technology in the engineering industry: cases of control and constraint', *Work, Employment and Society*, vol. 2, no. 3, 366–80.

WINTERTON, J. and WINTERTON, R. (1985), *New Technology: The Bargaining Issues*, University of Leeds/IPM.

WOOD, S. (ed.) (1983), *The Degradation of Work? Skill, Deskilling and the Labour Process*, London: Hutchinson.

WOOD, S. and KELLY, J. (1983) 'Taylorism, responsible autonomy and management strategy', in S. Wood (ed.).

WOOD, S. (1988), 'Between Fordism and flexibility? The US car industry', in R. Hyman and W. Streeck (eds).

WOODWARD, J. (1958), *Management and Technology*, London: HMSO.

WOODWARD, J. (1965), *Industrial Organization: Theory and Practice*, Oxford University Press.

WOODWARD, J. (1970), *Industrial Organization: Behaviour and Control*, Oxford University Press.

WOOLRIDGE, E. (1982), 'Negotiating technological change', *Personnel Management*, October.

WYLPU (1988), *A Cause for Concern: Health and Safety at Work in West Yorkshire*, Batley: West Yorkshire Low Pay Unit.

YIN, R.K. (1989), *Case Study Research: Design and Methods*, London: Sage.

YOUNG, K. (1986), 'The management of craft work: a case study of an oil refinery', *British Journal of Industrial Relations*, vol. XXIV, no. 3.

ZEITLIN, J. (1979), 'Craft control and the division of labour: engineers and compositors in Britain 1890–1930', *Cambridge Journal of Economics*, vol. 3, no. 3.

ZIMBALIST, A. (ed.) (1979), *Case Studies on the Labour Process*, New York: Monthly Review Press.

Index

Abernathy, W. et al. 18, 20, 35, 205, 206, 209
Ackroyd, S., et al. 17
alienation 40
ASTMS 51, 57
Atkinson, J. 11
AUEW 50, 55, 67, 79, 116, 134, 148, 155, 186, 190, 192, 198, 212
automation 36, 38, 61

Bain, G.S. 48
Batstone, E. 1, 9, 14, 38, 53, 67, 94, 157, 190, 193, 217
Beechey, V. 39
Bendix, R. 208
Beynon, H. xiii–xv, 46, 91, 204
Blauner, R. 33
Braverman, H. 2, 40, 42, 112, 115, 210
Buchanan, D. 204, 209
Burawoy, M. 43, 91, 208, 216

case-study methodology 13–16, 73
CAD (computer aided design) 21, 38, 68, 75, 173–4, 207
cellular technology 17, 23, 34, 38, 76, 107, 118, 134–6, 144, 148, 163, 172, 174, 182, 192, 202, 210
Child, J. 43–4
closed shop 6, 94, 156, 198
Clark, J. 1, 43
CNC (computer numerical control) 14, 21, 38, 65, 68, 75, 83, 133, 148, 184–5, 212
coercive autonomy 186, 197, 209
collective bargaining 8, 57, 72, 218
computer-controlled autonomy 208
contingency theory 37
control 18, 21, 33, 37, 39, 40, 90–1, 113–14, 121, 142, 148, 172, 174, 180, 186, 191, 207, 210
core workers 11, 36, 169, 216, 218

Daniel, W. 48, 69, 80
decentralization 7, 8
demarcations 67
dependency relations 32–3, 214, 218
deskilling 35, 37, 81, 85, 101, 117–18, 125, 148, 203, 205, 206
de-recognition 8, 55
direct control 21, 42, 102, 111, 150, 159, 165, 186
Dickens, P. and Savage, M. 17
Donovan Report 7, 173, 190

Edwards, P.K. 9
EETPU 49, 55, 56, 64, 65, 196
employee commitment 33, 92, 187, 197, 208
employee participation 9, 22, 97, 188–89
enterprise unions 27, 30

Flexibility of labour 2, 11, 23–4, 36, 71, 81, 84, 110, 145, 163, 167, 178, 180, 195–6, 203, 216
flexible specialization 2, 35, 205–6
Fordism 20, 21, 35, 205–6, 211
Fox, A. 38, 91, 117, 121, 208
Friedman, A. 33, 42

Graham, I. 17, 189
Guest, D.E. 2, 9, 28, 31
group technology, see also cellular technology, 201

Hartmann, G. et al. 45, 81, 89
Hyman, R. 6, 36, 41, 56, 97, 120, 190, 203, 206
hierarchy, at work 64, 108, 143, 165–6

ideology 33, 91–2, 187, 208

Japanese management 27–35, 168, 206

Japanization 2, 17, 18, 31, 138, 151, 202, 211, 214, 217, 218, 219
Jaques, E. 180
job design 116, 120, 158, 194, 201, 204, 213
Jones, B. 44, 79, 184
just-in-time production 17, 24–6, 34, 76, 106, 113, 136–7, 170, 202, 205, 214, 219

Kelly, J. 42, 51, 72
Kinnie, N.J. 8, 48, 162
Knights, D. and Willmott, H. 41, 43

Labour Research Department 66
Lane, T. 129, 190
Leadbeater, C. 10
lifetime employment 28
Littler, C.R. and Salaman, G. 20, 42, 121, 201, 208
low-trust relations 117, 186

MacInnes, J. 12, 14
Manwaring, T. 59, 64
Marchington, M. 10, 217
Marx, K. 40
Massey, D. 5
McLoughlin, I. 43

new realism 10, 55, 73, 191–2, 219
Nichols, T. 14, 55, 91, 101, 169, 204
Noble, D.F. 41, 45
Norsk Hydro 71

Oliver, N. 2, 18, 30–1, 32, 201, 213, 217
Oi, W. 80
operating objectives 210

pay 122–3, 127, 171, 173, 183, 195, 217
peer group pressure 197, 209
Penn, R. 39
peripheral workers 11, 29, 36, 215
Piore, M. and Sabel, C. 35, 205, 218
Pollert, A. 11

postal surveys 13
product design 168, 174–5
productivity 62, 101, 112, 148, 172, 177–78, 210–11, 215, 217

quality, *see also* total quality control 105, 112, 117, 144, 151, 169, 203
quality circles 70
quality of working life movement 21
quasi-elite stewards 157

responsible autonomy 42, 101, 143, 150, 159, 205
restrictive practices 146, 154
reward system, *see also* pay 170
Robins, K. and Webster, F. 59, 64
robots 75, 105, 115
Rolfe, H. 39

Sayer, A. 36, 76, 92, 164, 182, 202, 216
Schonberger, R. 17, 22, 23, 25, 27, 136, 138
scientific management, *see* Taylorism
selection and recruitment 27, 28, 120
semi-skilled workers 67, 74, 77, 80, 115, 117, 133, 146, 177, 184, 196, 213
seniority pay systems 27
Senker, P. and Beesley, M. 101
shop stewards 54, 94–5, 124, 126, 129, 138, 157, 186, 190, 197, 212, 216
single union deals 56
skill 18, 37, 38–9, 42, 87–8, 90, 118, 149, 150–51, 179–85, 202, 206
Storey, J. 2, 10, 18, 42, 210
strategic objectives 141, 209, 210
strikes 57, 71, 127, 213, 214, 218
supervisor 78, 81, 107–8, 134, 165–6
supplier relations 34

TASS 51, 57, 63, 65, 134, 149, 184, 198
Taylorism 19–20, 37, 40, 118, 206
technological determinism 206
technology, definition 37–8
Thompson, P. 2, 34, 35, 36, 206, 216
total quality control 17, 26–7, 32, 137–9, 170
trade unions: attitude to innovation 67, 99, 101, 138, 152, 155, 189, 191, 194, 199, 212; density 48, 53–4, 95, 122, 198; influence 59–70, 97, 100, 123, 153–6, 193–8, 212, 214, 216, 219; organization 50–1, 56, 70, 93–5, 99, 122, 126, 156–8, 198, 212, 217
training 63, 80, 88, 109, 148, 154
TUC: technological change 60–4; quality circles 70
Turnbull, P.J. 2, 18, 36, 182, 190, 201, 206, 216

unorganized conflict 120
U-shaped work flow 135, 179

Whipp, R. and Clark, P. 41, 205, 209
Wickens, P. 17, 24, 28, 137, 168
Wilkinson, B. 1, 2, 15, 18, 30, 31, 32, 44, 89, 185, 195, 201, 213, 217
Williams, R. and Moseley, R. 66
Williams, R. and Steward, F. 68, 72
Willman, P. 48, 59, 67
Wilson, F. 204
Wood, S. 34, 36, 205
Woodward, J. 37–8, 45, 130
work intensification 124, 170, 184, 192, 205, 216–17

Zimbalist, A. 41